QUEER EXPECTATIONS

SUNY series in Contemporary Jewish Literature and Culture
Ezra Cappell, editor

Dan Shiffman, *College Bound:
The Pursuit of Education in Jewish American Literature, 1896–1944*

Eric J. Sundquist, editor, *Writing in Witness:
A Holocaust Reader*

Noam Pines, *The Infrahuman:
Animality in Modern Jewish Literature*

Oded Nir, *Signatures of Struggle:
The Figuration of Collectivity in Israeli Fiction*

Zohar Weiman-Kelman, *Queer Expectations:
A Genealogy of Jewish Women's Poetry*

Richard J. Fein, translator, *The Full Pomegranate:
Poems of Avrom Sutzkever*

QUEER EXPECTATIONS
A GENEALOGY OF JEWISH WOMEN'S POETRY

ZOHAR WEIMAN-KELMAN

Cover: René Magritte, Lola De Valance, 1948, used by permission of the Société des auteurs dans les arts graphiques et plastiques (ADAGP).

Published by State University of New York Press, Albany

© 2018 State University of New York

All rights reserved

No part of this book may be used or reproduced in any manner whatsoever without written permission. No part of this book may be stored in a retrieval system or transmitted in any form or by any means including electronic, electrostatic, magnetic tape, mechanical, photocopying, recording, or otherwise without the prior permission in writing of the publisher.

For information, contact State University of New York Press, Albany, NY
www.sunypress.edu

Library of Congress Cataloging-in-Publication Data

Names: Weiman-Kelman, Zohar, 1982- author.
Title: Queer expectations : a genealogy of Jewish women's poetry / Zohar Weiman-Kelman.
Description: Albany : State University of New York Press, [2018] | Series: Suny series in contemporary Jewish literature and culture | Includes bibliographical references and index.
Identifiers: LCCN 2017061601 | ISBN 9781438472232 (hardcover   ) | ISBN 9781438472249 (e-book) | ISBN 9781438472225 (paperback   )
Subjects: LCSH: Hebrew poetry, Modern—History and criticism. | Jewish lesbians—Poetry—History and criticism. | Jewish poetry—Women authors—History and criticism. | Hebrew poetry—Women authors—History and criticism. | Yiddish poetry—Women authors—History and criticism. | Lesbianism in literature. | Lesbians in literature.
Classification: LCC PJ5024 .W45 2018 | DDC 809.1/99287089924—dc23 LC record available at https://lccn.loc.gov/2017061601

10 9 8 7 6 5 4 3 2 1

CONTENTS

Acknowledgments vii

Introduction xi
What to Expect When You're Not Expecting

Chapter One 1
Queer Lines: Adrienne Rich and Kadya Molodowsky

Chapter Two 23
Vanished Hellas and Hebraic Pain: Emma Lazarus and Anna Margolin

Chapter Three 41
Waiting in Vain: Leah Goldberg and Anna Margolin

Chapter Four 65
Heys Haunting: Poetics of Lesbian History

Chapter Five 89
Community across Discontinuity

Chapter Six 107
Translating Generations: Irena Klepfisz

Coda 125
Queering the Present of Jewish Literary History

Notes 137

Bibliography 169

Index 185

ACKNOWLEDGMENTS

This book has been a journey, "looking inward and outward / at once before and after / seeking a now that can breed / futures," in the words of black, lesbian, mother, warrior, poet Audre Lorde. Before I invite readers to join this journey, I want to give thanks to all those who brought me here, home, now.

Thank you to my mother Paula, who taught me that women are not only an acceptable topic, but *the* topic. I was fortunate enough to find scholarly support for this approach thanks to Tamar Hess at the Hebrew University in Jerusalem, where I also found my way to Yiddish, thanks to Hanan Bordin; together they set me on the path of Yiddish women's writing. This led me to the Department of Comparative Literature at the University of California, Berkeley, which proved to be the perfect home for the queer comparisons I was compelled to explore as this project developed. My dissertation committee chair, Chana Kronfeld, taught me to reimagine the relationship between Hebrew and Yiddish, the relationship between scholarship and activism, and most importantly, the relationship between scholars, offering new models of creative collaboration. Naomi Seidman shared with me her rare academic cocktail of rigor, chutzpa, and creativity. Our conversations, whether in Berkeley, Warsaw, or Toronto, always keep me on my toes. Both Chana and Naomi generously read multiple drafts of this project in dissertation form, often giving opposite advice and always providing challenging questions steeped in love and encouragement. Daniel Boyarin showed me how queer Jewish studies could be, and helped me claim a place there. Judith Butler has been a true mensch, a source of support and inspiration for bringing together multiple lines of resistance.

Since becoming an academic grownup, I have been blessed with new mentors, who are also dear friends: Ayelet Ben-Yishai granted me the gift of her benevolent bossiness, which consistently pays off, and Anna Shternshis held my hand and had my back, keeping me kosher through the job-and-book market. My colleagues at Ben Gurion University, especially Yael Ben-zvi, Catherine

Rottenberg, and Eitan Bar-Yosef, cheered me on through the final stages of this book project, and have given me a reason to stay in the game.

This project became a book thanks to the Anne Tanenbaum Postdoctoral Fellowship at the Centre for Jewish Studies at the University of Toronto, where I received warm and enthusiastic support for two years. Prior to that, the Department of English at Haifa University provided me with a teaching fellowship, and gave me hope for the power of scholarship as a tool of connection and empowerment in Israel/Palestine. The Townsend Center for the Humanities' Discovery Fellowship, the Berkeley Fellowship and Dean's Normative Time Fellowship supported four blissful years of concentrated study and writing at the University of California, Berkeley. The Foundation for Jewish Culture's Maurice and Marilyn Cohen Dissertation Fellowship gave me a much-needed year of dissertation completion funding. The Posen Foundation summer workshop, the Women and Gender Studies Dissertation writing seminar, and the Center for the Study of Sexual Culture's dissertation retreat all gave me precious feedback at different stages of the writing process. Grants from the American Council of Learned Societies, the Max Weinreich Center, the Center for Jewish History, the Helen Diller Family Foundation, and the Taube Foundation funded my many research trips to New York, Poland, Germany, and Israel/Palestine.

My father, Levi, read every single word of this book and offered invaluable edits—proving that being a radical rabbi and being a queer academic are much closer than I expected. Marty Fink and Monica Pearl read the first version of the manuscript, enacting the cross-generational dialogue this book imagines: they pushed me to make both my rage and passion come through. During the final stages of writing, Laura Portwood-Stacer's bird's-eye view helped me refind my voice and ensured that I was getting my points across. Ri J. Turner dove into the man-uscript with astonishing skill and zeal, making my arguments sharper, and saving me from many potential blunders. I'm also grateful to the many online friends who helped me pick the title, and reminded me that someone was waiting for my book in the real world. Thanks to Rafael Chaiken, Ryan Morris, and Ezra Cappell at SUNY Press for making the book a reality, and to the reviewers who made that reality better.

For countless conversations, comments, and cups of coffee, I want to thank my elders, colleagues and coconspirators: Elizabeth Abel, Sarrah Alghamdi, Asaf Aharonson, Salma Al Atassi, Michael Allan, Suzi Andreis,

Acknowledgments

Inbal Arnon, Michal Aronzon, Nadia Awad, David Biale, Ella Ben-Hagai, Chana Bloch z"l, Brenda Cossman, Ruby Cymrot-Wu, Carolyn Dinshaw, Deema Darawshy, Rachel Epstein, Sidra Ezrachi, Maura Finkelstein, Leora Gal, Coco Guzman, Ettie Freifeld, Galit Hasan-Rokem, Nayrouz Abu Hatoum, Noa Hever-Polak, Kathryn Hellerstein, Alex Jaunait, Orev Reena Katz, Martin Kavka, Natalie Kouri-Towe, Vivi Lachs, Tamir Lederberg, Laura Levitt, Lital Levy, Heather Love, Barbara Mann, Krystyna Mazur, Ana Minian, Sarah Anne Minkin, Durba Mitra, Anat Moses, Yigal Nizri, Noki, Anita Norich, Dana Olmert, Ilana Pardes, Jake Payne, Eddy Portnoy, Yosefa Raz, Ariel Rokem, Naama Rokem, Hershel Russel, Allison Schachter, Esther Schor, Jeffrey Shandler, Maya Shapira, Davey Shlasko, Ivy Sichel, Andrew Sloin, Barbara Spackman, Dean Spade, Nicole Taylor, Evelyn Torton Beck, Pani Michelle Viise, Rachel Wamsley, Zoe Whittall, Shira Wolosky, Anna Zawadzka, Rawan Zaytoun, and Amalia Ziv.

    I want to give special thanks to Shaul Setter, Katrina Dodson, Max Strassfeld, and Anastasia Kayiatos, who have each played a formative role in my writing, thinking, and becoming. I also want to thank the stars and star guides, Julia Wawrzyniak-Beyer, Chani Nicholas, and Jessica Lanyadoo. To my feminist aunts, especially Claire Burch of blessed memory for her vision and compassion. To my uncle Mark, my great uncle Ralph, and my grandfathers Jerry and Wolfe, for the love of words and people. To my grandmothers Hassie and Jacky, for always telling it like it is. Thank you to my younger siblings, Benji and Rafa, who are both role models I look up to for doing their own unexpected thing. No matter what that thing was, our parents granted all of us ridiculous amounts of shameless love, curiosity, and pride that make everything seem possible. Thanks to Eden Segev Simsolo, who is with me (whether near or far), and found the perfect cover image, which just happens to be our portrait. Finally, at long last, thanks go out to my partner in love, academia, and activism, Ido Katri, for making life an adventure with a future I queerly look forward to.

    I dedicate this book to Irena Klepfisz, a gift of backward future *hemshekh*.

INTRODUCTION
What to Expect When You're Not Expecting

* * *

אַתְּ לִי בְּשׂוֹרָה נִפְעָמָה, מְצַוָּה
עַל מַהוּת אַחֶרֶת לִשְׁמֹר.
אַתְּ לִי פְּגִישָׁה לֹא-צְפוּיָה, צוֹהֶלֶת,
בְּטֶרֶם עוֹד רָאֲתָה אוֹר.

אַתְּ לִי גָּלוּי סַף רָחוֹק וְנֶעְלָם
שֶׁל וַדַּאי הַחוֹלֵם לִהְיוֹת,
שֶׁל הֲזָיָה עוֹרֶגֶת, מִתְעַטְּפָה,
עַל מַה שֶּׁלֹּא יוּכַל הֱיוֹת.

אַתְּ קוֹרֵאת, חוֹזֶרֶת לֹא-נִרְאֵית
וָאַעַן לִקְרִאָתֵךְ אֲנִי.
טוֹב לִי הֵעָלְמֵךְ מִפָּנַי,
טוֹב לִי הִתְעַטְּפֵךְ בְּדָמִי.

טוֹב לִי בְּסִתְרֵי מֶרְחַקִּים
אֵלַיִךְ לַחֲכּוֹת בִּכְדִי.
אַתְּ תִּקְוַת דָּם לִבִּי הַשְּׁלוּחָה
אֶל אֲשֶׁר לֹא יָבוֹא עוֹד לִי.

* * *

To me you are enraptured annunciation, commanding
Another essence to keep.
To me you are un-expected encounter, rejoicing
Ere still the light it did see.

To me you are a discovery's distant vanishing verge
Of a certainty dreaming to be,
Of a yearning delusion, enwrapped
By that which cannot be.

You call, repeat un-seen
And answering you is me.
Good for me your vanishing from me
Good for me your enwrapping silently.

Good for me in secrets-distance
To wait for you in vain.
You are my heart's blood sent hope
For that which will no more come to me.[1]

This poem, written in Hebrew by Yocheved Bat-Miriam in 1930, stages an "un-expected encounter" at the same time as it insists on the impossibility of encounter, foreclosing future fulfillment. The hyphen in the word *un-expected* in the Hebrew (*lo-tsfuyah*) perfectly holds this paradoxical combination, bringing together the expectation and its negation, which would otherwise be two separate words. In my translation the hyphen separates what would otherwise be a single uninterrupted word, *unexpected*, placing emphasis on the negation, while also making it a homophone for its opposite, inviting *an*-expected encounter. It is in this intricate combination of anticipation and preemptive negation that I recognize this poem as a queerly expectant text. This expectancy is queer in that it resists the future it expects. However, it is the expression of resistance that gives voice to those expectations. Moreover, this queer expectancy works not only forward, but also backward. Texts expressing resistance to the past's expectations refuse to fulfill those expectations, while bringing them into being. Queer expectancy, then, is generated not by looking forward, but by looking back, to, and through the past's unfulfilled desires. Challenging biology, linearity, and other hegemonic norms and dictates, queer expectancy creates a backward continuity.

This backward continuity, the act of turning back, my turn and the turn of the writers I read, forges a new kind of lineage, constituted not by generative texts (say, like an expectant parent), but by what Christopher Nealon calls "foundling texts"[2]—orphan texts waiting to be adopted, not by the prior generation of parents but by future generation of (queer) readings and readers, who will adopt them across time. Despite this dependence on future readers, an essential aspect of the queer lineage I construct is rooted in resisting futurity. By "futurity" I do not mean the progression of time toward the future, but rather, I am referring to a current emphasis on the value of the future, with a particular set of dictates and goals to be fulfilled in the service of this future to come. If the future is what comes, futurity is the present orientation toward that future. While this is perhaps most easily comprehended in relation to pressures of biological reproductive normativity, undermining futurity is about more than the choice whether or not to reproduce. What is at stake is a subversion of the symbolic order derived from the reproductive imperative, put bluntly by queer theorist Lee Edelman: "Fuck the social order and the child in whose name we're collectively terrorized [...] fuck the whole network of Symbolic relations and the future that serves as its prop."[3] Reproductive futurity, structuring the social order far beyond actual reproduction, renders both the present and the past dependent on bringing about a future to come. Queer expectancy undoes this dependence, replacing future fulfillment with a backward-looking present resistance.

Writing in the interwar period, Hebrew poet Yocheved Bat-Miriam offers a resistance of futurity while setting up her own foundling status by naming herself "backward." Born Yocheved Zhelezniak, in Belarus in 1901, the poet took on the name "Bat-Miriam," daughter of Miriam.[4] She thus connects to the poetic legacy of Miriam the Prophetess, who sang the Song of the Sea with her brother Moses in Exodus. But in so doing, she also reverses the order of Biblical lineage, making the Biblical Yocheved (mother of Moses and Miriam) the daughter of Miriam.[5] Here, as Naomi Seidman writes, the "biological affiliation and the respect and authority traditionally invested in the older generation give way to a fluid model of imaginative and voluntary affiliations."[6] Such alternative affiliations were strategically deployed in the three historical moments this book turns to: the emergence of Jewish American women's writing in the late nineteenth century, Hebrew and Yiddish women's writing in the interwar period, and the Jewish lesbian writing of the 1970s–'80s. As writers from these diverse moments subvert simple biological or linear notions of lineage, the texts themselves become expectant, inviting future readers to make use of their texts in ways they could not yet imagine.

Besides this backward foundling adoption, Bat-Miriam also adopted a language, Modern Hebrew, which was not her mother tongue. She was born to a religious Hasidic Jewish family, where Yiddish was spoken in the home, and was educated in Russian, from childhood through studies at the universities of Kharkov, Odessa, and Moscow. She became involved with the communist literary group "The Hebrew Octoberists" in 1918, and began writing Hebrew poetry. She immigrated to Paris in 1926 and then to Palestine in 1928, where she lived until her death in 1980. Bat-Miriam was part of a generation of Jewish writers who chose Hebrew as a literary language, only later expanding it to a fully functional vernacular. Her poetic efforts are in fact part of the normalization of the language, at the same time that her poetic language is uniquely dense and far from conversational. Indeed, a major challenge to a fulfilling encounter with Bat-Miriam's poetry in general, and specifically with the poem here, is the challenge of translation. The most significant aspect lost in translation is the fact that the poem speaks in first-person feminine, to a grammatically female-gendered addressee. Another challenge lies in the fact that the poem is constructed almost entirely in the present tense, veering from this norm only in two instances (which I will discuss below). Both aspects, of time and of sexuality, are part of my reading of the poem as a queerly expectant text. In fact, time and gender are both key to my understanding of queerness in this book.

Attending first to sexuality, via Bat-Miriam, we can read queerness as an expression of desire between women, which this poem stages using a female speaker and female addressee. While the longing (*'ergah*) described is not explicitly sexual, the fact that the speaker insists on its impossibility underscores a reading of this desire as forbidden lesbian desire. The fact that historically such desires could only be alluded to is fundamental to the backward adoption of foundling texts. Speaking from one woman to another, Bat-Miriam's poem sets up this desire and its impossibility. The first stanza speaks of an "un-expected encounter" that has not yet happened ("ere still the light it did see"). The second stanza invokes "a certainty that dreams to be," yet declares it "will not be able to be." These paradoxical statements thus narrate a promise and its negation. In the third stanza, Bat-Miriam opens a dialogue: "you call, repeat, unseen / and answering you is me." But as the speaker says in the next verse, she prefers her addressee in her preemptive vanishing, her hiding ("*tov li he'almekh mipanai, tov li hit'atfekh bidmi*"). The fourth stanza reveals that the speaker herself is also hiding, in the realm of "secrets-distance" ("*besitrey merḥakim*"). It is there that she chooses to wait for her, the addressee, who will not come, as the poem tells us in its closing line.

To retroactively read this desire as queer or lesbian when Bat-Miriam herself did not claim such an identity exposes my role as queer reader, the one

Nealon calls a "hermeneutic friend," who can identify (and identify *with*) desires that were not, or could not be, intelligible to authors in the past.[7] However, I want to emphasize that this interpretation does not seek to claim any sort of "truth" regarding Bat-Miriam's lived experience or desires. My queer reading of Bat-Miriam is not anchored in her sexual practice. Similarly, my use of Bat-Miriam to discuss a resistance to heteronormative futurity and reproduction does not rely on her biography. For the record, Bat-Miriam bore two children to two men while still in the Soviet Union. Her daughter Mariassa Bat-Miriam Katzenelson (1925–2015) has left us a beautiful account of her mother.[8] Her son, Nahum (Zuzik) Hazaz (born 1928), was killed in the war of 1948. Ironically, the strongest evidence for reading "actual" lesbian desire in the poem might be the staunchness with which the speaker denies the possibility of its fulfillment. The foreclosure described in the poem fits well with the likelihood that at the historical time of Bat-Miriam's writing, in the early 1930s, lesbian desire, if expressed, would also likely be disavowed. Indeed, it is the depiction of same-sex love as impossible, tragic, and doomed to failure that makes it recognizable to us across history. If early work in Gay and Lesbian Studies tended to deny the significance of these depressing accounts, according to Heather Love, queer studies have turned to them.[9] Suggesting a queer model of "feeling backward," Love shows how the fact that queers have historically felt outside of progress, positivity, and productivity can serve as a point of connection, by way of our own ability to feel backward (in time and across time), creating an affective genealogy and a "backward future."[10] This backward future is echoed in Bat-Miriam's cementing of the future impossibility into the present of her poem.

The collapse of the future into the present heralds another form of queerness, queerness in relation to time. When the speaker prefers her addressee to disappear, when she chooses to wait in vain, and to see in her addressee the revelation of that which "will come no more to me" (or: already will not/will not come again/will no longer come—*asher lo yavo od li*), she generates a queerly impossible time of expectancy that resists futurity in its narrative, as well as in its grammatical structure. The lack of fulfillment is written into the poem's adherence to the present tense. The two instances which veer from the present do not represent past or future alternatives, but rather construct the temporal complication of the poem; the first case is the statement indicating the foreclosure of what "will not be able to be," which uses the future tense *will*, but only in the form of a preemptive negation. The second case is the use of the verb *to answer*, "*va'an likratekh ani*" ("And answering you is me"). The statement could indicate a future answer, "and I will answer," as is the case in Modern Hebrew. However, the same verb can be read as an answer past, using the "conversive *vav*," a Biblical aspectual form, which implies a completed action: the answer has already been given. Drawing on Biblical Hebrew, Bat-Miriam was taking on a linguistic and literary history from which women were traditionally excluded. Drawing on Modern Hebrew, Bat-Miriam was participating in the creation of a future language for poetry. Activating the tension between the modern tense, according to which Bat-Miriam's speaker *will answer*, and Biblical aspect, according to which the speaker *has answered already*, creates an ahistorical time. Combining expectancy and foreclosure, queerness emerges as a category transcending sexual practice; rather, it is a relation to time itself.

However, it is precisely this ahistorical time that makes the impossible encounter available for my present queer reading. Indeed, if the addressee won't come, the reader will; each time the speaker utters the word *you* (*at*), a female reader is also implicated; as she repeats the phrase "you are to me" ("*at li*") this reader is brought into an unmediated encounter with the female speaker. This address is, however, as direct as it is impeded and impossible, by the very nature of the poetic address (which has already taken place and cannot receive an answer),[11] but also by the impossibility of encounter thematized here and in much of Bat-Miriam's poetry.[12] The reader is further implicated here by the verbal/textual nature of the nonencounter. The addressee's only (reported) address to the speaker is her "calling," a word that means also "to read," thus: "you call/read" ("*at koret*"). Furthermore, the encounter has *not* come into being in the same words used in Hebrew for publishing: "to see light" (here: "*beterem od ra'atah or*"). In fact, the poem's publication history plays directly into the complex expression of desire and temporality under discussion here, revealing an un-expected queer intertextual dialogue, which I only discovered after many years of working with the poem.

My own encounter with Bat-Miriam entailed looking for a history outside the canon of Hebrew Literature. Even though she was critically acclaimed in her time, receiving the Bialik Prize in 1968 and the Israel Prize in 1972, her poetry did not continue to circulate in the years since. This can be attributed to the often complex and even opaque nature of her poetry,[13] and to Bat-Miriam's own vow of literary silence after the death of her son Zuzik in the war of 1948, as well as to the fact that works of many women (and others) who did not enter the literary canon were not passed down through the generations. Bat-Miriam's poetry was out of print and hard to find for the most part of the past decades. The text of the poem produced above originates in the 1972 reprint of the 1963 edition of Bat-Miriam's collected poetry, which was until recently the most accessible edition of her work. It was only in 2014 that her complete works were collected and published. This collection offers a different version of the poem, based on Bat-Miriam's first book, *Meraḥok*, published in 1932. In addition, the meticulous critical apparatus of this new edition leads to an even earlier version of the poem, published on August 21, 1930, in *Moznaim*, an Israeli literary journal active to this day. This original version of the poem, as well as the 1932 version (which the 2014 collection relies on), reveals that this poem was originally part of a cycle, and only stands alone in the 1963 edition. This stark difference between a stand-alone poem and a cycle makes the two other versions appear identical. However, there is one significant point of difference: the later poem is dedicated to the Hebrew poet Rachel Bluvshteyn (1890–1931). If my initial reading of Bat-Miriam saw the reader (that is, myself) as the addressee, the hermeneutic friend needed to bring the encounter in the poem into being, the dedication, "To Rachel" (as the poet herself signed her poetry, with no last name), offers a very different history.

The dedication does not appear until the 1932 version. Because the 1932 version was published shortly after Rachel's death in 1931, it has been taken to be a response to her death, explaining the impossibility of the address in the poem itself: "In the cycle '*Pelekh dmama*' ['realm of silence'] (whose name speaks for itself)," writes Dan Miron, Bat-Miriam addressed "the dead Rachel Bluvshteyn to announce she would soon be joining her in the kingdom of silence and death."[14] While this interpretation fits the date of Rachel's death, the fact that the poem itself was originally published *before* Rachel's death precludes using her death as the ultimate key to deciphering the poem. Instead, following the publication trail of the poem itself, predating Rachel's death, we discover an intricate literary exchange between the two poets, complicating my initial queer interpretation by offering textual traces of dialogue and distinctly erotic echoes.

If Bat-Miriam initiates this dialogue in the poem we read, inviting an encounter (even as she declares it impossible), Rachel actually answers her in a poem of her own to Bat-Miriam, just three months later. Rachel's poem, "*Ivria*" [a combination of "Hebrew" and "Jewess"], was published in the Hebrew paper

Davar on November 14, 1930, and was dedicated to Bat-Miriam.¹⁵ It is only after receiving the dedication and poem from Rachel that Bat-Miriam added the dedication to Rachel. We cannot know if this addition happened before or after her death, since the poem does not appear again until 1932 (after Rachel died). Yet in tracing this intertextual dialogue, it becomes clear that the initial desire Bat-Miriam expresses is not for death (via Rachel's death), and furthermore, that whatever desire it expressed was answered by Rachel. Finally, adding the dedication to Rachel forms a recognition of this response, creating a queer dialogue that extends beyond death.

Rachel's poem, probably more known than any of Bat-Miriam's poetry, is powerful and erotic. In it a female speaker describes standing "enraptured" ["*nif'emet*"] before another woman (perhaps Bat-Miriam herself), who appears "as if she emerged from the Bible," with "antiquity's grace, blackness and flaming-passion" ["*beḥen kedumim, bish'ḥor velahat altah min hatanakh*"]. The word *enraptured*, used by Rachel twice to describe her speaker's state, is very similar to the word Bat-Miriam uses to describe her addressee in the first line of her poem: "to me you are enraptured annunciation." Bat-Miriam uses the word in an unusual form, *nif'amah*, which is then echoed in Rachel's repetition of the word in its more common form, *nif'emet*. The repetition of this unusual word together with the direct dedication by Rachel to Bat-Miriam and later by Bat-Miriam to Rachel gives flesh to the possibility of actual dialogue, while the poems themselves tell two different stories of the (im)possibility of encounter.

If Bat-Miriam's poem sets up the impossibility of encounter, Rachel sets up its inevitability; where Bat-Miriam proclaims a desire for hiding and vanishing, Rachel stages the ultimate gaze and revelation. To quote the closing stanzas of the poem,

אַךְ אִם מָעַלְתִּי—לֹא לָנֶצַח,
כִּחַשְׁתִּי—לֹא עַד תֹּם.
וְשַׁבְתִּי שׁוּב כְּשׁוּב הַהֵלֶךְ
אֶל כְּפַר מוֹלַדְתּוֹ.

כֹּה אֶעֱמֹד פֹּה לְפָנַיִךְ
נִפְעֶמֶת אֲחוֹתִי,
בְּחֵן קְדוּמִים, בִּשְׁחוֹר וְלַהַט

אָזוֹן עֵינַי תְּכָלְתִּי.

> If I betrayed—not forever,
> Denied—not to the end.
> And I return again like the wanderer
> to the village of his birth.
>
> So I stand here before you,
> my sister, enraptured
> by antiquity's grace, blackness and flaming-passion
> I feed my eyes of blue.[16]

Here Rachel sets up the encounter as a compulsive, inescapable return, underscored in the Hebrew by the repetition of versions of the word *shuv* three times, employing an intricate alliteration of "shin" sounds in the third line of the penultimate stanza: "*veshavti shuv keshuv hahelekh.*"[17] The return, staged in the present tense, results in the speaker standing before her addressee, but as in Bat-Miriam's poem no dialogue takes place. Still, there is an encounter, and instead of the disappearance Bat-Miriam stages (and prefers), here the speaker "feeds" her eyes on the vision of her addressee. If Bat-Miriam's poem stages a call and response while foreclosing encounter, here there is meeting with no dialogue. But taken together, both meeting and dialogue materialize in a delayed back and forth, enacting the literary dialogue Bat-Miriam's poem describes: reading, returning, responding. Moreover, my own hermeneutic role suddenly becomes clearer, for these poems have awaited the reader, her archival work, her queer desire; She has the task of bringing this call and response into being, thus queerly joining it.

My ability to join this history derives from what Carolyn Dinshaw defines as the queer historical impulse, which simultaneously seeks to historicize and to reach cross-temporally. The drive toward historicism is derived from the fact that what is considered queer is dependent on the norms of each given time and place. In this sense queerness is a "relation to a norm, a relation that can be historicized *and* traced across time," to follow Dinshaw.[18] Dinshaw's understanding of queerness thus generates a historical awareness that is deeply embedded in individual disparate times. At the same time, the queer historical impulse is based in the possibility of moving across time, allowing past and present (each activated by historicist endeavors) to pleasurably touch. The need to define a relation to norms in time forces me to simultaneously historicize my own time and the time of the historical subjects I turn to, placing the queer both in the past and in the present. Yet it is also an antihistoricist endeavor, where the very idea of connection across time undermines the separation between past and present, undoing notions of linear progression. Anachronistically moving between disparate historical groundings, queer time undermines binary separation between past and present, undoing linear, teleological and progressive notions of history. If my initial reading of Bat-Miriam staged the queer encounter as purely a product of my anachronistic interpretation, the work of historical research revealed a dialogue that exceeded my queer fantasy. After I discovered the back-and-forth exchange with Rachel, the encounter seemed far more real, undermining my queer fantasy. The truth of this story is, however, relegated to "*sitrey merḥakim*," the hidden realms of history, for we will never know what actually transpired between the poets. Instead, this story enacts the combination of historicizing and anachronistic reading at the heart of my queer methodology. Somewhere between the traces that Rachel and Bat-Miriam left, the clues I collected, and the time of my own reading, the story of queer desire becomes possible, inevitable, undeniable.

∗ ∗ ∗

"We must strive, in the face of the here and now's totalizing rendering of reality to feel a *then and there*," writes José Esteban Muñoz. The *then and there* Muñoz offers is queer futurity, where "queerness is a structuring and educated mode of desiring that allows us to see and feel beyond the quagmire of the present."[19] Over and against Muñoz's futurity, this book searches for a way out of the predicament of the present by way of the past. Looking back to Jewish women's writing in the nineteenth century and in the interwar period, and to Jewish lesbian writing from the 1970s to the 1980s, I find writers wrestling with their limited access to history, with their circumscribed role in their disparate presents, and consequently, with the ultimate value of futurity—the same conditions that force me to look back to the past rather than forward to the future. Aiming to intervene in my present, I am in search of alternative pasts offered to me by Jewish women's poetry and politics. I turn to poems from 1880 to 1990, in English, Yiddish, and Hebrew, and show how Jewish women writers have used poetry to draw genealogical lines of continuity that connect themselves to Jewish women of the past. This continuity resists heteronormative imperatives of biological reproduction, inheritance, and futurity, and offers instead queer expectancy, breeding connection by disrupting expected models of gender, time and history. By looking back, the looking back of the poets and my own looking back, a queer continuity is formed.

This project began in West Jerusalem, when my love of Hebrew women's poetry became my official subject of study at Hebrew University. It was as part of that all-Hebrew and overwhelmingly male curriculum that I was exposed to Yiddish women's poetry as well. In *Imahot meyasdot, aḥayot ḥorgot* (Founding Mothers, Stepsisters) (1991), one of the first books on Hebrew women's poetry, Dan Miron rejects the idea that Hebrew poetry was inhospitable to women's writing, citing the glorious past of Yiddish women writing at the same time.[20] While my political education taught me better than to take the success of one part of a minority as a refutation of the struggles of others from that same minority (in this case, Jewish women), I was stunned by what this comparison revealed: that women wrote poetry in Yiddish. My Israeli education taught me next to nothing of modern Yiddish literature, and I had certainly never heard of women writing modernist poetry in Yiddish. This erasure was not accidental; rather, it was very much tied to the association of Yiddish with women (as *mama loshn*/mother-tongue, not as literary tongue) and with the Diaspora/*goles* (to be negated). What I encountered in my studies was not only Yiddish as a language of Jewish diaspora, but also a different, Diasporic Hebrew. Through nineteenth-century Hebrew literature I realized how deeply anchored the language had been in Diasporic life and literature, long before it was naturalized and nationalized. The fact that Hebrew was also being written by Jews outside of Europe was not part of the curriculum in Israel, nor was Jewish creation in Ladino, Judeo-Arabic, or any non-European vernacular. Still, my two discoveries, of Hebrew as a language of Jewish diaspora and of Yiddish as a language of modern Jewish culture, both deeply unsettled how I understood the history that led to the present I was living in, a present I was struggling with. It was 2001, a moment of extreme violence in Israel/Palestine, and especially in Jerusalem. This is not the place to recount how quickly everything deteriorated over those first years of the Second Intifada, or to trace my own process of disillusionment. Rather, I want to highlight how in those rather desperate times, discovering a new Jewish history was the one thing that gave me hope, by proving to me that the reality I lived in was but one option the past had held for the Jewish future. Today, when Yiddish can no longer be considered a competitor for *the* Jewish language, and Hebrew reigns as the language of Jewish nationhood, I choose to go back to moments when neither of these realities had come to be. I connect to all those possibilities past, and recognize the existence of new possibilities for my present, and even for my still unforeseen future.

When Bat-Miriam began writing in the 1920s, the future, which is our present, was anything but expected. The interwar period was a time of past potentiality for the future in/of Jewish literature, culture and life, for men and women alike. At the time both Hebrew, the language Bat-Miriam adopted, and Yiddish, her mother tongue, were still nascent modern secular literary vehicles, emerging from a long past of largely religious textual orientation; these years of Jewish history were rich with possibility. Linguistically and culturally, Jewish writers could choose between Jewish languages such as Yiddish, Hebrew, or Ladino, and local languages such as Polish, Russian, Arabic, or English, and even had the ability to inhabit multiple positions at once, or move fluidly among them.[21] No writer could anticipate the effect of her linguistic choices in relation to how Jewish literary history would evolve, yet these choices proved critical for the lives of writers and for the course of Jewish literary history. As Dan Miron writes, the choice of language had momentous implications, "for the choice of language amounted to a choice of a cultural Jewish future."[22] But the choice of a future was deeply embedded in the choice of a past as well, as Miron suggests: "In nothing did the new literatures convey their sense of troubled awareness of their newness more than in this need to choose and justify the selection, its choice of a past or pasts."[23]

As much as men and women shared uncertainty about the future, the available pasts to choose from were significantly different for women.[24] Most significantly, women were largely denied access to the sacred tongue, Hebrew, and to religious textual heritage in that language.[25] The religious past of Jewish letters meant there was hardly a long or continuous tradition of women writing in Jewish languages. Moreover, because women had limited access to the religious texts, they were also less likely to produce modern literature. While Jewish men could repurpose the Hebrew of the Bible and the Talmud to create a new secular literature, women came to writing Hebrew and Yiddish without the cultural and linguistic inheritance that traditional male education afforded.[26] Even outside the realm of Jewish tradition, women had to contend with a historical disadvantage, for they were writing without an acknowledged tradition of women writing before them, a predicament feminist literary criticism names as one of the fundamental challenges for women's writing.[27] In terms of "women's history," the problem was first the fact that it was less likely for women to come to writing, and even when they did, their texts were less likely to be saved, circulated, and passed down. The force of these dynamics left women outside of history and without access to history. Indeed, the "newness" Miron invokes as conditioning the turn to the past was particularly acute for women, for without a past, what could women's writing-future be?

While Jewish women were recognized as readers of Yiddish literature, they were not meant to be producing it.[28] Their access to Hebrew was even more limited; the few who were taught Hebrew being the exception rather than the rule, an exception very much dependent on the disposition of unique fathers rather than the product of a cultural norm.[29] Jewish women thus faced not only a lack of access to the production of a textual past and a lack of access to women's history, but also a one-track future that would perpetuate their present marginalization. Therefore, for women, to choose a "cultural Jewish future" depended not only on challenging past and present norms, but entailed a struggle against a particular form of future, by gaining access to a past. Looking backward worked simultaneously against women's past erasure and against their future imperative of reproduction.

Despite or possibly due to Jewish women's historical disadvantage, they were deemed an essential part of the Jewish future, as agents of reproduction producing future Jewish (male) scholars (and later, Jewish soldiers).[30] Whereas men metaphorically birthed texts, Jewish women were meant to be birthing babies, not writing. Discussing these conditions, I do not mean to evoke an essentialized notion of "womanhood" as stable and unchanging across history. On the contrary, I think of gender, through Judith Butler, as an "identity tenuously constituted in time,"[31] and argue that in order to understand women's history (and lack thereof), we must account for the way gender is socially constructed in any given time, and what role that allowed women in society, and consequently in history. Women's childbearing capacities have been perhaps the most deciding factor in women's social positioning, linking them to the (re)production of the future, while limiting their role in the present. It is my contention throughout this book that Jewish women writers have had to undo the imperative of reproduction, as well as the normative history structured by that imperative, in order to become writers.

This undoing demands not only reclaiming and inventing histories, but also generating alternative modes of queer history and temporality alike. If "the modern sense of linear temporality with the celebrated logocentrism of Western thought" assumes "that history is a chronological development through linear time," [32] it also uses the present outcome to justify this development, "selecting past material so as to identify a tradition leading to the present."[33] This, according to Jewish historian David Myers, is historicism's success, and has come to dominate our way of thinking about the past as a justification of our present. [34] The manner in which we have been conditioned to place the single event in context and then link it to a chain of other contextually bound events thus constructs historical narratives that appear to be both natural and inevitable, thereby erasing the very act of construction. Queer theory, on the other hand, is invested in exposing the act of construction of the very ideas of "natural" and "inevitable," from the individual level of gender (questioning the very category of "woman"), all the way through to society at large, including our understanding of history, and of time itself. Bringing together gender and temporality, queer histories undermine the heteronormative dictates structuring time as consecutive, progressive, and reproductive teleology.

Jewish lesbian literature serves as a leading model for this mode of intervention: when the radical lesbian movement emerged in the 1970s, it had to (re)create a lesbian history, for there were very few forerunners to be found. At the same time, this movement rejected heteronormative reproduction (or at least demanded alternatives modes of reproduction). Unable or unwilling to be measured by the sons they produced (or did not produce), the Jewish lesbian poets of the 1970s challenged the role relegated to them by finding their *hemshekh*, their continuity, not in the children to come, but through the women who came before them. As a result, this literature constructed continuity by producing a past rather than a future, offering a model of queer history. Indeed, this ties together my approach to women's writing and to Yiddish writing as bound by the challenges of history, for reaching the history of Yiddish, in my personal experience and in the experience of so many others, entailed overcoming our own historical disadvantage; it meant uncovering a history very much repressed by the Israeli literary establishment where I received my early training, and by the American Jewish establishment as well. It was a past that had to be forgotten,[35] a past without a future. But even this lack of future has a past, connecting not just to the current state of Yiddish, but to the entire (short) history of modern Jewish literature, in relation to the language politics, policy, and poetics of Yiddish and Hebrew alike, for neither language represents uninterrupted continuity.

If the lesbian lineage I trace—and ultimately, join—offers new nonnormative ways of looking forward, by challenging the default mode of heteronormative reproduction (that you have to have children, and that they have to be made one certain way), Yiddish offers a similar challenge to the future, because of the way it is, for the most part, no longer transmitted as mother tongue outside of ultra-Orthodox circles. In order to have a future, it must be actively (queerly) chosen rather than (heteronormatively) produced and inherited. Turning away from the languages of my present (Hebrew and English) to Yiddish means adopting a past I did not inherit, making Yiddish itself a foundling language, rather than a normatively generative one.

The turn to Yiddish was itself part of the lesbian history project that emerged in the United States in the 1970s. While many women in the lesbian movement went in search of lesbian histories, and women's history more broadly, some Jewish lesbians sought their own history through Yiddish literature. Consequently, Jewish lesbians played a major role in discovering, translating, and publishing a significant portion of the Yiddish women's poetry available today. While none of these Yiddish poets (none discussed here and none that I know of) lived or identified as lesbian, in the lesbian model of history and its queer temporality, new connections were drawn by lesbian authors looking back to the past, retroactively making these Yiddish women writers part of a lesbian lineage—whether or not they would have wanted to be included. Similarly, many lesbian authors of the 1970s would have, or actually have, resisted the label "queer," which was only reclaimed in the 1980s.[36] Just as lesbian authors made Yiddish women writers part of their lesbian lineage, I, in turn, make lesbian writers, and Yiddish women writers, part of my own queer genealogy. This genealogical move proves to be most challenging in places where the past is indeed not quite gone. Accounting for the privilege of having lesbian foremothers who can—and do—talk back, and Yiddish foremothers whose voices are no longer heard, in its complications of linear temporality and transmission, the queer genealogy I draw insists on affective and erotic continuities, even in points of contest and conflict.

This complication is manifested in my own accesses to the lesbian and the Yiddish past. If for many readers the lesbian history project provided the first encounter with Yiddish women's poetry, for me, the Yiddish component is what gave me full access to this lesbian project at a time when I was still trying to understand it, and myself. As I negotiated my own sexuality and identity in my first years of graduate school, lesbian literature was my guilty pleasure. It was only through Yiddish—and through the sage advice of one of my teachers, Elizabeth Abel—that I realized that this lesbian literature did not have to be my (nonacademic) mistress (as Abel put it). Rather, it was part of what was connecting me to the past, and to the very act of searching for new pasts that Yiddish had always represented for me. Legitimizing my interest in lesbian literature also entailed making English a central language of my investigation. This choice brought me back to my mother (and father's) tongue, and to my surprise, brought me back to Israel/Palestine, where I was hired as a scholar of American literature.

For Jewish American lesbians of the 1970s, the turn to Yiddish was not only a turn to the past, but also served as a present intervention, for it was the very frustration with the Zionist focus of American Jewish politics in the 1970s to the 1980s that led Jewish lesbians backward toward Yiddish, positioning it again over and against Hebrew, past and present. The (limited) lesbian turn to Hebrew, which is also represented in lesbian letters, was not as a turn backward, but across, connecting to the story of the nascent lesbian movement in Israel rather than to historical Hebrew-speaking figures. The connection with the Israeli women's movement is based not only in lesbianism and Judaism but also in a shared politics against the Occupation.[37] Similarly, my own turn to the Yiddish past reflected a frustration with contemporary politics. In both cases, the past is recruited to rethink and indeed reconfigure the present; turning to the past, as Blanche Cook wrote in 1979, gives us "the resources and the evidence to name and analyze our world" so we "may begin to change its very contours."[38] The project of lesbian history, and the project of Yiddish are, then, contemporary political projects.

In the present, where Yiddish is no longer a widely circulating language of Jewish literature, (hetero)normative history would only tell the story of its demise, especially once we take into account the way the rise of Hebrew has been cemented into a national narrative. Linguistically speaking, then, the queer histories I identify and create resist a deterministic retrospective reading by which Yiddish was fated to vanish into English or Hebrew. Concurrently, this nonteleological thinking is also crucial for reading Hebrew poetry beyond the national lens, as part of the *Jewish literary complex* (a term I borrow from Dan Miron, and which I ultimately take issue with, precisely for its failure to undo Hebrew's ultimate supremacy).[39] Moreover, I take up the idea of language choice as a temporal choice—of past and future alike—recognizing the role language choice has in the construction and transmission of history. I look at the surprising acquisition of languages outside of the heteronormative model of mother tongue, whether in the choice of certain poets to adopt Modern Hebrew in its process of becoming a vernacular language, or in the choice of certain poets to use Yiddish when it was only just becoming a literary language. Positioning languages *in time*, while reaching for their histories *across time*, renders language a tool of queering temporality.

I also seek to interrogate the process of translation from new angles. When providing translations for the Hebrew and Yiddish texts in this book, I often analyze both the translation and the significance of the act of translation itself (for example, looking at translation as a major aspect of the feminist project of recovering unknown texts of women past). At times, however, I was forced to create my own translations. More than anything, this experience provoked frustration, where more often than not the aspects that drew me to a certain poem were the first ones lost in translation (for example, issues of gender, which are so central in Hebrew and Yiddish and become invisible in English). At the same time, I have come to understand this frustrating exchange as a form of dialogue, where the meaning of the poem and the meaning I mean to make of it, where languages and histories, are activated and negotiated. Finally, through the bilingual Yiddish-English poetry of Irena Klepfisz, lesbian activist and scholar living and writing to this day in New York, I was also able to see translation itself as a site where meanings are queerly undermined and new ones queerly produced. I have thus come to understand translation as a potentially queer process of transition and transformation between languages and between generations. Over and against translation as a naturalizing process that erases difference and construction, I adopt a notion of translation as transgression, creating affective relationships between texts, writers, and readers.

***

As I bring together Yiddish, English, and Hebrew poems seldom if ever before read side by side, the literary history that emerges undoes the linear narratives of each single literature and of the movements between them. Consequently, I am also generating a different mode of literary history. The book's structure reflects this mode, as I move between time and language queerly rather than chronologically. Each of the six chapters brings together poems from multiple times and multiple languages, which I read in relation to their disparate contexts, in relation to their potential connections (whether actual or imagined), and in relation to my own, also ever-shifting moment. Together, poetry, historiography, and theory, create queer connections based in nonlinear cultural transmissions, affective affinities, and cross-temporal encounters, in which I invite the reader to join.

Chapter 1 reads Kadya Molodowsky's Yiddish "Froyen-lider" (Women's Poems/Songs) (1927/28) as answering the expectancy of her foremothers, not by fulfilling their expectations, but by staging a dialogue with them and questioning their power over her. Examining multiple versions of the original poem, as well as multiple instances of its translation, I extend the line Molodowsky draws to the 1970s lesbian poetry of Adrienne Rich. The encounters discussed in this chapter, in life and in text, in conversation and translations, join together to offer queer models of intergenerationality and intertextuality, threading different moments and moments of difference, in multiple queer lines.

Chapter 2 puts queer continuity into practice by setting up nineteenth-century American poet Emma Lazarus as an origin of Jewish women's poetry. Choosing Lazarus, a Sephardic poet writing in English, challenges the Ashkenazi focus of modern Jewish literary scholarship and reverses the dominant narrative describing a unidirectional movement from Yiddish to English. Bringing Lazarus together with Yiddish poet Anna Margolin, who wrote in New York during the 1920s, I identify in the works of both poets a shared strategy of collapsing temporality. Together, the poets construct a queer history extending from Ancient Greece to Mandatory Palestine, while distinctly transgressing borders of identity and chronology, undoing binary divisions and opening up new routes to the Jewish past.

Chapter 3 connects this transgressive approach of Margolin's to the early work of Hebrew poet Leah Goldberg, writing in the 1920s in Eastern Europe. Like Margolin, Goldberg turns to the dominant European culture and to the history of Christianity to carve out a space for Jewish women's poetry. Looking back at Goldberg and Margolin together reveals a moment of multilingual potential, while embracing the pessimism of the poems themselves becomes a mode of connection between past and present. Linking disparate poetic moments together, the chapter connects to the past by virtue of a shared future-resistance.

Chapter 4 brings together historical traces of queer desire in Jewish poetry (in poems by Emma Lazarus and Anna Margolin) and poems of cross-temporal haunting (also by Margolin, as well as Kadya Molodowsky). It explores haunting in general, and lesbian ghosts in particular, as enabling an otherwise impossible movement across time, as well as otherwise forbidden (lesbian/queer) desires. Between absence and presence, ghosting and being ghosted, this chapter creates a lesbian Jewish history that moves queerly across time.

Chapter 5 looks at two moments of community: Ezra Korman's 1928 anthology *Yidishe dikhterins* (Yiddish Women Poets), and the first collection of Jewish lesbian writing, *Nice Jewish Girls* from 1982. Distinguishing the stakes of each of these moments, I also expose overlooked connections between them, while recognizing the challenges posed by actual encounters, including my own encounters with 1970s lesbians. While many feminist projects have aimed to recover women's lost pasts, I explore what it means to write without a past, what the stakes are in recovering the past, and what complications arise when the past is not quite gone. Confronting moments of queer contiguity and contemporaneity, this chapter complicates straight lines of lineage.

Chapter 6 reads the bilingual poetry of Irena Klepfisz, written in New York in the 1980s, as a queer mediation of Yiddish invention and reclamation. We will see Klepfisz writing *as* a lesbian Yiddish woman poet, first using the voice of a Yiddish poet past, and then creating her own original Yiddish poetry. Allowing Yiddish as well as English to voice her poetic and political concerns, and using the English/Yiddish encounter to undermine dominant norms in both languages, Klepfisz invents a model of temporal translation that undoes the borders between past and present, English and Yiddish, creating a poetics of queer historiography.

The closing coda asserts that even if "it is unwise during periods of stress / or change to formulate new theories" (in the words of Irena Klepfisz),[40] the theoretical avenues opened by the material realities of language and sexual politics explored throughout the book all call for a reconsideration of Jewish literary thinking, recognizing the vitality of the alternative pasts and alternative temporalities revealed through Jewish women's poetry.

Like the map of these chapters, my own movement has been equally nonlinear; beginning with a movement from Jerusalem to Berkeley, it follows a circuitous path back through Poland, where instead of searching for Jewish history I joined a nascent lesbian movement, to Tel Aviv where I discovered a queer politics of resistance, to archives in New York, to the Universities of Toronto and Pennsylvania (the very same institutions where each of my grandfathers received their degrees), and finally back to Israel/Palestine, where the situation seems, as always, worse than it has ever been. As I go about building my queer home (familial, academic, political, spiritual), I think of Dareen Tatour, Palestinian citizen of Israel under house arrest for a poem she published online. I think of all of the voices of dissent and cries for justice struggling to be heard, here and worldwide, as the far right's powers continue to rise. It is then that the histories offered by the poems in this book become all the more vital. Not because they are hopeful (you will see, they are not), but because their existence gives me something to look back to, without knowing what to expect.

Looking back in time to and through the poems, I encounter a past very different from the present. In the interwar period, when Hebrew and Yiddish women's writing was emerging, the balance between Hebrew and Yiddish was about to tip, just before Yiddish inherited Hebrew's role as the hallowed language of the Jewish past, a language whose future is in question, much like Hebrew's was. Today one is incredulous at reading Hebrew national poet H. N. Bialik's statement made in 1905 that those invested in the resurrection of Hebrew are also those willing to admit the possibility of the language's final demise.[41] Our distance from this statement is the result of both a century of literary history (and what has been termed the *revolution*[42] of the Hebrew language within the Zionist project), and of the particular way that history has been told. How differently might we read Hebrew today if we reinscribe the fact that its present and future were once highly insecure, that it was not the obvious, natural, or only choice? Embracing Yiddish through its present precariousness can bring back the past precariousness of Hebrew and open a space for future precarious potentialities of a Jewish literature that we cannot yet imagine. Rather than investing in future viability, this literary thinking resists futurity, showing that if we are to rethink Jewish literature, perhaps the future is not where we should be looking at all. Instead, I look back to a past I did not know existed, one so often erased "ere still the light it did see," to quote return to the words of Bat-Miriam. Here I find the "un-expected encounter" of Bat-Miriam's poem, forming a community across time. This book explores such encounters with the past and in the past to generate a genealogy that is not an expression of, but a resistance to biology, linearity, and other hegemonic norms and dictates, offering instead an alternative history of resisting futurity through Jewish women's writing. Taken together, the various chapters of this study share a strategy of turning backward rather than forward; they offer new models of lineage and of potential continuity. Between the pasts that never happened, or whose stories I never knew, and the futures that did not come to be, I find new possibilities for my present. Finally, I recognize that the future I inherited was only one possibility, and I encounter another past, one accessible to me precisely because it already holds the seeds of my disappointment over how the future has turned out, and "over that which will come no more to me," in Bat-Miriam's words. It is in this queer time and place of possibilities foreclosed preemptively and retrospectively that a meeting space is formed. It is there that we may find what Bat-Miriam calls "another essence," which is incumbent on us to keep. Whether or not it ever really *was*, here it is, expectantly waiting.

ONE QUEER LINES
Adrienne Rich and Kadya Molodowsky

> And what was I invoking
> but the matrices we weave
> web upon web, delicate rafters
> flung in audacity to the prairie skies
> nets of telepathy contrived
> to outlast the iron road
> laid out in blood across the land they called virgin
> nets, strands, a braid of hair
> a grandmother's strong hands plaited
> straight down a grand-daughter's back.
>
> —Adrienne Rich, "For Julia in Nebraska"

I take these words from Adrienne Rich, and use them to formulate my own search for a model of queer Jewish literary lineage. What are "the matrices we weave"? Rich offers a series of images: webs, rafters, nets, connections of the body (hair, blood), and of the mind (telepathy). These images are active—they are woven, flung (in audacity!), contrived. They are vast, and will "outlast the iron road," and they are intimate: "a braid of hair / a grandmother's strong hands plaited / straight down a grand-daughter's back." Omitting the possessive pronouns of both the grandmother and (her) granddaughter, Rich casts these women in their respective roles, positioned on a matrilineal matrix of their own making. Coming to this poem, and to the larger history of Jewish women's writing, I too join in the making of this matrix, and offer a queer model of intergenerationality and intertextuality. Drawing out queer connections and conversations within individual texts, among texts past, and between these texts and myself, I thread together different moments and moments of difference, in multiple queer lines.

The women's poems I read (and my reading of them) speak to women past as they speak for them, and often, also, against them. Staging one such encounter in "Froyen-lider" (Women's Poems/Songs), Yiddish poet Kadya Molodowsky negotiates her own model of continuity; as a poetic speaker, she stands up to the women who came before her, while in fact bringing them into being and giving voice to their complaints against her, which she places alongside her defiance of their expectations.

פֿרויען־לידער

I

עס וועלן די פֿרויען פֿון אונדזער משפחה בײַ נאַכט אין חלומות
מיר קומען און זאָגן:
מיר האָבן אין צניעות אַ לויטערע בלוט איבער דורות געטראָגן,
צו דיר עס געבראַכט װי אַ װײַן אַ געהיטן אין כּשרע קעלערס
פֿון אונדזערע הערצער.
און איינע װעט זאָגן:
איך בין אַן עגונה געבליבן װען ס׳זײַנען די באַקן
צװײ רויטלעכע עפּל אויף בוים נאָך געשטאַנען,
און כ'האָב מײַנע צײנער די װײַסע צעקריצט אין די איינזאַמע נעכט פֿון
דערװאַרטונג.
און איך װעל די באָבעס אַנטקעגנגײן זאָגן:
װי האַרבסטיקע װינטן יאָגן נאָך מיר זיך
ניגונים פֿאַרװעלקטע פֿון אײַערע לעבנס.
און איר קומט מיר אַנטקעגן,
װוּ די גאַס איז נאָר טונקל,
און װוּ ס׳לינגט נאָר אַ שאָטן:
און צו װאָס אָט דאָס בלוט אָן אַ טומאה
ס׳זאָל זײַן מײַן געװיסן, װי אַ זײַדענער פֿאָדעם
אויף מײַן מוח פֿאַרבונדן,
און מײַן לעבן אַן אויסגעפּליקט בלאַט פֿון אַ ספֿר,
און די שורה די ערשטע פֿאַרריסן?

The women of our family will come to me in dreams at night
and say:
Modestly we carried a pure blood across generations,

> Bringing it to you like well-guarded wine from the kosher
> Cellars of our hearts.
> And one woman will say:
> I am an abandoned wife, left when my cheeks
> Were two ruddy apples still fixed on the tree,
> And I clenched my white teeth throughout lonely nights
>   of waiting.
> And I will go meet these grandmothers, saying:
> Like winds of the autumn, your lives'
> Withered melodies chase after me.
> And you come to meet me
> Only where streets are in darkness,
> And where only shadows lie:
> And why should this blood without blemish
> be my conscience, like a silken thread
> Bound upon my brain,
> And my life, a page plucked from a holy book,
> The first line torn?[1]

In these lines of the 1927 poem "Froyen-lider," Molodowsky defiantly turns to the women of her family asking why "this blood without blemish" should be her conscience, why her life should be "a page plucked from a holy book, the first line torn." Invoking lines of blood and of text, Molodowsky opens questions of continuity and disruption, offering in fact a queer model which holds both continuity and disruption as inextricably linked, for her connection to the past, and for our connection to her, and through her to the past she conjures; without the struggle with the tradition of the past, without the poem, there would be no *seyfer*, no "holy book" that included the women of her family, whose lives remained unnarrated by the same Jewish tradition. Resist this bloodline though she might, the speaker/poet brings this line into being in her writing.

Of all the Yiddish women poets, Molodowsky is perhaps the most well-known outside of Yiddish-speaking circles, but not as a modernist Yiddish writer. Instead, it is her children's poetry in Hebrew translation that continues to be reprinted and circulates as a staple in many Israeli homes.[2] This is certainly an unexpected legacy for a writer who distinctly chose Yiddish over Hebrew. Born in the shtetl Bereza Kartuska, Belarus, in 1894 to a Yiddish-speaking family,

Molodowsky was educated in Russian and Hebrew.[3] She was part of both Yiddish and Hebrew educational endeavors in interwar Warsaw and Odessa, where she also began publishing Yiddish poetry. She immigrated to the United States with her husband in 1935. The two attempted to settle in the newly established State of Israel in 1949, but after only three years they returned to the United States,[4] where Molodowsky continued publishing poetry and prose, and edited the Yiddish literary journal *Svive*, until her death in 1975. As much as Molodowsky's modernist poetry, children's writing, and Yiddish publishing projects separate her from the kosher lives of her foremothers, for today's reader these endeavors now serve as a link, allowing us to connect both to Molodowsky and to her predecessors.

Transgressing borders of language and time, Molodowsky's poem stages a queer cross-temporal encounter and enacts its own form of queer dialogue. Molodowsky stages an imagined encounter between the speaker and her foremothers, where the women implicitly demand that the speaker continue their pure bloodline. The poet/speaker resists this demand in the lines quoted above, asking "*tsu vos?*," "why?," or even, "to what end?" their demands should dictate how she leads her own, apparently divergent, life. The tentative nature of the encounter is emphasized by the future tense *veln* [will], and even there it is relegated to the space of the speaker's dream. This dream realm, the place of meeting, is also cast in the poem as the "dark street," "*vu di gas iz nor tunkl*"—not where a nice Jewish girl should be, but rather the dark streets where immodest female sexuality is performed (and indeed in a later poem in the same cycle she invokes these "*gasn-meydlekh*," "streetwalkers"). This marginal space is where the speaker can come *antkegn* (toward but also against), meeting the grandmothers halfway and asserting herself against them. As they berate her for all the hard work they put into keeping their bloodline kosher for her, she retorts that their very piety and the price they paid for it was what drove her out onto the streets, away from their legacy.

In answering the women, the speaker disidentifies herself from them, but in the same move also binds herself to them. For she is not only haunted by their *nign*, the sacred song of their life/story, she is also the one writing it. If patriarchal history denied much of women's cultural transmission, she re-creates it, at the same time as she attempts to reject it. For Molodowsky and the Jewish women of her time, becoming a woman writer meant breaking with tradition, but it is also what transmits to us the history of women, transforming the unwritten *farvelkte nigunim*, the "withered melodies" of their lives, into poetry. The *nign* is a perfect image for this move, for it is a wordless melody. For the *nigunim* were not meant to be, nor could they be, written. Furthermore, women could sing these melodies despite not knowing the Hebrew words of other prayers. Putting the *nigunim* in the mouths of women takes them out of the realm of male-dominated religious tradition, while exposing how aspects of this tradition are already aligned in many ways with female experience.

The poet looks back to question Jewish tradition's hold on her, as well as her stake in it. At the same time, she refuses to be detached from it, as she rejects the notion of her life being "a page plucked from a holy book, the first line torn," by posing a defiant question to her foremothers. Of course, a page plucked from a holy book is still holy, and in Jewish tradition such a page would receive sacred burial in the *gnize*, marking Molodowsky as still inextricably linked to the tradition she cannot be torn away from. Similarly, the bloodline she questions is also one that promises continuity regardless of whether its pure state is upheld, insuring a specifically matrilineal form of bequeathal and belonging.[5] By invoking the bloodline and the line of text in this one verse, Molodowsky establishes the thread as a connection, challenges its necessity and continuity, and questions the inevitability of severing its binding ties, ties with the past, with tradition, with the history of women. Queerly combining modalities of lineage, lineage of blood and lineage of text, she complicates the concept of the pure, continuous, and compulsory line of blood, which would demand a certain type of biological continuity that she refuses. At the same time, she challenges the idea of the complete break embodied in the ripped line of the *seyfer*'s text.

My reading here is itself a page ripped out of the eight-poem sequence within which it was originally published. Beautifully reading the entire sequence, Kathryn Hellerstein draws out the speaker's complicated position toward reproduction. If in the poem read above, the resistance to reproduction is implicit in the speaker's refusal to continue the kosher bloodline, Hellerstein shows that taken together, the poems of the sequence "exclude the dramatic speaker of 'Froyen-lider' for whom conventional female fertility seems impossible."[6] Offering one of the earliest feminist interventions in Yiddish scholarship,[7] and indeed preempting the queerest aspects of my own reading, Hellerstein suggests that "the speaker is engaged in a creative act that requires no man."[8] In this sequence, writes Hellerstein, "the poem itself becomes a metaphor for childbearing, and that childbearing a metaphor for creating in general."[9] Hellerstein positions this metaphor as an expression of, and resolution for, the conflict between women's productivity and their creativity. Hellerstein traces the inheritance of this conflict in the feminist movement and literary scholarship of the 1970s and 1980s,¹⁰ writing that "the conflict that Molodowsky faced was, in fact, only reformulated in 1972 by the American poet Adrienne Rich: 'To be a female human being, trying to fulfill traditional female functions in a traditional way, is in direct conflict with the subversive function of the imagination.'"¹¹

Rich not only "reformulated" Molodowsky's conflict, she also translated it from Yiddish into English for the *Treasury of Yiddish Poetry*, thereby linking herself back to Molodowsky.¹² When I first encountered Rich's translation, I was struck by how different it was from the translation I was familiar with, that of Kathryn Hellerstein. On first encountering Rich's translation, I ascribed the difference between Rich and Hellerstein's texts to their sensibilities as translators. My assumption was bolstered by how well the differences in translations seemed to correlate to the difference in the poetic politics of each of the translators. While literary scholar Kathryn Hellerstein pioneered the feminist study of Yiddish literature, she is also a meticulously attentive translator, attempting to remain loyal to the different linguistic and poetic elements prioritized by the poet herself,¹³ while theorizing the implications of feminist translation.¹⁴ Adrienne Rich's translation, on the other hand, did not match the Yiddish original I was familiar with. And though it seemed jarring to imagine a translator altering Molodowsky's text (and I assumed Rich had) the fact that the translator of this version was Adrienne Rich, radical lesbian poet, certainly seemed to account for the changes she made. It was not until I opened Ezra Korman's 1928 anthology *Yidishe dikhterins*, the first anthology of Yiddish women's poetry¹⁵ (which chapter 5 will discuss extensively) that I realized the two translations actually reflected two separate original versions. Following this discovery, I was faced with the irreducible multiplicity of women's history, not only in the form of multiple translations, but also in the multiple versions of the original Yiddish poem.¹⁶ In what follows I will trace these multiple texts as another incarnation of the queer historical model for which I am arguing.

The first version appeared in 1927, in Molodowsky's debut book of poems, *Khezhvndike nekht*,¹⁷ and the second followed closely, appearing in 1928, in Korman's *Yidishe dikhterins*. The proximity of these publication dates makes it hard to determine which was the first to be written, as one would need to know when Molodowsky's manuscript was submitted to her Warsaw publisher, and then to Korman.¹⁸ Without knowing which came first, a brief comparison of the final stanzas of each version and of their translations will illuminate two markedly different modes of encounter set up by the poet.¹⁹

פֿרויען-לידער

I

עס וועלן די פֿרויען פֿון אונדזער משפחה בײַ נאַכט אין חלומות מיר
קומען און זאָגן:
מיר האָבן אין צניעות אַ לויטערע בלוט איבער דורות געטראָגן,
צו דיר עס געבראַכט ווי אַ ווײַן אַ געהיטן אין כּשרע קעלערס
פֿון אונדזערע הערצער.
און איינע וועט זאָגן:
איך בין אַן עגונה געבליבן ווען ס'זײַנען די באַקן
צוויי רויטלעכע עפּל אויף בוים נאָך געשטאַנען,
און כ'האָב מײַנע ציינער די ווײַסע צעקריצט אין די איינזאַמע נעכט פֿון
דערוואַרטונג.

און איך וועל די באָבעס אַנטקעגן גיין זאָגן:
אייערע זיפֿצן האָבן וי פֿאַכיקע בייטשן געאָטעמט
און האָבן מיין לעבן מיין יונגן געטריבן פֿון שטוב צום אַרויסגאַנג,
פֿון אייערע פּשרע בעטן אַנטלויפֿן.
נאָר איר גייט מיר נאָך, וווּ די גאַס איז נאָר טונקל,
וווּ ס'פֿאַלט נאָר אַ שאָטן.
און אייערע שטילע פֿאַרשטיקטע געוויינען יאָגן נאָך מיר זיך וי
האַרבסטיקע ווינטן,
און אייערע רייד זיינען זיידענע פֿעדעם אויף מיין מוח פֿאַרבונדן.
און מיין לעבן אַן אויסגעפֿליקט בלאַט פֿון אַ ספֿר
און די שורה די ערשטע פֿאַרריסן.

The faces of women long dead, of our family,
come back in the night, come in dreams to me saying:
We have kept our blood pure through long generations,
we brought it to you like a sacred wine
from the kosher cellars of our hearts.
And one of them whispers:
I remained deserted, when my two rosy apples
still hung on the tree
and I gritted away the long nights of waking between my
    white teeth.
I will go meet the grandmothers, saying:
Your sighs were the whips that lashed me
and drove my young life to the threshold
to escape from your kosher beds.
But wherever the street grows dark you pursue me—
wherever a shadow falls.

Your whimperings race like the autumns winds past me,
and your words are the silken cord
still binding my thoughts,
My life is a page ripped out of a holy book
and part of the first line is missing.
(Trans. Adrienne Rich)

און איך וועל די באָבעס אַנקעגנגייןן זאָגן:
ווי האַרבסטיקע ווינטן יאָגן נאָך מיר זיך
ניגונים פֿאַרוועלקטע פֿון אייַערע לעבנס.
און איר קומט מיר אַנקעגן,
ווו די גאַס איז נאָר טונקל,
און ווו ס'ליגט נאָר אַ שאָטן:
און צו וואָס אָט דאָס בלוט אָן אַ טומאה
ס'זאָל זייַן מייַן געוויסן, ווי אַ זייַדענער פֿאָדעם
אויף מייַן מוח פֿאַרבונדן,
און מייַן לעבן אַן אויסגעפֿליקט בלאַט פֿון אַ ספֿר
און די שורה די ערשטע פֿאַרריסן?

The women of our family will come to me in dreams at
    night and say:
Modestly we carried a pure blood across generations,
Bringing it to you like well-guarded wine from the kosher
Cellars of our hearts.
And one woman will say:
I am an abandoned wife, left when my cheeks
Were two ruddy apples still fixed on the tree,
And I clenched my white teeth throughout lonely nights
    of waiting.
And I will go meet these grandmothers, saying:
Like winds of the autumn, your lives'
Withered melodies chase after me.
And you come to meet me
Only where streets are in darkness,
And where only shadows lie:
And why should this blood without blemish
be my conscience, like a silken thread
Bound upon my brain,
And my life, a page plucked from a holy book,
The first line torn?
(Trans. Kathryn Hellerstein)

The first Yiddish version presented here is from Kadya Molodowsky's *Khezhvndike nekht*, and the second one is from Korman's *Yidishe dikhterins*. Kathryn Hellerstein's translation is based on the version from *Khezhvndike nekht* whereas Adrienne Rich's translation is based on Korman's version. Neither translation is entirely accurate, yet each highlights interesting aspects of Molodowsky's poetics while revealing the translators' position in the poetic politics of translation. Both Yiddish versions open with the *bobes*, the grandmothers, coming to the speaker, yet in each version the encounter and its implications play out differently: In the version from *Khezhvndike nekht* the speaker goes to "meet these grandmothers," and they "come to meet" her, repeating the adverb *antkegn* (against/toward) for the speaker and foremothers alike, thereby creating a meeting space in the middle. In the Korman version, the speaker goes toward the women in an identical verse, "*ikh vel di bobes antkegn geyn*" (I will go meet the grandmothers), yet instead of coming to meet her they "pursue her" (*ir geyt mir nokh*). Their "sighs like whips" (*ziftsn vi fokhike baytshn*), and their silent cries chase her, driving her from their (and her own) kosher beds, highlighting the unkosherness of the speaker and marking the dark streets where they meet as sites for potential sexual impropriety. The image of the *koshere betn* is strikingly absent from the *Khezhvndike nekht* version, downplaying the centrality of sexuality in comparison to the Korman version. On the other hand, the Korman version does not include the metaphor of "blood without blemish" (*blut on a tume*), limiting the centrality of the blood metaphor overall.[20]

The *Khezhvndike nekht* version represents blood simultaneously as biological and religious regulation, both of which the speaker can, and does, reject—the women may have toiled to keep their blood *kosher*, but neither *tume* (impurity) nor *tsnies* (modesty) will define the speaker's blood as it does theirs. Defiantly asking *tsu vos?*, "why should this blood without blemish / be my conscience, like a silken thread . . . ?," the speaker questions the idea that this blood must define her actions. Instead of blood, the Korman version offers speech, *reyd*, as that which is still binding: "and your words are the silken cord / still binding my thoughts." Whether blood or words, both versions construct the binding through the image of a silken cord or threads. However, as opposed to the singular *fodem* (thread) of the bloodline in the *Khezhvndike nekht* version, Korman's version portrays the binding words in the plural, *fedem* (threads, which Rich then translates as the singular "cord"), serving as a multivocal chorus of ever-haunting cries and sighs. Instead of these sighs, cries, and most importantly, words, the version in *Khezhvndike nekht* represents the women's voices only as "withered melodies" ("*farvelkte nigunim*"). While the *nign* can be read as a possible image of women's continuous nonverbal tradition (as I suggested above), the fact that it is withered implies not only that it is ancient, but also a lack of tending, care and use—by the women, their *svive* (environment, also the title of the literary journal Molodowsky edited) and later their descendants. For the speaker, these *nigunim* no longer hold the power of prayer. Like the kosher blood, they are not enough to hold her.

Perhaps the most significant difference between the two versions and the respective models of encounter they portray lies in the closing line, posed as a defiant question in the first version and a definitive affirmative statement in the second. If in one the speaker questions why the ancestors' pure blood should bind her, in the other she declares herself bound by their words. The two versions thus set up alternative modalities of genealogy, that of words and that of blood. When it comes to blood, the speaker can defy the tie, along with the religious injunctions it carries. It is because the bloodline is controlled by oppressive religious categories that the speaker can and must rebel against it. However, posing the final statement as a question, why, to what end (*tsu vos*) should her life be a "page plucked from a holy book / The first line torn?" simultaneously undermines the ties that bind her, as well as the necessity of a break from these ties. Similarly, the version that declares that her "life is a page ripped out of a holy book / and part of the first line is missing"[21] also works against its own definitiveness, opening a bond that is not biological, but textual. The women's words cannot be rebelled against like the bloodline, which implies that the biological bloodline, however immutable, is more open to challenge than the constructed textual one. For indeed, the textual line needs the speaker to bring it into being before it can be rejected. The sighs and cries, as well as the *nigunim*, must become words, as they finally do through the poem, ventriloquized by the poet/speaker, making the bond one of narrative transmission. The foremothers will haunt the speaker until she gives them voice, thereby finding her own voice, so that she can take a stand against them. She renders them expectant, at the same time she insists on becoming a future that resists their expectations.

If each of the Yiddish versions offers different models of encounter, the translations themselves also differ, with Rich's translation accentuating the distance and conflict more extremely than Hellerstein's, and more extremely than both Yiddish versions as well. Therefore, even if my initial suspicion that Rich had altered the poem was refuted when I discovered the second Yiddish original, the mark of Rich's poetics, as well as of her politics, is striking. This is apparent in the first line, which is the same in both Yiddish versions: "*Es veln di froyen fun undzer mishpokhe / Bay nakht in khaloymes mir kumen,*" translated by Rich as "The faces of women long dead, of our family, / come back in the night, come in dreams to me," as opposed to Hellerstein's: "the women of our family will come to me in dreams at night." Metonymically replacing the women with their faces, and inserting the adjective "dead," doubly differentiates the specters from the speaker. This is not a happy family reunion but an external invasion, repeated as the women "come back in the night," as opposed to Hellerstein's "will come"—a singular, tentative, even hypothetical projected (future) encounter.

Moreover, Rich's version accentuates the physicality and sexuality of the poem. In the Yiddish line "*kh'hob mayne tseyner di vayse tsekritst in di eynzame nekht / fun dervartung,*" instead of the speaker clenching her "white teeth throughout lonely nights," as in Hellerstein's translation, which closely mirrors the Yiddish, the speaker in Rich's translation "gritted away the long nights of waking between my white / teeth." Rich not only translates the Yiddish into English, but also converts the physical symptoms of frustration into poetic metaphor. Rich also makes changes to the layout of the poem, isolating the word *teeth* from the rest of the line and placing it in a line unto itself, thereby recasting the physicality she poetically converts, opening it to implicit sexual innuendo, and making the space "between" not the space between teeth but between white thighs or other body parts. The sexualizing aspect of the translation is also evident when Rich translates Molodowsky's metaphor in the previous line: "*s'zaynen di bakn / tsvey roytlekhe epl oyf boym nokh geshtanen.*" What Hellerstein closely translates as "my cheeks / Were two ruddy apples still fixed on the tree," Rich translates as "my two rosy apples / still hung on the tree," leaving just the apples hanging at the end of the line. Again using enjambment, and omitting the tenor of the metaphor (the cheeks), the rosy apples seem much more readily read as breasts than as cheeks. However, the heightened sexualization of Rich's translation also bring her closer to other elements in the original text, namely Molodowsky's choice to describe the apples as standing (*geshtanen*), rather than hanging, much like young breasts would. Rich's interpretation by way of translation therefore retroactively highlights the ways the original was already anything but *tsniesdik* (modest).

Rich herself did not have direct access to the Yiddish original, for, as we know from much of her writing, she had little contact with Jewish texts during her upbringing, and had less exposure to Jewish languages such as Yiddish or Hebrew than writers who came from a more traditional Jewish background.[22] Trying to reclaim and then contain both Jewish and lesbian/feminist histories, Rich "redefines her view of her own past and the history of women: the two cannot be separated," as Kathy Rugoff writes.[23] Focusing on the familial drama, Rugoff explores how Rich positions herself in relation to the legacy of her father, both as a representative of Jewish patriarchy and as a victim of internalized anti-Semitism. She goes on to note how, "ironically, after rejecting the language of her father, she enters into a dialogue with the poetry of the Jewish fathers."[24] However, through Yiddish, Rich engages not just with the poetry of the fathers, but also with women's poetry, written in a tongue that has long been identified with feminine creativity. "If Hebrew presents itself as the 'Name of the Father' within the family drama of language acquisition," writes Naomi Seidman in her pioneering work on the sexual politics of Yiddish and Hebrew, *A Marriage Made in Heaven*, "Yiddish is even more strongly linked to maternity or grand-maternity."[25] "Froyen-lider," in Rich's translation, brings this matrilineal story into English, missing lines, languages, and all.

According to Hellerstein, Rich arrived at Molodowsky's poems through Irving Howe[26] and needed to work with more literal prose translations out of which she fashioned her own poetic (and political) rendition, linking "Froyen-lider" not just back to the *sforim*, the holy books, but forward, to the tradition of radical lesbian poetry and queer reading, in its irreverent and transgressive relation to norms of translation. But of course, these translations were done before Rich was out as a lesbian on the front lines of the women's liberation movement, making this reading of mine anachronistically queer, as well as a queer anachronism. For what is anachronistic here is not just treating Rich as lesbian before she was out, but enacting the type of queer temporal transgression I perform throughout this book, the same way I term the staging of Molodowsky's encounter as queer. Yet in deeming Rich's translations as queer, I have an additional goal: to undermine the traditional male-centered (and indeed misogynist) sexual politics of translation, as well as the heteronormative intergenerationality within which they are embedded.

Critiquing the sexual politics of translation metaphorics, Lori Chamberlain summarizes George Steiner's four-part model:[27] the translator begins with "initiative trust" in the text, moving toward an aggressive "penetrating" and "capturing" of the text; followed by making the text "naturalized" in the translator's language, literally incorporated or embodied in it; and finally—in order to compensate for the "appropriative 'rapture' "—reciprocity and restitution, as the translator attempts to make amends for the act of aggression. According to Chamberlain, Steiner's model shows that the metaphorics of translation "is a symptom of larger issues of western culture: of the power relations as they divide in terms of gender" (465). In the case of Yiddish translation, the sexual politics of translation are particularly acute, if we consider the language's position both historically and geographically, taking into account the ways it has been historically feminized even before coming to be translated (or not translated), in relation to Hebrew and in relation to other "proper" languages. However, as Chana Kronfeld notes, Chamberlain shows that "the power relation between source and target texts (and their attendant cultures) determines who is gendered female ('marked,' in linguistic terms) in the marriage/translation contract";[28] that is, there are no stable hierarchical relations between "original" and "translation," for their disparate contexts play a crucial role in determining the power relations in each case. For "translation as a practice shapes, and takes shape within, the asymmetrical relations of power that operate under colonialism,"[29] writes Tejaswini Niranjana, and indeed we can apply this critical positioning to many other contexts within which power is unequally deployed, such as the case of Hebrew/Yiddish, as well as Yiddish/English.

In today's context, the precarious state of Yiddish renders it doubly susceptible to annihilation by translation, for the status and the survival of the original are themselves in question. Accordingly, Anita Norich posits that the discourse on Yiddish translation "suggests that, in the original, these texts will no longer be read by anyone but will, like their intended audience, disappear."[30] At the same time, however, Norich rightly observes, "translation is also an act of resistance to history, an act of defiance that preserves a culture whose transformations should not be met with silence."[31] Setting up a tense dichotomy between source and target text, Norich reminds Yiddish translators, following Steiner, of the etymological links among translation, transgression, and aggression: "Translators literally carry something over from one place (or language) to another. In doing so, they necessarily transgress—step beyond their point of origin. And the act of aggression—attack—thus performed is inevitable."[32]

Hellerstein, on the other hand, formulates a notion of feminist translation of Yiddish "where each translation continually converses with its original, which does not vanish, but shimmers beneath the second language. A fluid interpretation, the translation talks. Rereading, answering, querying, it keeps the text in motion."[33] Let us not, she writes, "close off a Yiddish text in a 'definitive' translation. Let us not condemn translators as traitors. Rather, let us strengthen the fluid, reciprocal conversation between Yiddish poems and English poems."[34]

I want to continue "the text in motion" as my model for reading across languages and historical moments, while questioning the inevitable attack Norich invokes by undermining the linearity of the movement from source to target text. As Barbara Johnson writes, it is by miming "the process of departing from an origin" that translation "enhances the belief that there *is* an origin."[35] Or in Judith Butler's framing of the same point from the opposite direction, "The origin requires its derivations in order to affirm itself as an origin, for origins only make sense to the extent that they are differentiated from that which they produce as derivatives."[36] That is, we only know something to be an origin if it has copies, which we can then describe (only retroactively) as deriving from it. In this framework, both the notion of copy and the notion of origin are equally dependent on each other, and are therefore deeply unstable. This instability "confounds the possibility of stably locating the temporal or logical priority of either term."[37] While it might be easy to point to a translation's status as a derivative of the original, Butler and Johnson offer a framing that undermines the power dynamic between original and translation, and specifically the need for the translation's act of aggression against the original. This opens space for the recognition that this aggression might be less inevitable outside of heteronormative metaphorics.

The notion of translation I am proposing here is in fact a manifestation of the queer intergenerational model I am in search of. If feminist notions of translation already open up not only a sexualized/gendered dynamic, they also deploy metaphorics of kinship, as Naomi Seidman writes: "Translation and paternity announce a relation, between source and target texts, between father and child, that is open to disruption by the very conduit—the translator/mother—through which this relationship is established."[38] But of course, the queer intergenerational model cannot adhere solely to this nuclear family model, and must therefore undo "the legal and contractual apparatus that hedges kinship and translation."[39] Combining Seidman's challenge to kinship with the Hellerstein's notion of motion, alongside Johnson and Butler's undermining of the linear trajectory between source and target texts, I argue for a queer intertextual and intergenerational dialogue model that is, as Jack Halberstam suggests, "outside the frameworks of conflict or mandatory continuity."[40]

Instead of aggression, I embrace transgression, translational, temporal, and otherwise. If Molodowsky herself begins this transgression by simultaneously invoking multiple voices in her Yiddish poem and resisting both conflict and continuity, we can see her translators as joining her queer line, bringing her voice into English, while making it also their own. Specifically, I want to focus on Rich as queering translation. By virtue of *not knowing* Yiddish, Rich undermines the binary between original and translation. In so doing she challenges the conservative privileging of native fluency, which relies on (heteronormative) intergenerational transmission. This challenge to transmission is also a challenge to the blood-based framework of identity transmission that dominates hegemonic conceptions of Judaism, according to which Rich would not be considered Jewish because her mother was not Jewish. Rich's translations, writings, and life story all offer an alternative narrative of movement and multiplicity. Translating Molodowsky, Rich queers translation itself, generating a new conversation between English and Yiddish poetry.

In her own poetry, Rich herself continued to grapple with the same dichotomy of continuity and discontinuity we saw in Molodowsky, employing the very same figures of grandmothers and blood. As opposed to the unmarked grandmother and granddaughter from the poem "For Julia in Nebraska," which opened this chapter, Rich's poem "Granddaughter,"[41] published in the same collection, is a triptych telling the story of Rich's two grandmothers, for whom the first two poems are named: "Mary Gravely Jones" and "Hattie Rice Rich." The third poem is dedicated to the granddaughter herself.

3. Granddaughter

Easier to encapsulate your lives
in a slide-show of impressions given and taken,
to play the child or victim, the projectionist,
easier to invent a script for each of you,
myself still at the center,
than to write words in which you might have found
yourselves, looked up at me and said
"Yes, I was like that; but I was something more . . ."
[. . .]

> Born a white woman, Jewish or of curious mind
> —twice an outsider, still believing in inclusion—
> in those defended hamlets of half-truth
> *broken in two by one strange idea,*
> "blood" the all powerful, awful theme—
> what were the lessons to be learned? If I believe
> the daughter of one of you—amnesia was the answer.
>
> 1980

In this poem, Rich explicitly formulates the task I attributed to Molodowsky of bringing her foremothers into being through writing, and confesses that she has chosen the easier task easier of inventing a script for them. This invention is part of her struggle against amnesia, represented in the poem by in the solution of the daughter (who is the speaker's mother). Instead, here and throughout her long poetic career, Rich turns to the project of remembering: "routine remembering. Putting together, inch by inch / the starry worlds. From all the lost collections."[42] Far from amnesia, she uses recovery, invention and translation of the past as a thread connecting a community of women within the political moment of women's liberation, and across history, creating what she defined elsewhere as a "lesbian continuum."

Offering a parallel model of continuity, Jewish historian Yosef Haim Yerushalmi coins the term "continuum of memory." Interestingly, he insists this continuum is *not* a silken thread, thereby joining Molodowsky's resistance to the image of binding continuity. Instead he offers his own version of the "Chain of Tradition" ("*shalshelet hakabalah,*" which can be translated as the chain of transmission, or even more accurately, the chain of reception). Turning back to the model found in *Pirkey Avot*, Yerushalmi understands the chain to be comprised of a "dual movement of reception and transmission, successively propelling itself towards the future." This dual movement, he writes, renders "the continuum of memory" as "links in a chain," rather than a "silken thread."[43] Through the complications offered by Yerushalmi, Rich, and Molodowsky, I suggest that a concept of queer transmission allows for multiple and simultaneous links, not only backward and forward, but every which way, at any given time. This model refigures the image of the singular, continuous chain within Jewish tradition, endowing it with new spatiotemporal movements and multiplicity, much like the mixed metaphor of web and scaffolding Bonnie Kime Scott employs to reorganize women's modernist writing, allowing for exploration of various attachments while considering their difficulties.[44] Chana Kronfeld proposes her own metaphor for the complex transmission of literary history—the image of a rope, following Wittgenstein:[45] "... as in spinning a thread we twist fibre on fibre. And the strength of the thread does not reside in the fact that some one fibre runs through its whole length, but in the overlapping of many fibres."[46] This rope serves Kronfeld "as a visual enticement to reconfigure the literary trend as an open-ended category that maintains a culturally structured family resemblance among its members rather than being defined by a series of necessary and sufficient conditions."[47] If Kronfeld asks us to complicate the interactions that define familial resemblance, Michael Gluzman shows how the very reliance on familial models has been detrimental to women's writing, as the very theories that use family models for the description of literary history manage to exclude women from the one place patriarchy has traditionally reserved for them: the family.[48] Gilbert and Gubar similarly sought to rewrite Harold Bloom's male-centered theory of literary influence as father/son struggle.[49] Both Adrienne Rich and Kadya Molodowsky poetically enact alternative models for literary transmission, by bringing into being pasts, and specifically female pasts, with which they can negotiate. Beyond invoking her own images of web, rafter and braid connecting the female line of grandmother and granddaughter (as we saw in the epigraph), in her introduction to Irena Klepfisz's poetry, Rich writes that having "as birthright a poetic tradition that everyone around you recognizes and respects is a privilege,"[50] not because of what you get to continue, but because of what you can negotiate, inhabit and reject: "like a family from which, even in separation, you bring away certain gestures, tones, ways of looking: something taken for granted, perhaps felt as constriction, nonetheless a source, a point of departure." Rich thus formulates a version of the complex combination of continuity and disruption, much like we saw in Molodowsky's poetically defiant dialogue.

I am acutely aware of the privilege of having a past with which I must negotiate, specifically in terms of lesbian history, a history far too new to be taken for granted. The lesbian movement has made tremendous effort to make visible the lines of lesbian history, and women's history more broadly, and Jewish women's history more specifically, as this book argues. Part of my claim is that women have been denied access to history—whether participation in its events or in its record. This,

I argue, is even truer for lesbians, making the creation of history a central project for the lesbian movement. In the Jewish case, I tie women's disenfranchisement to the patriarchal nature of Jewish ritual and textuality (and specifically, maybe, to denying them access not just to sacred texts but to the Hebrew language). But it is not just Jewish women who "take issue" with history; rather, it has been suggested that Jews themselves "find the work of the historian irrelevant." Indeed, Yerushalmi's book *Zakhor* offers a stunning reading of the Jewish entry into history in the nineteenth century. While it is not my concern here to trace the dynamics of traditional Jewish approaches to history, or of modern Jewish historiography for that matter, there is one element from each (the traditional and the modern) that shapes the lineage this book goes in search of/creates: (1) the traditional concept of "contemporaneity" and (2) the idea of history of/as rupture, respectively.

Conceptualizing contemporaneity is key to the discussions in this chapter and this book, as should be clear from the type of cross-historical encounter we've been reading within, as well as the encounter between poems and languages. According to Yerushalmi, those inside the "enchanted circle" of Jewish tradition "seek, not the historicity of the past, but its internal contemporaneity." This internal contemporaneity is about *feeling* the past, and more—about feeling as though we were in the past, or as if the past was *now*. For example, to this day, for Jews celebrating Passover, the imperative is to see themselves as if *they* were coming out of Egypt. In this sense, writes Yerushalmi, "the historical events of the Biblical period remain unique and irreversible," while psychologically "those events are experienced cyclically, repetitively, and to that extent at least, atemporally."[51] Another fascinating example Yerushalmi gives is temporality in rabbinical literature, where famous figures (such as Moses) appear anachronistically across history.

Bringing together anachronism (across history), contemporaneity (within multiple histories), and atemporality (beyond/outside history), this complex mapping fits squarely within Carolyn Dinshaw's definition of queer history: "What it feels like to be a body in time, or in multiple times, or out of time, is a *queer* history—whatever else it may be."[52] Through Dinshaw's queer history, the dichotomy Yerushalmi poses between "historicity" and "contemporaneity" is refigured: an experience of contemporaneity is the basic condition that makes historical understanding possible.[53] Over and against an assumption that historicity would foreclose contemporaneous connections, queer history uses bodies to make connections, implicating bodies past and present, making them pleasurably touch. This corporeal activation undermines the linearity of time not with a repetitive psychological cycle, but with a fluctuating simultaneity that recognizes sameness and difference, altering both past and present in the process. It is through bodies in time—"their pleasures, their agonies, their limits, their potentials"—that a queer temporality can emerge, enlarging "singular narratives of development."[54] Considering bodies generates a historical awareness that is deeply embedded in individual disparate times, while the very idea of connection across time undermines the separation between past and present, undoing notions of linear progression. Thus, embodied time offers a contemporaneity that is noncontemporaneous, "a queer historical awareness of multiplicity."[55] It is this approach that enables me to read Molodowsky's poem as cross-temporally queer, and to stage a conversation between Molodowsky and Rich, by way of translation and by way of imagination. However, history has also offered moments where noncontemporaneous contemporaneity are embodied events, as evidenced by way of one rare image, of none other than Kadya Molodowsky and Adrienne Rich.

Courtesy of Arnold Chekow

This photograph was taken by Arnold Chekow on November 2, 1969. The occasion was the publication of Rich's translations of Molodowsky's "Froyen-lider" in the anthology *A Treasury of Yiddish Poetry*.[56] The two women mirror each other, both sitting cross-legged, each clasping her own hands. Molodowsky's white hair radiates around her face under her dark hat, in contrast to Rich's shining long dark hair, soon to be replaced by short hair, once she came out. Molodowsky's light dress is finally *tsniesdik* in the manner her foremothers demanded, covering her elbows and knees, while Rich's short dress, barely covering her thighs, marks the height of fashion of the moment, also soon to be replaced by less feminine clothing, in line with the particular 1970s lesbian fashion dictates that were marked by a turn to a more androgynous style (departing not just from heterosexual fashion, but also from earlier lesbian butch/femme fashion). Both women turn sideways, gazing at a source absent from the image, presumably the person reading at the front of the stage, while the third figure, John Hollander, stares blankly forward.[57] Hollander was also one of Molodowsky's translators for this anthology. Like Rich, Hollander was a recipient of the Yale Series of Younger Poets award (he in 1958, and she in 1951). This award distinguishes them both as notable English-language poets celebrating the beginning of their careers, and though the photo comes long after they received this recognition for their poetic promise, for the fleeting moment of this photo, they still both represent the "Younger Poets" in comparison with the aging Yiddish poetess. Neither of them spoke Yiddish fluently,[58] and neither continued publishing Yiddish translations beyond that point.[59]

In the moment we glimpse here, Yiddish and English, as read by Molodowsky and Rich, coexisted even if they could not talk to each other. Their encounter thus materializes the intergenerational dream encounter of Molodowsky's "Froyenlider" poem, if not Rich's *Dream of a Common Language*. But even if Rich and Molodowsky do not share a language, these two very different women can share a page and the stage, creating a community of Jewish women's poetry that transcends the rushing currents of history, even as, or precisely by, diving into them. The simultaneity exposed here does not open a dialogue; rather, it exposes the opposite trajectories of English and Yiddish poetry, embodied in the poets—Molodowsky's body tells the story of her impending death in 1975; a year later, in 1976, Rich came out as a lesbian, becoming a radical voice who would no longer be invited to share the spotlight of mainstream Jewish literature (at least not until much later in her life, and then too with a set of strings attached).[60]

Taking into account this very real encounter, alongside the imagined encounters this chapter has read, I want to ask how we might imagine a historical model that builds at once on historicity and contemporaneity, on blood and text, a narrative that refuses to be trapped in or relegated outside of tradition but rather generates new modes of continuity through the very breaks with and in history. "Perhaps," writes Yerushalmi,

> the time has come to look more closely at ruptures, breaches, breaks, to identify them more precisely, to see how Jews endured them, to understand that not everything of value that existed before a break was either salvaged or metamorphosed, but was lost, and that often some of what fell by the wayside can become, through our retrieval, meaningful to us. To do so, however, the modern Jewish historian must first understand the degree to which he himself is a product of rupture. Once aware of this, he is not only bound to accept it; he is liberated to use it. (101)

Taking Yerushalmi's suggestions into a history of Jewish women's poetry, by way of queer theory, I want to offer those left outside Yerushalmi's "enchanted circle of tradition" (Yerushalmi himself included), through Carolyn Dinshaw, "a post-disenchanted—that is to say, queer—future."[61] This future refuses to be excluded from tradition, but rather connects to the very breaks in tradition, choosing what to salvage and recognizing what was lost. Accordingly, Molodowsky's poem rejects continuity while creating it, telling the story of what existed and what could, therefore, be lost. As Molodowsky's own image of a ripped page with a missing first line implies, the text itself embodies the losses it is embedded in, *it is* the loss involved in the fracturing of Jewish women's history, the same loss that enables the text to exist and tell the story of the fracture. Reading today, the torn text is not just the disrupted story of Jewish women, but also the rupture in the history of Jewish language, resulting in the precarious present of Yiddish. Queerly enacting Yerushalmi's model of retrieval reveals that what must be recovered is not only the Yiddish history that was not passed down, but also all of the other past possibilities that did not come to be the future we live in. It is in these queer times and places of possibility, which were foreclosed preemptively and retrospectively, that a meeting space is formed. Retrieving the *loytere blut*, the luminous bloodline of Molodowsky's *froyen-seyfer* (women's holy book) by connecting to Molodowsky's Yiddish poem through my own queer choice to learn Yiddish, and through the feminist and queer translation projects of Hellerstein and Rich, the multilingual cross-temporal conversation can finally continue.

TWO VANISHED HELLAS AND HEBRAIC PAIN
Emma Lazarus and Anna Margolin

> Late-born and woman-souled I dare not hope,
> The freshness of the elder lays, the might
> Of manly, modern passion shall alight
> Upon my Muse's lips, nor may I cope
> (Who veiled and screened by womanhood must grope)
> With the world's strong-armed warriors and recite
> The dangers, wounds, and triumphs of the fight;
> Twanging the full-stringed lyre through all its scope.
> But if thou ever in some lake-floored cave
> O'erbrowed by rocks, a wild voice wooed and heard,
> Answering at once from heaven and earth and wave,
> Lending elf-music to thy harshest word,
> Misprize thou not these echoes that belong
> To one in love with solitude and song.[1]

"Late-born and woman-souled" is how Emma Lazarus identifies the first-person speaker of her sonnet "Echoes," qualifying her ability to speak "the might of manly, modern passion." But much like the poem ultimately reverses this modest position in favor of a female and even feminist poetics, so too can we reverse the claim of being "late-born." Born in the middle of the nineteenth century, Lazarus is rather a precursor of Yiddish poetry, of American Jewish poetry and American women's poetry, as well as lesbian poetry. Though she "dare not hope," Lazarus's poem holds the queer expectancy for what will come after her. This undoing of progressive time, reversing early and late, reveals a poetic tradition that mobilizes historical specificity in order to undo normative constructions of temporality, and open avenues of queer history.

This chapter, and the one following it, will read this tradition across times and across languages, turning to Lazarus, to Yiddish poet Anna Margolin and to

Hebrew poet Leah Goldberg, who all employ a strategy of queer transgression, as they use poetry to cross a variety of boundaries—between historical eras, between gender binaries, between languages, between Jewish women and the spaces that would have excluded women and/or Jews. Each of these poets maps the multiplicity they invoke within the space of a single poem, enacting what Carolyn Dinshaw has termed *noncontemporaneous-contemporaneity*.[2] Dinshaw offers this multiplicity as an epitome of queer history, by way of the body, asking what it means to be a body not just in one time, but in multiple times. It is this multiplicity that activates both historical difference and connection across time, what Dinshaw terms the "queer historical impulse" to make "pleasurable connections in the context of postmodern indeterminacy."[3] Rather than simple indeterminacy, the poems in this chapter activate the distinct difference of each space and identity, while linking them inextricably to each other. Indeed, these connections are thus invited by the shared poetic strategy; as their poems undo divisions of past and present, Jewish and non-Jewish, male and female, so too are the divisions between the poets undone, generating a queer continuity.

As I go in search of these women's histories, I am reminded by Lazarus herself that "the epochs of our life are not in the visible facts, but in the silent thought by the wayside as we walk." I read this line as a future warning, one especially valuable to those about to embark on a journey into the histories of Jewish women's writing. But this line is not Lazarus's own, rather it is an epigraph to her poem "Epochs," published posthumously in the 1889 collection of her poems, quoted from Ralph Waldo Emerson's 1841 essay. This essay, "Spiritual Laws," does not read exactly as Lazarus quotes it. Instead, Emerson writes,

> We call the poet inactive because he is not a president, a merchant, or a porter. We adore an institution, and do not see that it is founded on a thought which we have. But real action is in silent moments. The epochs of our life are not in the visible facts of *our choice of a calling, our marriage, our acquisition of an office, and the like*,[4] but in a silent thought by the wayside as we walk.[5]

In their full original context these lines clearly do not apply to Lazarus, poet though she may be. If Emerson is defending the life of poetry in the face of other life choices, Lazarus entirely omits the mention of "a choice of a calling, our marriage, our acquisition of an office." Indeed, these choices are far less relevant for a nineteenth-century Jewish woman, even one from the relatively high society of New York City, for the choice of marriage would very likely have negated her career as a poet, and the acquisition of office was hardly realistic. In Lazarus's use of Emerson's lines as I read them, what comes into question is not the role of the poet, but rather the role of the literary historian who would hope that facts found in writing can reveal a life's epochs, and is instead told they are lost in silent thought by the wayside. How we might access lost facts, and equally importantly, reckon with their absence, is part of the queer methodology of this book overall. This chapter, however, will use what we *do* have: the poems, the histories invoked by the poems, and the known histories of the poets themselves, to show how women overcome their limited history (and the history of their limitations) to create their own modes of queer temporality.

To explore Lazarus's queering of history, we should first pinpoint some aspects of her own history. Lazarus, born in New York in 1849, is one of the first Jewish American authors, and certainly one of the most famous ones, though her history is often only partially engaged. Critics have tended to focus on her "Jewish writing," more often than not in relation to her encounter with the massive waves of Jewish immigration following the pogroms of the 1880s. In fact, her writing engaged a wide span of material and used sophisticated and innovative forms, positioning her as an important American literary figure. Despite multiple existing studies of her writing, and even more studies of her biography,[6] many aspects of her life and work remain untouched or unresolved. The question of Lazarus's sexuality is key among these. The most tangible historic trace left of Lazarus's life is certainly her 1883 poem "The New Colossus," etched at the base of the Statue of Liberty, "A mighty woman with a torch turning" to welcome the "huddled masses" to the American shores.[7] Lazarus herself was not an immigrant, but was born to a family descended from the first Jewish settlers to colonize America. The family was Sephardic on her father's side and Ashkenazi on her mother's side. The historical rupture of the expulsion from Spain and Portugal that shaped the legacy of her Sephardic side remained a key moment for her poetry, pervading her concept of Jewish history as expressed in poems such as the 1887 "By the Waters of Babylon."[8]

The poem exemplifies Lazarus's expansive and transgressive deployment of historical narrative. Beginning with what she titles "the Exodus (August 3, 1492)," Lazarus conflated the Biblical narrative of the Exodus from Egypt with the story of Spanish-Jewish exile. Imitating Biblical structure, the poem is divided into chapters and verses. But this is not simply an act of imitation; it is, rather, an act of unique poetic creation. According to Michael Weingrad, this may be the first English-language prose poem, gesturing to Baudelaire's "Little Poems in Prose."[9] As in the conflation of the Egyptian/Spanish Exodus, throughout the poem Lazarus brings together disparate times and places, generating a new history: for example, "The herdsmen of Canaan and the seed of Jerusalem's royal shepherd renew their youth amid the pastoral plains of Texas and the golden valleys of the Sierras."[10] The poem as a whole weaves a tale crossing the threads of Jewish history and geography, moving between Moses Mendelsohn, Jesus, Ibn Ezra, the Prairies, Kiev (which she spells as "Kief"), the Kabbalah, and more. Significantly, the poem's entire swooping historical scope is focalized via a first-person speaker, speaking both to and for "the Soul of Israel," who is finally transformed into the angel of Jewish history.

> But when the emancipating springtide breathes wholesome, quickening airs, when the Sun of Love shines out with cordial fires, lo, the Soul of Israel bursts her cobweb sheath, and flies forth attired in the winged beauty of immortality.[11]

Within the multiplicity woven through the poem, one figure that stands out in the poem is "the enchanted magician, heart-broken jester," Heinrich Heine. Heine, who "more than any other writer outside of Emerson, was her spiritual and aesthetic guide,"[12] made his first appearance in Lazarus's earliest book (published for private circulation in 1866). Lazarus later published an entire volume of translations and a biographical sketch of Heine in 1881,[13] as well as another essay about Heine in 1884,[14] which included the poem "Venus of the Louvre." This poem creates a unique monument to the poet Heine, to Western culture and history, to art, and to the poet herself.

> Down the long hall she glistens like a star,
> The foam-born mother of Love, transfixed to stone,
> Yet none the less immortal, breathing on.
> Time's brutal hand hath maimed but could not mar.
> When first the enthralled enchantress from afar
> Dazzled mine eyes, I saw not her alone,
> Serenely poised on her world-worshipped throne,

As when she guided once her dove-drawn car,—
But at her feet a pale, death-stricken Jew,
Her life adorer, sobbed farewell to love.
Here *Heine* wept! Here still he weeps anew,
Nor ever shall his shadow lift or move,
While mourns one ardent heart, one poet-brain,
For vanished Hellas and Hebraic pain.[15]

This poem is set in the physical space of the Louvre Museum ("down the long hall"), while invoking the history of Greco-Roman mythology of the goddess Venus, the story of the artifact "Venus de Milo" and the historical moment of Heine's exile in France.[16] "Transfixed to stone," Venus becomes immortal, writes Lazarus, "breathing on." Like her, Heine too is relegated outside of time: "Here *Heine* wept! Here still he weeps anew." Just like the art of sculpture is responsible for Venus's transfixed immortality, so too is Heine's immortality anchored in art: "Nor ever shall his shadow lift or move, / While mourns one ardent heart, one poet-brain." This mourning poet can be read as Heine, but also as Lazarus herself, for she is indeed the one who transfixes Heine's image to the sculpture in the Louvre, conflating "vanished Hellas and Hebraic pain." Like the conflation of time and space in "By the Waters of Babylon," this poem also constructs queer continuities transgressing categories of difference; in this case otherwise insurmountable differences not just of time, but also of gender and religion—moving from Greek mythology to French Revolution European Jewry to Victorian Europe and America. These multiple differences get mapped onto one singular moment, all by way of art.

* * *

Some fifty years later, Yiddish poet Anna Margolin's 1929 poem "*Ikh bin geven a mol a yingling*" ("I Was Once a Boy") offered its own version of historical multiplicity poetically conflated.[17] Margolin (pen name of Rosa Lebnsboym) was born in 1887 in Belarus, and spent her early years in Königsberg, Odessa, and Warsaw. She moved to New York twice, once in 1906 and again in 1913. In the interim she traveled to Paris and Warsaw, got married, and moved to Tel Aviv where she bore a son. Shortly thereafter she left her husband and child in Palestine, returning to New York via Warsaw. Though her archive contains correspondence in Russian, English, Hebrew, and Yiddish, she is only known to have published in Yiddish.¹⁸ Immigrating to the United States did not lead her to English; in fact, it was this immigration that led her to join the American Yiddish literary scene, serving on the editorial staff of the *Fraye arbeter shtime*, where she also published her first piece of fiction. She is best known for her poetry, which she began publishing in the 1920s. "*Ikh bin geven a mol a yingling*"¹⁹ is one of the most famous Yiddish poems written by a woman, and is strikingly similar to "Venus of the Louvre" in its movement between, and even conflation of, very different historical moments, as well as the Jewish and the Hellenic, male and female.

איך בין געוועזן א מאָל א יינגלינג

איך בין געוועזן א מאָל א יינגלינג
געהערט אין פּאָרטיקאָס סאָקראָטן
עס האָט מײַן בוזעם־פֿרײַנד, מײַן ליבלינג,
געהאַט דעם שענסטן טאָרס אין אַטען.

געוועזן צעזאַר. און א העלע וועלט
געבויט פֿון מאַרמאָר, איך דער לעצטער,
און פֿאַר א ווײַב מיר אויסדערוויילט
מײַן שטאָלצע שוועסטער.

אין רויזנקראַנץ בײַם ים ווײַן ביז שפּעט
געהערט אין הויכמוטיקן פֿרידן
וועגן שוואַכלינג פֿון נאַזאַרעט
און ווילדע מעשׂיות וועגן יידן.

I Was Once a Boy

I was once a boy, a stripling
Listening in Socrates' portico,
My bosom-buddy, my sweet darling,
Had Athens' most beautiful torso.

Was Caesar. And from marble constructed
A glistening world, I the last there,
And for my own wife selected
My stately sister.

> Rose-garlanded, nursing wine all night
> In high spirits, hear tell the news
> About the weakling from Nazareth
> And wild tales about Jews.[20]

The speaker of this poem enters the most prized spaces of masculinity, including its positions of power, at the heart of Western culture and scholarship, and has access to the ultimate male privileges: exclusive male bonding and the right to take a wife. To maintain the gender indeterminacy Margolin sets up, I will use the gender-neutral pronouns *they* for the rest of the discussion.[21] But gender fluidity is not the only indeterminacy at play here, for the speaker imagines themself not only in the privileged position of a man, but also in that of a non-Jew, who looks down on the Jews of the "wild tales." In a unique move, Margolin aligns Jesus (the "weakling from Nazareth") and early Christianity in general with the weak effeminate Jewish males of her present, for "weakling" was the dominant stereotype of diasporic Jewish masculinity of the time.[22] She thus manages to conflate past and present Christian and Jewish men, equally belittling both groups, which have historically held more power than Jewish women. Margolin allows herself to access the realm of power, the realm of philosophers and rulers, Pagans, Jews and Christians. Furthermore, she does so to pass criticism on it, undermining the way history and power operate. Instead of investing in dominant power and looking forward to the future, Margolin shows these powers as destined to fall, by weaving a queer history that resists heteronormative futurity.

The very language of the poem, a markedly Germanized and internationalized Yiddish, allows Margolin to trespass into the realm of non-Jewish cultural capital through the idiom of European "high culture." Yiddish is inherently a composite language in which elements of German, *loshn-koydesh* ("holy tongue/language," that is, Hebrew and Aramaic), Slavic languages and Romance languages are fused together.[23] Yiddish is able to absorb form and content, grammar and vocabulary, from its geographical and intercultural encounters, at times integrating the foreign elements, and in other cases leaving them unfused, still marked as foreign. In the meeting of these various elements, different emphasis can be given to each component, for different reasons—addressing certain audiences and excluding others.[24] The language of Margolin's poem is striking in its general avoidance of Judaic components, except for one word, *mayses*, which I discuss below. It relies particularly heavily on the Germanic and international components, and what is most unusual, on Greek words (*torso, portico*), making the language of the poem itself an "othered" form of Yiddish, and yet another way for Margolin to usurp power and privilege that are not her own. Margolin juxtaposes these disparate linguistic elements in her rhyme scheme, which both highlights their difference (e.g., *shpet/nazaret*—late/Nazareth) but also unites them in the strictly structured poetic product.[25] Barbara Mann has insightfully deemed the rhyming strategy of this particular poem as "a prosodic representation of the impossibility of isolating a singular narrative concerning 'Jewish history.' "[26] Before examining the notions of "Jewish history" set forth and intertwined by this poem, I will turn to the way the speaker themself enters history and invites us to join them. If the Jewish female poet's initial position is being barred from history, the queer history Margolin weaves puts her speaker at the center of multiple histories, and offers queer ways to look back to them and move between them.

The speaker is marked from the outset as both male and non-Jew by the word *yingling* (*boy* in Hellerstein's translation), which is a distinctly German word, rather than a fully fused Germanic word in Yiddish (such as *yingl*). If we could simply take the speaker of this poem to be male, then the statement "I was once a boy, a stripling" could be taken at face value, but reading the feminine signature complicates this in advance. What is at play here is the presumption that in the lyric poem the *I* of the poet and the *I* of the speaker are of the same gender, until the text signals otherwise. The opening of the poem could have been taken as such evidence, but the particularities of the sentence, especially around the phrase *a mol* (*once*), activate all of the statement's possible ambiguities. Consequently, instead of being read simply as coming from a male speaker referring to his childhood, the statement can be read "I used to be that way, namely male," opening the possibility that a female speaker is describing herself as having once, previously, for her whole past or at a certain point in that past, been a boy. Many translations have attempted to mask this ambiguity by translating the word *yingling* in nongendered forms such as "I was once a youth,"[27] or even the romantic-sentimental "Once I was young,"[28] erasing the gender-bending complexities the poem so distinctly opens up.

The transgression, as we shall see, is not limited to gender, but extends also to transgressions of temporality, allowing for an understanding of gender not as fixed but as shifting over time, and in relation to time. This can be seen to prefigure, literalize, and mobilize Judith Butler's treatment of gender not "as a stable identity or locus of agency from which various acts follow," but rather as "an identity tenuously constituted in time."[29] Margolin's use of the shifting gender of her speaker, together with multiple shifts in historical epochs, expose the ways in which gender is embedded in the temporal and social, the way in which it *is* the time of society, what Butler calls a "constituted social temporality."[30] The temporality of gender as I understand it through the poem addresses not just the manner in which gender is constituted in the temporality of one's own life, but also the way it is constituted in different historical periods, directly linking the shifts in personal story and the phases of Western history. This contextual grounding is crucial for the move undertaken by both my reading and Margolin's poem itself, which attempts to understand and utilize gender and identity across disparate material and discursive realities. In this poem, the temporal shifts are part of what enables the poem's explicit gender-bending and homoeroticism. Furthermore, the disruption of sexual and gender norms seems to be what propels the historical shifts themselves. For example, midpoem, the speaker refers to themself as "the last" ("*der letster*"), shifting away from a reproductive, heteronormative concept of historical progress while showing a distinct obliviousness about possible phases of history to come. Such obliviousness fits well within the logic of the poem, in which the progression of generations is executed outside the logic of reproduction; for the move from one empire to another, from Greek to Roman, does not take place through a reproductive succession of generations, but rather happens through the body of the male lover, the "bosom-buddy" of the speaker. We shall see this both thematically and syntactically.

To return to the opening line of the poem, "I was once a boy" sends us back in time, to a past soon proven to be not just a simple biographical past, but a distant classical non-Jewish past, that of Socrates, and later of Caesar and Jesus. Through Socrates's portico we enter an all-male scholarly space. The fact that it is not a space of Jewish learning is significant, for as a Jewish woman Margolin was barred mainly from Jewish scholarship, and not from the realm of secular learning. Indeed, since the Enlightenment, Jewish women had been important agents of secular learning precisely because they were not barred from non-Jewish texts the way they were forbidden even to touch the rabbinic ones. In the classical sphere of secular learning the speaker invokes, however, both women and Jews would have been excluded.

Moreover, this space is distinctly homoerotic. The potential homoeroticism of this space is activated by the speaker's declaration of having a "*buzem-fraynd*," a male-gendered friend or lover, who could be read either as Socrates or as a fellow listener, for he is brought into the poem directly after the mention of Socrates, and has no further introduction or even punctuation to distinguish him from Socrates. Reading him as Socrates being admired by the young speaker poses an interesting inversion in terms of power dynamics, since in the ancient Greek pederastic model of love the old is the one courting the young. The only description given of the "bosom friend" is his torso, in what Mann has termed a "visual pun" between the idiomatic expression *bosom buddy*, a term borrowed either from German or from English, and his chest, represented via synecdoche as an isolated torso.[31] Mann notes: "it may seem strange to describe a living person as having a nice torso, which perhaps explains why one translation reads 'chest' instead."[32] However, marble torsos and other incomplete sculptures are precisely the way in which we know Greek bodies, the fragmented material trace through which we encounter the corporality of the ancient past. The fact that only the artistic representation of the body can (more or less) survive the perils of time serves as parallel to the poem itself and its ability to travel through time.

The fragment itself marks the poem as a product of its time, very much in line with Margolin's modernist sensibilities. The specific focus on the Greek sculptures also ties this poem both to contemporary Yiddish modernist experimentation, and to German and Hebrew modernist poetry.[33] These sculptures represent the forbidden "graven image" of Judaism. Having a Greek statue as the love object therefore counters an entire history of Jewish martyrology based on refusing to bow down before such idols, for example, the tale of the woman who preferred to have her seven sons killed rather than to bow before idols.[34] Evoking this form of idolatry connects Margolin to Jewish imagism, which according to Mann "exemplified modern Jewish culture's larger revolution regarding the Second Commandment taboo on graven images."[35] By exploiting and collapsing the divide between image and text, Mann writes, "Jewish imagism simultaneously announced its participation in international modernism and its engagement in internal Jewish debates."[36] The ability to speak to two separate spheres, alongside mobilizing and blurring the distinction between image and text, join Margolin's thematic transgression of boundaries within the poem itself.

Of course, in and of itself a torso does not necessarily connote marble sculpture.[37] Instead, the marble is made clearly present in the next phase of history and the next stanza of the poem, with its "glistening world" constructed of marble. Reading back in time, from the (Roman) marble world, highlights the echo of marble already present in the synecdoche of the lover's torso. Reading forward, from the Greek lover toward the following phase of history, links the homoerotic love to the progress of history. This link propels the move from one empire to another not through a reproductive succession of generations, but rather through the body of the lover, through his torso.

From the Greek we then move to the Roman, introducing the figure of Caesar. But both the Yiddish and the English allow us to read doubly: there was Caesar, or, I was Caesar. This ambiguity, like the one regarding the speaker, is based in grammatical indeterminacy, focused in the concept of the word *was*. Here it is the fact that the poet presents the verb elliptically, leaving out the conjugated auxiliary verb ("Was Caesar"—*gevezn tsezar*), which opens the dual possibility that the elided pronoun is the intimate *I* (was Caesar) or the distancing *there* (was Caesar). Omitting half of the verb form, the very half that would distinguish between "I was" ("[*ikh*] *bin gevezn*") and "there was" ("[*es*] *iz gevezen*") opens the sentence to ambiguous interpretation. At the same time, it also definitively marks the shift in subject (whether between Socrates and Caesar, or in the speaker's own identity), by way of its declarative tone as well as its rich sound pattern, created by using the form *gevezn* instead of the more commonly used form *geven* (the form of *was* that appears in the opening line). Finally, starting this sentence elliptically with a past participle accelerates the pace of the historical movement. If this structure pushes the historical narrative forward, it is indeed the torso of the lover, if not his very existence, which we must read as propelling the move from one empire to another.

The speaker themself, whether or not it is Caesar, has the power to use the marble (and thus the homoerotic love signaled through the lover's torso) to create a "glistening world" in this second phase of non-Jewish history, which is introduced by the second stanza. In addition to this power of construction, the speaker gets to choose a wife, but calling her "sister" implies an incestuous bond, which would fit Hellerstein's presumption that the emperor being referred to here is Claudius I, who married his niece against Roman law, which he then changed.[38] The combined naming of sister and wife could also gesture to the Biblical epithet, "my sister, my bride." Pointing out the repeated metaphorical use of *brother* and *sister* in the Bible in general (for example, Genesis 19:7; 2 Samuel 1:26; Job 30:29), and the prevalence of the combination "sister" and "bride" in the Song of Songs in particular (4:9,10,12, 5:1), Chana Bloch explains in her translation of the Song of Songs that this combination is meant to signal intimacy, and "is not to be taken literally as implying a wedding ceremony, though it may well convey a hope for marriage in the future."[39] Finally, *sister* could be a figure of speech to mark a deeroticized bond with the wife, over and against the homoerotic bond between the male scholars, which furthers our reading of the first stanza, highlighting the homoerotic aspects of the poem.

The next phase of Western history, the rise of Christianity, seamlessly enters through the final stanza, hinting at the speaker's future downfall. First, we have the *royznkrants*, the rose garland that conjures distinctly Christian imagery invoking Mary's crown of roses. This Christian connotation is then further materialized when Jesus is actually alluded to, though not as a prominent figure (as opposed to Caesar or Socrates), but rather as "the weakling," an effeminate Jew, part of "wild tales about the Jews." Using the Hebraic word *mayse* brings us, for the first time in the poem, into the realm of Jewish discourse, and more specifically, an internally Jewish discourse that marks the tales as "wild" and thus clearly fictitious. We might even read these "wild tales" as holding concrete accusations against the Jews, the notorious European blood libel, echoing one of the most marked expressions of Christian oppression that has shaped Jewish history. But the poem opens this traumatic memory by transposing the Jewish discourse about Christian persecution onto the lips of the Romans, who were themselves persecuting the early Christians. Notably, however, the *mayses* (tales) also allude to *bobe-mayses*, the Yiddish term for tall tales, not to be taken seriously, told in "high spirits," negating the dramatic history of suffering and redemption alike.[40] In this case it is the progression of religious (rather than reproductive) time that we can see as being disrupted, and though Christianity will come to rise, and *der letster*, he who is last, will be first, the poem also implies that Jesus, like Socrates and Caesar, is ultimately destined to fall. Margolin thus conflates Jew and Christian, oppressor and victim, at the same time that she transgresses boundaries between self and other, male and female, homo and hetero. Margolin also transgresses normative temporality, writing herself back into the past and out of Jewish society. In this realm of otherness, in which otherness itself is replaced by fluidity, Margolin is not a bystander but rather an active participant who overcomes the limitations of her contemporary male-dominated society.

Seeing how similar images shift between Lazarus and Margolin bolsters the complication of temporality set forth by each of the poems, but also brings them together through their transgression of difference, to generate a queer history ranging all the way from Greek myth to Yiddish poetry. Tracing the links that construct this queer poetic history reveals it to be anything but linear. Lazarus's marble hall of the Louvre becomes Socrates's portico in Margolin's poem, and then a "glistening world, built from marble," linking the early and later bastions of Western culture. Lazarus's "pale, death-stricken Jew," Heine, becomes the "weakling of Nazareth," Jesus. In both examples the later poem directs us to a history that precedes that of the earlier poem. The complication of temporality is also evident on the level of individual images. For example, Venus de Milo, who stands at the center of Lazarus's poem, is already a conflation of Ancient Greek, Roman, and nineteenth-century European histories. This Greek sculpture, originally named Aphrodite of Melos, was brought to Paris in 1820 and became famous under her Roman name, as was common French practice.[41] The maimed sculpture hails back to the same moment of Ancient Greece that the bosom buddy comes from. As we saw, this bosom buddy facilitates the conflation of Greek and Roman Empires. Like the isolated torso, Venus too is an incomplete body materialized in the art of sculpture. Both historical relics physically travel across time until they are fixed in poetry. But if the maimed Venus arrives in a complete sonnet (as Lazarus's poem is a classic hybrid sonnet, rhyming ABBA ABBA CDCD EE), Margolin's poem is itself fragmented, for despite its three rhyming quatrains (alternately rhyming ABAB CDCD EFEF), it is missing the rhyming couplet that would make it a complete sonnet. The lack of couplet leads to a heightened emphasis on the closing line, which ominously links the rise of Christianity and the history of anti-Semitism.

By 1946 the meaning of the closing line had changed dramatically, so much so that Margolin requested that Leyb Feinberg, who was translating this poem into Russian, change its order: "I only ask that in the final stanza you transpose the order of the last two lines, because I wrote the poem so that its entire weight should rest on the last line ('And strange stories about Jews'). A line which I could not lift my hand to write in the present era of our great catastrophe."[42] And yet the rise of catastrophe seems to me to be already written into the poem itself, where Margolin's own art constructs a cyclical image of history, repeatedly striking a celebratory tone that holds the seeds of downfall yet to come. Together with Lazarus's moment of multiple mourning frozen in art, both poets can then be seen to agree on "time's brutal hand." Interestingly, the historical pessimism of both poems only fully comes to light in retrospect (for Margolin with the rise of Nazism, for Lazarus with her impending illness).

Reading Margolin's poem together with Lazarus's also highlights the American (and specifically New York) context within which Margolin, the

Eastern European Jew, was writing—for 1929 was the same year the stock market crashed, causing panic on Wall Street, a short walk from the Lower East Side where Margolin lived, and not far from the Lazarus family home on West Tenth Street. In another America/Europe reversal, Lazarus's poem was written in Europe, on her first of two visits. By the time she made her second visit, she herself was "the death-stricken Jew": "Once again," writes Richard Watson Gilder, editor of *Century Illustrated Monthly Magazine*, in his obituary of Lazarus, "came the lifelong analogy, which she [Lazarus] herself pointed out now, to the German master [. . .] She too, the last time she went out, dragged herself to the Louvre, to the feet of Venus, 'the goddess without arms, who couldn't help.' "[43]

This moment of utter helplessness stands at the dramatic closing of Kadya Molodowsky's Yiddish screenplay about Lazarus.[44] This screenplay, titled *Emma Lazarus*, is found in Molodowsky's archive at YIVO, and seems to have been intended for television production as it includes camera instructions and dramatic animation of a portrait of George Eliot come to life.[45] Molodowsky generates a lineage back from Lazarus to George Eliot, tied through a depiction of Jewish suffering. Despite this political setup, focused on the plight of Jewish immigrants (a pressing issue certainly on the minds of Lazarus and Molodowsky alike), the concern behind the play is in fact art, and more specifically the relationship between life, art, and history, as evidenced in the script's final scene:

> EMMA: [Pointing to Venus] She won't let me go. She is telling me about her severed hands. [To Venus] You are wounded, Venus. You are, perhaps, as sick as I am, yet your shining beauty never ceases. Maybe like you, torn out of life, I, too, will remain standing in beauty? But I wouldn't want to be in a museum. It is so cold here. I would like to be among living people. I want to go back to the teeming lively homely shores of America. New York, my city, city of light, goodhearted city. [Camera picks up Statue of Liberty. We see Emma Lazarus's poem "The New Colossus" on the base of the statue.]

> HOST: Emma Lazarus died in America on Nov. 19, 1887. Her song remained engraved in eternal beauty on the Statue of Liberty. [Close up on the torch of the Statue for Finale.]

In this scene, reproduced here from Zvee Scooler's translation found in Lazarus's archive (as well as in his own),[46] the focus is on the extreme helplessness of the Greek goddess, echoing Lazarus's poem. Over and against Venus's helplessness, Molodowsky casts Lazarus as another sculpture, the Statue of Liberty, the "mighty woman with a torch" from Lazarus's poem "The New Colossus." Returning to this poem through the helpless encounter of Venus-Heine-Lazarus-Molodowsky, what stands out is not the might of "the mother of exiles," but rather the way she is constructed over and against the Greek, masculine all-powerful.

> Not like the brazen giant of Greek fame,
> With conquering limbs astride from land to land;
> Here at our sea-washed, sunset gates shall stand
> A mighty woman with a torch, whose flame
> Is the imprisoned lightning, and her name
> Mother of Exiles. From her beacon-hand
> Glows world-wide welcome; her mild eyes command
> The air-bridged harbor that twin cities frame.
> "Keep ancient lands, your storied pomp!" cries she
> With silent lips. "Give me your tired, your poor,
> Your huddled masses yearning to breathe free,
> The wretched refuse of your teeming shore.
> Send these, the homeless, tempest-tost to me,
> I lift my lamp beside the golden door!"[47]

This poem embraces the static nature of the statue to create a feminized form of action, which is, surprisingly, passive. Speaking with "silent lips" and lifting the lamp of "imprisoned lightning," this figure commands an entire harbor ("between two cities") with her "mild eyes."[48] The figure rejects the "storied pomp" of ancient lands, the same histories Margolin later turns back to. And yet Margolin could hardly be considered to be enthusiastically embracing these histories, nor does she await the promise of the particular future they hold, for impending disaster seems to retrospectively echo back onto Margolin's poem. Reading the rise of Nazism into Margolin's poem, much like reading Lazarus's death into "Venus of the Louvre," would certainly be anachronistic. Yet both cases seem to invite such anachronism, invite a disruption of temporality, as the history set up by the poems themselves serves to prefigure the inevitable, and indeed inevitably tragic, future into their own art.

Answering both Venus and Lady Liberty, let us close with one final statue, depicted by Margolin and placed on her own marble headstone.

זי מיט די קאַלטע מאַרמאָרנע בריסט

זי מיט די קאַלטע מאַרמאָרנע בריסט
און מיט די שמאָלע ליכטיקע הענט,
זי האָט איר שיינקייט פֿאַרשוועגדט
אויף מיסט, אויף גאָרנישט.

זי האָט עס אפֿשר געוואָלט, אפֿשר געגלוסט
צו אומגליק, צו זיבן מעסערס פֿון פּייַן
און פֿאַרגאָסן דעם לעבנס הייליקן ווייַן
אויף מיסט, אויף גאָרנישט.

איצט ליגט זי מיט אַ צעבראָכן געזיכט.
דער געשענדעטער גייַסט פֿאַרלאָזט די שטייַג.
פֿאַרבייַגייער, האָב רחמנות און שווייַג—
זאָג גאָרנישט.

She with the cold marble breasts
and the narrow light hands,
she squandered her life
on garbage, on nothing.

Perhaps she wanted, even desired
misfortune, seven measures of pain,
and poured out life's holy wine
on garbage, on nothing.

Now she lies with a shattered visage.
The disgraced spirit has quit the cage.
Passerby, have pity and be silent—
say nothing.[49]

This poem is one of Margolin's last published poems, and appeared in 1932 when Margolin was forty-five. It is one of about six poems that Margolin published after her first and only book, *Lider*. Margolin is said to have spent the twenty-some remaining years of her life as a recluse, in deep depression. It is only by way of future work with her archives, writes her final partner, Reuven Ayzland, that we might find a key to her poetry and to the "tragic life-entanglement (*lebns-plonter*) of her final years."[50] Margolin left instructions to have the poem etched on her gravestone, in a final instance of marble, following the portico, the Roman world, the halls of the Louvre, as well as Venus and the Statue of Liberty. Margolin requested that the first two lines be omitted on her gravestone.[51] In so doing, the figure described is no longer a statue with cold "marble breasts," and her "shattered visage" becomes an even more violent image of destruction. But the real violence here is directed against her life's work of poetry, referred to twice in the course of one short poem as "garbage" and "nothing." The word *nothing*, *gornisht*, appears a third time, as an injunction to the reader: "Passerby, have pity and be silent—say nothing." However, in the idiom of this poem, to "say nothing" is not tantamount to silence, but rather to poetry, for that is the "nothing" that Margolin "squandered" her life on. Giving poetic voice and shape to the "silent thoughts by the wayside," Margolin and Lazarus resist silence, proving that "some of what fell by the wayside can become, through our retrieval, meaningful to us," to return to Yosef Haim Yerushalmi's injunction for Jewish historians. Retrieving and rewriting Jewish history within their own narrative, these poets transcend the brutal hand of time, reaching out to us, in silence and poetry alike.

THREE WAITING IN VAIN
Leah Goldberg and Anna Margolin

> There is no comfort looking forth nor back,
> The present gives the lie to all her past.
> Will cruel time restore what she doth lack?
> Why was no shadow of this doom forecast?
> [. . .]
> Yea, she hath looked Truth grimly face to face,
> And drained unto the lees the proffered cup.
> This silence is not patience, nor the grace
> Of recognition, meekly offered up,
> But mere acceptance fraught with keenest pain,
> Seeing that all her struggles must be vain.[1]

There may be "no comfort looking forth nor back," as Emma Lazarus writes in her poem "Epochs," but as we saw in the last chapter, poets like Lazarus (in English) and Anna Margolin (in Yiddish) collapse the very distinctions between forth and back, instead "looking inward and outward, at once before and after," to quote another poet, Audre Lorde.[2] Poetically disrupting the linear sequence of (hetero)normative temporality, these poets create queer histories that conflate multiple times and transgress categorical boundaries. These conflations and transgressions are also what enable me to link the poems to each other, drawing unexpected lines of continuity between them. The current chapter will focus on one particular way in which these queer lines are drawn, the mode I have termed *queer expectancy*. As part of the complication of temporality I have been discussing, queer expectancy is a position that already preemptively holds within it multiple future alternatives, including those that will not (or have already not) come to fruition. The act of waiting in vain epitomizes this mode of expectancy, as it holds both hope and its disavowal simultaneously, preemptively and retrospectively (while you are still waiting, before you know you will not get what you are waiting for, after you know it has been in vain). Despite the inevitable disappointment this "waiting in vain" holds, it is also a form of expectancy, and therefore of invitation. I use disappointments past to identify the possible futures that did not come to be, at the same time that I identify my own disappointment in the inheritance that came to be the future I live in. The continuity formed by this queer expectancy can be read as "backward future" (to borrow Heather Love's term), generated not by hope, but by disappointments and disavowals, future and past.

The poetic expression of preemptive disappointment has offered Jewish women writers a mode of resisting their present conditions and the demands of participation in dominant discourse and progressive history. I will focus specifically on the dictates of both nationalism and heteronormative reproduction, to show how these dictates are resisted through the poetic histories constructed in the Hebrew poetry of Leah Goldberg and the Yiddish poetry of Anna Margolin. The question of language is key in this investigation, as I read these poets' linguistic and poetic choices against the future-oriented politics and poetics of their time, and against the present status of Hebrew and Yiddish today.

Though separated by nearly a generation (Margolin b. 1887, Goldberg b. 1911), by language, and by geographical trajectory, the poetic and political affinities between the two writers prove striking. Indeed, despite their difference, Barbara Mann reads both as existing "at the canonical center of modernist literary production in Hebrew and Yiddish—both for its formal innovation and for the multiple cultural affiliations that emerge through a close reading of their work."[3] The queer theoretical framework I have been developing will highlight further connections between them, and these connections will offer a distinctly queer multilingual genealogy of Jewish literary history. In this queer multilingual genealogy, Hebrew and Yiddish are presented as contemporaneous and parallel literary possibilities. Neither viewed as natural nor inevitable, both are traced to their shared tentative status within the Eastern European past into which Goldberg and Margolin were born. Each poet deliberately chose which language to write in. Although (or rather because) neither of the two writers could anticipate the place of her choices in relation to how Jewish literary history would evolve, their choices, the very act of writing, their language, and the particular themes they explored, can all be seen as modes of queer expectancy that serve to disrupt a progressive history that could follow the Jewish past, or in fact, bring the Jewish past into the future. Instead, these writers queerly disrupt history and resist futurity.

Looking beyond Jewish history and away from a Jewish future, both poets in this chapter offer their own version of queer history, one that I read as constructed in order to challenge dominant history, which they were denied access to, while resisting a future that would equally circumscribe their participation.[4] Of course, women were not the only ones engaging history head on, for they were participating alongside their male colleagues in the general project of creating a new type of modern, secular Jewish literature. The difference I am identifying, however, is in the discontinuous history of women's writing (as opposed to men's writing). This is not, however, to say that Goldberg or Margolin were writing with no history whatsoever. Goldberg even had direct contact with one of her forerunners before she started publishing poetry. This encounter, with Hebrew poet Elisheva Bikhovska (1888–1949) who was touring Eastern Europe, is described in Goldberg's journal entry from April 23, 1924. Through Hebrew journals, Goldberg also had access to poems by Rachel Bluvshteyn, Yocheved Bat-Miriam, and Esther Raab, who preceded her, but also became her contemporaries as they continued publishing. Other female poets she may have read are unfamiliar names for today's readers. For Margolin, female contemporaries could be encountered more easily on the pages of Yiddish journals and in the literary scenes she moved through in Odessa, Warsaw, and New York. However, access to a concrete textual past of women writing consolidated in print would become available only in 1928, when Ezra Korman published his monumental anthology *Yidishe dikhterins*. Consequently, it is safe to say that both Goldberg and Margolin were embarking on a new tradition, without knowing what kind of continuities they could expect.

Between the discontinuous past and the unexpected future, the interwar period offered Jewish writers, and especially Jewish women writers, a new range of linguistic, cultural, and geographical possibilities, opening movement between the literary centers such as Odessa, Warsaw, Berlin, Tel Aviv, and New York, and between Jewish languages and local vernaculars. However, within this field of cultural fluidity, the choices open to men and women were very different; while they were largely left out of traditional Jewish education, women had far more access to local vernaculars.[5] Women's access to Jewish languages was also different, even once Hebrew became more accessible to women, a difference evident in the fact that very few women wrote in both Yiddish and Hebrew, whereas many of their male contemporaries did.[6] Instead, women's literary biographies frequently note a single transition from a vernacular to Hebrew or Yiddish.[7] The

Leksikon fun der nayer yidisher literatur (the Biographical Dictionary of New Yiddish Literature) repeats that "this particular writer began writing in Russian/Polish and then switched to Yiddish" in numerous biographies of women writers, rarely providing references to actual published texts, yet generating a kind of prototypical biography for a woman's journey to writing. Anna Margolin, who switched from Russian to Yiddish (and that only after arriving in America) is but one example of many.[8]

Though surrounded by speakers of Russian, Lithuanian, German, and Yiddish, Leah Goldberg actually began her literary career by writing in Hebrew and is thus exceptional among Jewish women writers. Born in 1911, she spent her early years in Lithuania and then Germany. There she found her place within the emergent milieu of Hebrew language proponents, starting with the teachers at the Hebrew gymnasium she attended.[9] The poems under discussion in this chapter are some of her first publications, appearing when she was less than twenty years old, while she was still living in Europe. By age twenty-four she immigrated to Palestine, where she gained prominence as a leading literary figure of the *Modernah*, the dominant prestate modernist movement in Hebrew poetry.[10] Goldberg's first attempts at Hebrew writing are found in her childhood diary, which was published in Israel just over a decade ago.[11] Goldberg began keeping the diary in 1921, when she was ten years old. The deliberate choice to use Hebrew (rather than Russian, Lithuanian, or Yiddish) is not only enacted in the diary, tracking her growing mastery of the language; it is also a frequent topic discussed in it.

The stories of becoming a woman, a Hebrew speaker, and a writer are all constructed as intertwining processes of identity formation. One example of this confluence of formations can be found in an entry from August 19, 1925, where Goldberg creates an analogy between her personal choice of a love object and the national choice of the Hebrew language, expressing great frustration in both choices. Of the loved one she writes: "I don't know who needs this, I love him, I don't know why this is, he certainly doesn't need this, and neither do I. But nobody asked me for an answer."[12] These deep doubts mirror exactly those she expresses regarding the choice of language in the very same diary entry: "I don't understand for what or for whom it is necessary that an entire folk speak a language it doesn't know, which is hard for the people to learn, and is not the one in which they think." By using the same term—*necessary* (*naḥuts*)—to discuss personal choices of the heart and collective national considerations, the two become inextricable. Indeed, conducting this very discussion in Hebrew in the private genre of the diary personalizes the collective language choice as a difficult and even absurd one, at the same time as it renders the most intimate of expressions part of the collective project, thereby contributing to its success. This joint struggle of language and love diverges as Goldberg comes of age. Whereas her choices of love object continued to be a source of pain and frustration throughout her life, as reflected in her work, her fraught inchoate attempts at Hebrew self-expression proved fruitful as she took on an active role in shaping Hebrew poetic language as we know it.

* * *

Taking on Goldberg's early Hebrew poetry, before the Hebrew linguistic project came to fruition, I want to focus on the places where she resists the forward-looking gaze, creating her own queer history. Following the model of the previous chapter, I will identify this queer history according to the widest meaning of the term *queer*—that is, disrupting of normative identity, desire, and temporality—while considering the poetic and political resonance of doing so in Hebrew. The previous chapter explored Margolin's self-fashioning of herself as a non-Jewish male in the poem "*Ikh bin geven a mol a yingling*" ("I Was Once a Boy"), transgressing boundaries of sexuality, temporality, and religion. If Margolin ended by mocking the "weakling of Nazareth," Goldberg offers us her own projection of herself as male, while leading us to read her speaker as none other than Margolin's "weakling of Nazareth": Jesus.

חֲלוֹם נַעֲרָה

"מגדלנה הקדושה"—תמונה מאת קרלו קריוֶלי
נמצאת ב-Kaiser Friedrich Museum בברלין

אֲנִי חָלַמְתִּי שֶׁאֲנִי—אַתָּה,
וּמַגְדְּלֶנָה שֶׁל קְרִיוֶלִי
לִי מַגִּישָׁה מַשְׁקֶה רוֹתֵחַ, זַךְ
בִּגְבִיעַ-בְּדֹלַח מְצֻפֶּה זָהָב,
וְתַלְתַּלָּהּ—נָחָשׁ נִפְתָּל וָרֹד—
מִדֵּי עָבְרָהּ, נוֹגֵעַ בִּלְחָיַי,

וְכָל גּוּפִי שִׁכּוֹר מֵרִיחַ טֻבָּרוֹזָה.
אֲנִי חָלַמְתִּי שֶׁאֲנִי—אַתָּה.
וּפַרְצוּפָהּ שֶׁל נַעֲרָה חִוֶּרֶת
נִמְחָה מִזִּכְרוֹנִי לְעוֹלָמִים
וְאָנֹכִי צָמֵא לְמַגְדָּלֶנָה.

וְלֹא הָיָה מוֹצָא מִתּוֹךְ זְוַעַת-חֲלוֹם,
וְלֹא הָיָה מִפְלָט מִמַּגְדָּלֶנָה.

Dream of a Girl
"Saint Magdalene"—a painting by Carlo Crivelli, in the
    Kaiser Friedrich Museum in Berlin

I dreamt that I was—you,
and Crivelli's Magdalena
was serving me a steaming drink, pure
in a gold-plated crystal goblet
and her curl—coiled soft snake—
as she passes, touches my cheek,
and my entire body drunk with the scent of tuberose.
I dreamt that I was—you.
And the face of a pale girl
was wiped from my memory forever.
Now I thirst for Magdalena.

And there was no way out of horror's dream,
and there was no escaping Magdalena.[13]

Both the poem itself and its title, "Ḥalom na'arah" ("dream of a girl"), hold the ambiguity of "girl" as object of the dream and girl as dreamer. This ambiguity is present in translation and in the original Hebrew title's genitive construct (*smikhut*), which ties the girl and dream into one interdependent term. It also plays on the idiom *ḥalom balahah*,[14] meaning nightmare. If we understand the poem to be a girl's dream, then we can assume the speaker of the poem is female. However, the poem opens with the statement "I dreamt that I was you," using the second-person address *atah*, which in the Hebrew original is distinctly gendered as male. Besides indicating that the speaker dreamed she was a particular male, that is, the addressee (you/*atah*), the structure also opens the possibility of the pronoun *atah* (*you*) standing for what the female speaker dreamt she was in general (i.e., "I dreamt I was an '*atah*' "—"I dreamt I was a 'he' ").[15] The only other distinctly gendered word used for the speaker is *tsame*, thirst, which is gendered masculine. Just as the identity of the speaker is ambiguous, so too is the identity of this "you," the addressee. However, his identity can be inferred in relation to the woman who is named in the poem, Mary Magdalene, whose depiction in the poem invokes her Biblical encounters with Jesus.

By activating the Biblical context of Magdalene, Goldberg implicitly identifies the addressee with Jesus. And yet, the primary context is that of the speaker's dream and her poem, rather than the symbolic, collective, and religious resonances of the Christian narrative. The specificity of the particular Magdalene is part of this relocation of the collective symbol. For this reason, Goldberg insists on identifying her as "Crivelli's Magdalena," both under the poem's title and within the poem itself. Thus, it is not the Magdalene of Jesus, or even of Christianity in general, but rather that of one particular artist, and by extension, that of this particular poet. In this sense, the verbal narrative of history is mediated by visual art, which in turn is mediated by the verbal unfolding of the poem. At the same time, the dream context serves Goldberg as a realistic motivation for positioning her speaker in the role of Jesus, and can thus be differentiated from Margolin's self-fashioning in "I Was Once a Boy," which does away with, and even acts against, such realistic grounding.

Magdalene is the "other woman," not just in relation to the Virgin Mary, but also in the poem where she competes with the "face of a pale girl," the one who is supposedly erased from the speaker's memory in the dream-poem. This "pale girl" is easily identifiable with Goldberg's construction of self in other poems, writing for example (in an untitled poem): "You are a not pretty woman, twenty-two years old / an extinguished candle on the Sabbath table."[16] By erasing the trace of this girl from memory, but not from the poem, the speaker inscribes in the poem the very image (possibly her own image) that she is trying to disavow, creating a split. While the poem seems to set up a dichotomy between "the face of a pale girl" and Magdalene, Crivelli's image itself can be interpreted as a girl's pale face, leading to a further blurring between the figures in the poem. If this "other woman" can erase the speaker's *I*, and the male addressee can replace the speaker's *I* for the duration of the poem/dream, then perhaps they both stand in equally for the lyrical *I*, causing the speaker's desire to be Magdalene (instead of the pale girl), to mesh with her desire to have her, armed with the male persona of the Jesus of her dream. Staging the encounter with the dreamed woman in the name of a male persona still has a queer resonance, for the woman is the one who possesses the symbolic phallus (in the form of that curling snake) and imposes herself on the speaker, who is powerless against her. The entangling of desires *to be* and *to have*, a classical lesbian pathology as patriarchal discourse would have it,[17] is here complicated by the extreme negativity associated with both forms of desire, as expressed in the closing couplet: "And there was no way out of horror's dream, / and there was no escaping Magdalena."

Doubly distancing the discourse of forbidden desire to the realm of the past as well as to a non-Jewish discourse,[18] the queer narrative Goldberg writes joins the poetic tradition of Margolin and Lazarus. Like them she conflates differences of self and other, Jew and non-Jew, male and female, while mapping the haunting desire onto the experience of Jesus, originating in the New Testament narrative. Moreover, the New Testament becomes, in Goldberg's hands, a queerly expectant text. Activating the intricacies of Christianity's ambivalent relationship to female sexuality, Goldberg voices her own ambivalent experience. While the poem echoes Christianity's fear of female sexuality in general, it does so not through an anonymous woman, but through Magdalene, who is closely associated with sinful and demonized sexuality. In this move Goldberg is also reversing the original context she draws from, for in scripture Jesus repeatedly accepts Magdalene, alongside others who are labeled as sinners. The New Testament context alluded to is the scene from Luke in which a woman, who is generally identified as Mary Magdalene, a "known sinner," washes Jesus's feet with her tears, anoints them with oil, and kisses them. While the Pharisee criticizes Jesus for allowing this, Jesus condones her behavior and turns against the Pharisee accusingly: "You gave me no kiss, but from the time I came in she has not stopped kissing my feet" (Luke 7:45). This retort condones submissive sexuality in its juxtaposition with servitude, and opens a surprising space for homoerotic interaction. While we do not get to see the Pharisee kissing Jesus's feet in Luke, we do see Judas doing so in Goldberg's poem "Pieta."[19] Goldberg's poems thus activate a range of subtle intertextual interactions with the Christian texts, highlighting the sources' own ambivalence regarding sexuality, where heterosexuality produces as much anxiety as homosexuality, and sinful sexuality (like that of Magdalene) is condoned and homoeroticism (among Jesus and the apostles) is even invited. Goldberg does not adopt the Christian binaries, but rather engages them in a nuanced way that reflects her own ambivalence, writing both gay and straight panic into the poem. Both modes of panic, and the desire behind them, make Goldberg's poems fertile ground for my queer interpretation, as her poems themselves offer a queer hermeneutic of texts past.

We can see this queer hermeneutic both in individual poems and in the intertextual relations between the poems and other source texts. For example, we can follow the symbol of the drink from the poem across multiple texts. In Luke's narrative, and in Crivelli's painting, the woman carries an alabaster flask to anoint Jesus's feet. In the poem this becomes a drink in a "gold plated crystal goblet." The drink is tied to the thirst for Magdalene expressed by the speaker, but also to the words uttered by Jesus on the cross: "Later, knowing that all was now completed, and so that the Scripture would be fulfilled, Jesus said, 'I am thirsty'" (John 19:28). In Goldberg's queer rewriting of Jesus's final moments, as her poetic speaker thirsts for Magdalena, Goldberg shows that in fact not "all was completed," or perhaps, that another end is available. In this alternate history, the return, the resurrection, and the Second Coming, are not of Christ but of Magdalena. And rather than a messianic anticipation, Goldberg offers an ambivalent queer expectancy.

In another of Goldberg's Christian poems, "Beminzar Pazaislio" ("In the Pazaislio Monastery"),[20] the image of the drink stands at the intersection of temptation and transgression, between Christian and Jewish dictates and histories. "In the Pazaislio Monastery" is named for the monastery Goldberg visited east of Kovno while she was working for a Christian family that hired her to teach their children Lithuanian. Hebrew literature scholars Giddon Ticotsky and Yfaat Weiss, who have done extensive work with Goldberg's archives, write that this was Goldberg's first experience of total immersion in a Christian environment, and they claim, based on her letters to her friend Mina Landau from the decade leading up to the writing of this poem (1925–35), that this experience led to her disenchantment with the culture that she had earlier found particularly alluring.[21] "In the Pazaislio Monastery" indeed sets up the allure of Christianity, monastic life, and the pious ideal of motherhood, all of which the speaker ultimately rejects. In the poem, the speaker is served a drink by a "foreign god image." This drink is described as poisonous ("*kos kuba'at tar'elah*," alluding to Isaiah 51:17), and later on in the poem the speaker describes her blood as poisoned by "tales of foreign lands" ("*agadot nekhar*"). The effect of the poisoning words makes it impossible for her to resist the temptation of kneeling before the foreign deity. These foreign tales echo the wild tales, the *vilde mayses* of Margolin's poem, and here too they are words placed in the mouth of the non-Jewish other. In addition to the implications of idol worship in Margolin's poem, discussed in the previous chapter, here the kneeling is also tied to the Christian ideal of submission. It is clear that for the speaker of this particular poem, to kneel would be an act of defiance against, and betrayal of, her Judaism, for the Christian ideal of submission is not hers to fulfill. Unable to take this transgressive step, she heeds the Jewish "voice of generations," which whispers in the final verse: "let go of the folly; / Not for you Madonna's mourning tear, / and the mothers' laughter not for you." She must disavow Christianity, along with its venerated image of maternity, as well as its sanctified image of suffering. At the same time, the abdication of motherhood itself can be associated with a Christian tradition of celibacy, entirely foreign to Judaism, as the Jewish dictum is that women should bear children to produce future generations.

In an earlier version of the poem, published in 1928 (five years before the version included in Goldberg's first book, *Taba'ot ashan* [Smoke Rings]), the conflict posed by the temptation of the mourning Madonna is cast in national terms rather than personal ones: "not in the name of a mourning Madonna / did the best of your people burn at the stake" ("*lo beshem madona mit'abelet/alu tovey amekh al hamoked*"). Ticotsky and Weiss, who briefly mention this fascinating original version in a footnote, attribute the shift from the national to the personal to Goldberg's "understanding that she was not meant to be a mother."[22] Instead of this personal/national dichotomy, I would argue that both versions offer a complicated position vis-à-vis the national collective; in the original line the reference is to the best of *your* people (*amekh*, feminine), highlighting the speaker's personal role in relation to that collective; in the later version, even though she remains loyal to the Jewish faith ("Not for you Madonna's mourning tear"), she is also betraying the collective call to reproduce the nation by rejecting motherhood ("and the mothers' laughter not for you"). The voice of generations' whispering thus commands loyalty to (Jewish) generations past, while rejecting, via Christianity, participation in the (re)production of a Jewish future.

The juxtaposition of Christian imagery with themes of motherhood is consistent with much of Goldberg's early poetic vocabulary. Considering that the bulk of her so called Christian poems include a rejection of motherhood ("not for you the mothers' laughter"), the use of the Christian monastic discourse can be seen as facilitating this position, which pushes against both the Zionist and the Jewish reproductive imperatives.[23] But Goldberg does not merely adopt this possibility;

instead, as we saw above, she activates the complicated range of meaning found in the original Christian context, drawing on Christian dogma's venerated virgin motherhood together with its condemnation of female sexuality. Examining the activation of this binary and the way Goldberg utilizes its full complexity reveals the subtlety of Goldberg's engagement with this discourse. Expressing both queer desire and a rejection of motherhood via non-Jewish discourse serves Goldberg as a calculated displacement: by drawing attention first and foremost to the foreignness of her thematics, the full impact of her subversiveness appears to be mitigated. Allusions to the New Testament, though not uncommon in Jewish modernism, had a huge shock effect for a reading public forbidden to touch the "other" Christian texts. Thus, readers were (and still are) more likely to call these Goldberg's "Christian poems" than her "queer" or "anti-motherhood poems," when in fact the poems simultaneously weave together these multiple transgressive positions.

In one final reading of the image of the of the drink, I want to tie it not to its Biblical sources, but back to the epigraph of this chapter, where Emma Lazarus describes the "proffered cup" having been drained as a sign of "acceptance fraught with keenest pain / Seeing that all her struggles must be in vain." This (extremely pessimistic) acceptance is what denies Lazarus's speaker comfort from looking "forth" and "back," relegating her to the realms of the present. This form of acceptance leads us to one final Goldberg poem, "Madonot al parashat derakhim" ("Madonnas at a Crossroads"),[24] where the speaker declares not her struggles to be in vain, but rather her act of waiting. In both poems, success seems to lie in acceptance, where acceptance itself acts as a mode of queer expectancy, holding multiple temporalities in advance, while resisting future fulfillment.

מָדוֹנוֹת עַל פָּרָשַׁת דְּרָכִים

אֲנִי הִסְכַּנְתִּי לְחַכּוֹת לַשָּׁוְא
וּבְלִי יָגוֹן לִזְכֹּר יָמִים מְבֹרָכִים.
מָדוֹנוֹת עֵץ עַל פָּרָשַׁת דְּרָכִים
שְׁלֵווֹת כָּמוֹנִי בְּקֶרַח אוֹר הַסְּתָו.

מָדוֹנוֹת עֵץ בָּלוֹת וְדוֹמְמוֹת
יוֹדְעוֹת: הוּא לֹא יָקוּם עוֹד לִתְחִיָּה,
הוּא לֹא יָבוֹא לִמְחוֹת דִּמְעָה בְּדוּמִיָּה
עַל אֵם דְּרָכִים קְפוּאוֹת וְשׁוֹמֵמוֹת.

הֵן לֹא תִזְכֶּינָה לְנַשֵּׁק הֲדוֹם רַגְלָיו,
הֲהֵן שָׁמְעוּ אֶת צְחוֹק הַיֶּלֶד מִנְּצֶרֶת?
וּמַה גַּם אִם רָאוּהוּ עַל הַצְּלָב
וְעַל שְׂפָתָיו קָרְאוּ אֶת שְׁמָהּ שֶׁל הָאַחֶרֶת?

אַךְ הֵן זוֹכְרוֹת יָמִים מְבֹרָכִים
וּמַסְכִּינוֹת לְצִפִּיַּת הַשָּׁוְא—
כְּמוֹהֶן אֲנִי: עַל פָּרָשַׁת דְּרָכִים
קָרָה וְכֹה שׁוֹקְטָה בְּקֶרַח אוֹר הַסְּתָו.

Madonnas at a Crossroads[25]

I've resigned myself to wait in vain
remembering without anguish blessed days.
Wooden Madonnas at a crossroads
peaceful, like me, in the ice light of fall.

Wooden Madonnas, worn and silent
know: he will no more be resurrected.
He will not come silently to wipe a tear
at a crossing,[26] frozen and desolate.

They will not get to kiss his feet,
did they hear the laughter of the child of Nazareth?
And so what if they saw him on the cross
and on his lips they read the name of the other?[27]

But they remember blessed days
and resign themselves to vain expectation.
Like them, I—at a crossroads
cold and so quiet in the ice light of fall.

This Hebrew poem, written before Hebrew became normalized as a poetic and vernacular language, uses the nascent language to weave a Christian history rooted in an Eastern European landscape. This move continues the queer conflations this book has been following, as it brings together the Jewish and the Christian, the Eastern European and the Palestinian, the past and the present, conflating multiple categories and expressing antifuturity. This complex multiplicity is actually embodied in the writer's choice to write in Hebrew, which can be seen as simultaneously constructing a connection to the Jewish past, and as participation in the construction of a particular Jewish future. At the same time, Goldberg uses Hebrew to write against (Jewish) past and future alike.

Standing against the present orientation toward the future, the poem uses a concrete element in the present—an icon—to activate the discourse of a Christian past. The Madonnas of the poem mark the common practice of placing wooden representations of the Virgin Mary at rural crossroads in Eastern Europe. The focus on the iconic furthers the visual poetics of reappropriating idol worship that we recognized in the previous chapter as part of Margolin's "Jewish imagism," following Barbara Mann. Taking part in this Hebrew-Yiddish literary trend, Goldberg moves beyond a simple relocation of the symbol to utilize the multiple levels of meaning invoked by these Madonnas simultaneously, from their material qualities (wooden, worn, stationary, mute), through their symbolic power as icons (multiple representations, each possessing part of the sanctity of the original, and thus worthy of worship), and not least, their referents' narrative/biographical role in the life of Jesus. Goldberg thus both personifies and multiplies the single image of the Madonna, creating a group representation of women who share a similar fate. Goldberg gives the Madonnas a story, but not quite a voice, so the Madonnas serve as a silent chorus, collectively speaking to the poet alone, allowing her to join their ranks. That the speaker is able to position herself among them by the end of the poem is enabled only by her redefinition of their significance, rewriting both the Christian intertext and the dominant Zionist politics and poetics of Goldberg's time.

A central aspect of Goldberg's poetic rewriting lies in her rejection of the possibility of redemption, declaring the speaker's waiting to be in vain. This rejection, however, is intricately constructed between the feminine, the Jewish, the Christian, and the Zionist. Overtly subverting the Christian discourse she is borrowing from, Goldberg replaces the messianic anticipation of the Second Coming of Christ with a personalized, painful anticipation that is acknowledged in advance as futile. The commitment to eternal anticipation plays on stereotypes of female passivity, in line with Christianity and with the Biblical dictum that declares that "though it tarry, wait for it; because it will surely come, it will not tarry" (Habakkuk 2:3, KJV translation). At the same time, this waiting can also be read as a counter to the Zionist version of secular messianism that advocates actively bringing about redemption (of the land) rather than passively awaiting it (that is, the traditional belief that Jews should return to the land of Israel when, and only when, the Messiah comes, in fact the dominant rabbinic notion that "rushing" the footsteps of the Messiah along is a catastrophic transgression). Finally, however, the fact that the waiting is declared to be in vain (*lashav*) negates the messianic potential and the sense of ultimate purpose attached to it, together with all other forms of action and political hope.

Declaring explicitly that "he will no more be resurrected," or "revived" ("*lo yakum od lit'ḥiyah*"), Goldberg may be pointing directly to the Hebrew poetic movement that preceded her own period (the Modernah): the Teḥiyah, the revival period. This movement's name appropriates the term describing (messianic) resurrection for a linguistic Zionist context, while implying the messianic force of the literary movement itself. This period, ranging from the 1880s to the 1920s, is seen as marking both the revival of the Hebrew language and literature, and the return of the literary center—by the end of this period—to "the Land of Israel," with the first three major waves of immigration. While biographically Goldberg can be seen as an heir of the period, arriving in Palestine in 1935, this particular poem also marks her deviation from it. If Goldberg's resistance to redemption can be seen as anti-Teḥiyah (revival), the fact that Goldberg does not return the Madonnas to the land of Israel can be seen as subversive of the dominant Zionist poetics focused on a "return" ("*shivah*") to the Land (Zion) and its prediasporic Jewish/Israelite history. She is not returning the scriptural figures to their native Palestine, reinscribing Mary as a Jewish mother; and she is not using them to celebrate a sense of historical continuity and a renewed bond with the land, as her predecessors and contemporaries have done.

Indeed, there is a context to the Jewish turn to Christian figures,[28] and yet I will argue that both Leah Goldberg and Anna Margolin (whose invocation of Jesus in the poem "Once I was Boy" stood at the center of the previous chapter) transgress the norms of this context, and make very different use of it as Jewish women writers. Tracking the appearance of Jesus in Hebrew and Yiddish modernist writing by men, Matthew Hoffman emphasizes the national appropriations of the Jesus figure.[29] He describes the writers' use of Jesus as a prototypical modernist Jew to engage a wide variety of topics, from pogroms in Russia to Jewish nationalism in Palestine. The general trend of modernist Jewish writers of the time, writes Hoffman, was to transfer "ownership of the figure of Jesus, and all of the cultural patrimony that flowed from him, to the Jews." He asserts that in the modernists' views, "Christians had misunderstood Jesus's intrinsically

Jewish teachings and kidnapped their ancient Jewish brother, who now had to be returned home."[30]

Over and against this trend, I argue that both Goldberg and Margolin transpose themselves into the landscape of Christianity. This landscape is conjured to mirror the Eastern European Christian present they both grew up in, and stands in contrast to a future national or messianic return to the land of Christian and Jewish history.[31] In their poems, the Christian figures cannot simply be identified as being "reclaimed" by Judaism, perhaps because as women Judaism itself was not theirs to claim. Where the speakers identify with them, it is precisely their otherness that is foregrounded, whether as compelling or deterring. Activating the intricacies of their original context, whether in the New Testament or in Church dogma (and playing the two against each other), allows them to make subversive statements regarding their present and impending future. When Christian figures are identified with Judaism, as we saw in Margolin's description of Jesus as "the weakling of Nazareth," this serves a double distancing, allowing the female poet/speaker to express distance from Christian figures, and from the Jewish men they are like. This complex engagement of both Margolin and Goldberg may be due to the fact that for writing women, both Christianity and Judaism share something of a foreignness. At the same time these female poets utilize their own exclusion from the centers of Jewish text and life as enabling freedom of movement and cross-identifications,[32] across time and gender, and here, across culture and religion. This type of cultural fluidity was less accessible to Jewish men of their time, whose firm grounding in Jewish tradition placed them at odds with both Christianity and with Western culture as a whole. Just as the Christian figures used in Jewish literature stand both inside and outside Judaism, so too do the female poets occupy a liminal space, which they use to critique both Christian and Jewish hegemonic tradition while mobilizing gender against the normative nationalist concepts of Jewish identification that are set up as trumping all others.

The heart of Goldberg's critique and subversion can be read through two disruptions of temporality in the poem "Madonot," both relating to the rewriting of the time of the evoked Christian intertext. The first complicates the narrative of Mary's biography and the second defiantly challenges Jewish and Christian theology, negating the present promise of future redemption. The poem strikingly merges the roles of the different women in Jesus's life, and the different periods of his life and afterlife, collapsing the particular biographical chronology by deeming Mary mother, lover, mourner, and worshiper all at once. Cast as a chorus, the Madonnas are "post"—in the sense that they speak after the life of Jesus, and in that they are past their prime (even the word used for *worn*, *balot*, means menopausal in Biblical Hebrew)[33]—but they are also "pre"—before the resurrection, which will never come and yet is anticipated in its very negation. In this liminal space, the linear temporality of the narrative is collapsed, blurring the distinctions between what may have happened in the past ("did they hear the laughter?"), what happened but is disregarded or even disavowed ("so what if they saw"), and what may have occurred in the past but is now distinctly foreclosed ("They will not get to kiss his feet").

The collapsed temporality of the Madonnas is perhaps most extreme in their position of "resign[ing] themselves to vain expectation," and her speaker's resignation to "wait in vain." Goldberg's poem thus recasts expectancy, offering anticipation as an act of resignation, thereby invoking a queer time that resists future fulfillment. Choosing to wait can thus be read as a position of relinquishing the present in the face of the future, and choosing to wait in vain forecloses the future as well, for it suggests that the future will be a static continuation of the unfulfilled present. The active choice of passivity brings to mind the words of Yochved Bat-Miriam: "Good for me in secrets-distance / To wait for you in vain. / You are my heart's blood sent hope / For that which will no more come to me."[34] If Bat-Miriam declares an active preference for the lack of fulfillment she inscribes in her poem, Goldberg's Madonnas' waiting can be read as "a politics of passivity, queer, as only a passive politics could be said to be."[35] This passivity, writes Carla Freccero, is "a suspension, a waiting, an attending to the world's arrivals (through in part, its returns)." I see this not only as resistance to Christian messianism, but also as a counterpoint to Zionist messianism, embodied in the Zionist politics and poetics of action, epitomized in creating "facts on the ground" ("*uvdot bashetah*," the militaristic status of attaining and expanding control). Instead, it offers waiting, again in the words of Freccero: "not as a guarantee or security for action in the present, but as the very force from the past that moves us into the future."[36] Mapping the waiting onto the past, Goldberg's speaker is the future of those Madonnas whose (a)temporality she creates so that she can join it. But that, of course, is not what they are waiting for; she is not their redemption, since they are not hers.

Goldberg was only twenty years old when this poem was published, yet she already offers a distinct sense of what will happen in the future, or rather, what will not happen (including, in her own life: a foreclosure of heteronormative romantic fulfillment, namely in the form of marriage, and reproduction). This reading runs the risk of what Michael André Bernstein has termed "backshadowing,"[37] an anachronistic reading influenced by the outcome of certain events, mixed with the (often unfortunate) tendency to limit poetic interpretation to the biography of the poet, a risk particularly pertinent in the case of female poets. Furthermore, backshadowing presumes a deterministic view of historical progression, precisely the premise this study questions. Instead of deterministic progression, I identify anachronistic projection as Goldberg's own poetic strategy, enacting what Heather Love calls "proleptic mourning,"[38] when a loss is called into being by the mourning that would normally follow it. Goldberg herself stages the scene of proleptic mourning for the Madonnas, who mourn in advance the one who will not return again ("*lo yakum od*"). Placing her speaker as one of the Madonnas, Goldberg's text stages a proleptic mourning of the future, in what we might see as a queer form of *Imitatio Christi*.

Pushing the boundaries of Christian and Jewish messianic traditions while undoing religious and reproductive teleology, this poem continues the conflation of transgressions read in Anna Margolin's poem. As we saw, Margolin's poem "Once I was a Boy" creates a cyclical time that transgresses the model of development dictated by reproductive heteronormative history. Goldberg's transgression challenges not only this model of progression, but also the future orientation dictated by Christian and Jewish messianic teleology alike. Joining the ranks of the Madonnas, Goldberg, like Margolin, makes a claim about her place in the present of Jewish letters by refusing the idea of a "better future," in particular one generated by reproductive futurity and other models of teleological historical progression. These poets are using the past, in Love's words, "to imagine a future apart from the reproductive imperative, optimism, and the promise of redemption."[39] Both Love and the poets I discuss here argue against two modes of future: reproductive futurity and a version of messianic teleology. What Love offers instead is a "backward future,"[40] like the one the poems construct by turning to an imagined past, by disrupting linear temporal progression, and by denying the viability of futures produced biologically or through teleological ideology, religious or nationalistic.

I want to argue for the vitality of the backward future, as a means for these writers to carve out a space for themselves within and against the dominant discourse. Margolin uses her own hindsight regarding the ultimate fall of the Roman Empire in "I Was Once a Boy," ironically portraying the Pagans mocking the Christians, not knowing their own days as an empire are numbered. Using

Margolin's version of history to understand this backward future reminds us of the traditionally cyclical view of Jewish history, of the folly and dangers of trying to write the history of the victor, which is always shortsighted. Indeed, the historical centers of power with which Margolin aligns her speaker are those of greatness that did not last, though they are still regarded as the classical site of Western culture. Margolin may enter that site only with the knowledge that its power was temporary, pointing perhaps to the fleeting power of other dominant groups whose oppression she was still facing. While she may join the victors of the moment in mocking that "weakling from Nazareth," the joke, we can say, is on that past, which did not last, but also on the speaker "who once was" a non-Jewish boy, but is now (in the time of the poem) a Jewish woman, and is, after all, subjected to Christianity's often anti-Semitic rule, along with the oppressive patriarchy of Judaism itself. In this case, we might ask what, or, who is the future really good for?

Echoing this question, modernist writers have foregrounded resistance to futurity as a major poetic tenet. In her introduction to *On the Margins of Modernism*, Chana Kronfeld points out this resistance, highlighting the choice of Hebrew over German made by the first Hebrew modernist poet, Avraham Ben-Yitzhak (Sonne) (1883–1950), a choice that forced him to simultaneously assert and deny "the possibility of his project ever leaving a mark" by "refusing to constitute his modernist project as productive."[41] The poem Kronfeld reads, "Ashrey hazor'im" ("Happy Are the Sowers")[42] celebrates "the sowers that will not reap,"[43] and is, in fact, the last poem Ben-Yitzhak published, one of only a handful which were published in his lifetime. Even his complete works, published in 1992, amount to only a small sixty-page volume.[44] Hannan Hever, who edited the volume, identifies in this limited oeuvre "a clear declaration of a preference for resignation and becoming silent in order to achieve the real advantage in eternity."[45] Hever ties this antiproductive position both to his poetic sensibilities and to his ambivalence toward institutional Zionism.[46]

We can see the impact of this poetic and political resignation in Leah Goldberg's poetry. Furthermore, Goldberg also left a record of her actual encounter with Ben-Yitzhak in her 1952 tribute *Pegishah im meshorer* (*Meeting with a Poet*).[47] This text expresses her admiration for his minimalist poetic project, as well as her sense of responsibility to pass on the "precious treasure" ("*otsar yakar*")[48] she received from knowing him, a treasure she believes is too precious to keep private (*birshut hayaḥid*). In a poem she published the same year and dedicated to Ben-Yitzhak,[49] Goldberg returns to Christian imagery (significantly, Catholic and monastic, as Kronfeld stresses)[50] to valorize his position, which she cogently terms "the calm of refusal." Turning to Christianity to bolster an oppositional stance, specifically one of preemptive resignation, resonates strongly with the poem "Madonot." In fact, Ben-Yitzhak's poem "Happy Are the Sowers" shares a number of points of intertextual encounter with Goldberg's poem,[51] most evidently, the idiomatic expression for "crossroads," *em derakhim* (literally, "mother of roads," as I explained earlier in my reading). Additionally, the penultimate verse in Ben-Yitzhak's poem: "Happy are those who know what their heart calls from the desert / and on their lips will blossom silence" foreshadows the Madonnas' disavowal of the knowledge of both death and betrayal: "So what if they saw him on the cross / and on his lips they read the name of the other?" In the Hebrew original, Goldberg's text reads even more directly as an allusion to Ben-Yitzhak's, for the word for *call* and *read* are the same. The position adopted by Goldberg's Madonnas and speaker, by Ben-Yitzhak's idealized model, and by Goldberg's projected image of Ben-Yitzhak, all share a recognition of the futility of action, valuing inaction and silence, while the narration of passivity becomes the very message that has the power to generate future poetry.[52]

What distinguishes the male modernist writers' resistance to futurity is the degree to which they deploy "birth" as a trope for creative production, whereas female bodies' concrete birthing capabilities appear to be at odds with creative production.[53] Therefore, it is not surprising to see that part of the backward turn is tied directly also to questions of maternity, as we saw in Goldberg's queer/Christian poetry. Similarly, and at the same time, Margolin turned to the Virgin Mary, in a poetic cycle that also engages complicated themes of motherhood. The cycle, titled "*Mari*,"[54] revolves around the character Mari, creating a persona that relates to the Virgin Mary and activates Christian intertexts and culture more broadly.[55] The poem "Maris tfile" ("Mary's Prayer"), for example, relates directly to the New Testament's narrative of Mary's life, as Kathryn Hellerstein has shown,[56] while the poem "Mari un der prister" ("Mary and the Priest") invokes contemporary Christian religious roles and practice. Most significantly for the present discussion, two poems in the cycle resonate deeply with Goldberg's use of Christian imagery to portray a negotiation (and negation) of motherhood, as well as themes of waiting and unrequited love. In the poem "Vos vilstu, Mari?" ("What Do You Want, Mary?"),[57] the speaker generates a fantasy of a child napping in her lap, but this is not a beatific image of Madonna and child, but rather one of anticipation.

וואָס ווילסטו, מאַרי?

אפֿשר אַ קינד זאָל ליכטיק דרימלען אין מײַן שויס.
די טיפֿע שטומע אָוונטן אין שטרענגן הויז
אַליין, פֿאַמעלעך וואַנדערנדיק.
אַלץ וואַרטנדיק און וואַרטנדיק.
און זאָל מײַן ליבע זײַן צום מאַן, וואָס ליבט מיך ניט,
שטיל און ווי פֿאַרצווייפֿלונג גרויס.

וואָס ווילסטו, מאַרי?

What do you want, Mary?

Perhaps a child brightly drowsing in my lap.
Deeply silent evenings in the stern house
alone, wandering slowly.
Constantly waiting, waiting.
May my love be for him who loves me not,
quiet and like despair, immense.

What do you want, Mary?[58]

"*Pamelekh vanderndik / alts vartndik un vartndik*," the speaker is "slowly wandering / still waiting and waiting," for a man who does not love her. Constructed by words marking the tentative nature of the scene, *efsher* and *zol* ("perhaps" and "may"), the relation to fulfillment here, just as in Goldberg's "Madonot" poem, is one of negation and futility, where the fantasy of the child will not come to be. In another poem, "Mari un di gest" (Mary and the Guests), "the child" arrives:

און דו, און דו, און דו—אַ לאַנגע קייט.
און דאָס קינד איז דאָ.
עס איז געקומען צו דער מוטערס טיר פֿון זייער ווײַט.
עס האָט אין ווינקל זיך פֿאַררוקט, קליין און פֿול מיט טרויעריקייט.
עס איז אין זיך פֿאַרטיפֿט, דאָס קינד, און שטיל און ווײַס.
אויגן, קלאַנגט מיך ניט אָן, אויגן, קערט זיך ניט אָפּ.

> You, and you, and you—a long chain.
> And the child is here.
> It arrived at mother's door from a great distance.
> Crawled into a corner, small, suffused with sadness.
> This child, sunken into itself, silent and pale.
> Eyes, don't reproach me, eyes, don't turn away.[59]

This "guest" is described in eerie terms, "*kleyn un ful mit troyerkayt*" ("small and full of sadness"), "*shtil un vays*" ("quiet and white"). The speaker seems to speak silently, directly addressing the child's gaze: "Eyes, don't reproach me, eyes, don't turn away." Like Goldberg, Margolin uses Christian intertextually to construct an ambivalent position regarding romantic fulfillment and motherhood. But perhaps for Margolin the ambivalent and even negative mother-child relationship is less than surprising considering the child she left behind in Palestine.

As in Goldberg's case, here too I turn to the biographical not in order to produce a reductive reading of Margolin's poetry, but rather as a means to connect her poetry to the politics of her time, and to my time, through a letter I found in her archive.[60] The letter was written by her son, Na'aman, the child she bore and left in Mandatory Palestine with her first husband, the writer Moshe Stavski (Stavi). Eight-year-old Na'aman writes (in Hebrew),

> Your letter was read and translated for me by father and I was very happy about it. I don't understand and I also can't read "jargon," [a derogatory term for Yiddish] and I don't understand why you are so eager about your jargon. [. . .] Write to me in Hebrew so that I'll be able to read and answer you. *Shalom uvrachah* from me, your son, Na'aman.[61]

Margolin had little contact with the child after she left the Middle East, and this letter is a fascinating testament to a relationship marked by his not-so-subtle (if understandably passive-aggressive) revolt, not just against the abandoning mother, but also against Yiddish, the *mame-loshn*, the mother tongue that she uses, that she represents as a poet. The child's negation of Yiddish aligns him with the language of the father, his father, the author Stavski, who switched from Yiddish to Hebrew and wrote Orientalist tales in Hebrew. Following the Arabic model of naming the father for his eldest son, Stavski took on his son's name as a literary pseudonym, signing his works with the Arabic name *Abu-Na'aman* (father of Na'aman). As opposed to Yocheved Bat-Miriam's mother/daughter genealogical reversal and the complicated continuity it creates,[62] here the future replaces the past, in an attempt to erase the diasporic past through the native-born child, as well as through appropriative tactics, which reconstitute the immigrant author as a native of his adoptive land. Na'aman and the men of his generation indeed grew up to be the "New Jews," the generation their fathers yearned for, reshaping Jewish diasporic identity and culture. With the establishment of the State of Israel, the Hebrew language revolution came to fruition, forming a national Jewish language with its own geography and native speakers. Na'aman Stavi became the first military governor of the Galilee, appropriating not just Palestinian culture, as his father did, but taking control of Palestinian lives and land in the 1948 war and military rule (*mimshal tseva'i*) that followed it.[63]

Hebrew literature, according to the dominant literary historiography, emerged from the moment of uncertainty in the 1930s as the victorious Jewish language.[64] Israeli language politics, Jewish assimilation in the Diaspora, Stalinist purges, and the Khurbn (the Nazi extermination project), shaped the present and put into question the future of Yiddish as a Jewish language of secular culture. Reading Margolin's Yiddish poetry, which transgresses borders of temporality, gender and culture, we are reminded of the worlds Yiddish used to represent and create, expanding the boundaries of the language itself in doing so. Not yet knowing that the language of her modernist vision of history would itself become a thing of history, Margolin finally joins the ranks of the rulers and emperors among whom she imagined her poetic speaker, sharing their ultimate downfall. Falling silent shortly after her first and only book was published, Margolin stopped producing poems even before readers of modern Yiddish poetry stopped being reproduced.[65]

Reading Goldberg's early poetry reminds us of a world in which Hebrew played an entirely different role than it does today, when its future was far more in question than that of Yiddish. It is in this context that we can see Goldberg's turn to Christianity and the Eastern European landscape as a reflection of Hebrew's search for its own space of expression, as well as part of her search for her own (female) authorial voice. Furthermore, her resistance to action, to reproduction and to the premature celebration of redemption—all so characteristic of Zionism—not only distinguish her authorial voice from other voices of her time, they also offer today's reader a counterhistory to the present outcome of Jewish language politics. Reading these two poets together therefore serves to remind us that Jewish history had more than one inevitable future, geographically, linguistically, and politically. The importance of this reminder lies in the fact that it exposes the present moment as only one possible outcome, not the only necessary future, and not necessarily the best one. In the present moment, where Hebrew has come to represent the language of the State of Israel (and the State of Israel has come to represent the messianic teleological outcome of Jewish history), I cannot find hope in looking forward, if looking forward implies continuity. Turning to the histories offered by Margolin and Goldberg, I find not continuity, but rather queer possibilities of linguistic, poetic, and political multiplicity. For these writers, neither redemption (be it secular or religious) nor reproduction seemed much worth expecting. Instead, they let me look back at them, they let me look back with them, free from nostalgia (over the past) or utopian optimism (about the future). It is the backward future that spoke to their present ambivalence about the future, and it is that same tactic that allows me to turn back and find them waiting, perhaps not just in vain. This reading does not provide a happy end (of days), perhaps just the opposite, and yet it creates an unexpected genealogy and the promise that today's disappointments might hold the seeds of queer futures to come.

FOUR *HEYS* HAUNTING
Poetics of Lesbian History

> She responds, she understands.
> I have power on what is not,
> Or on what has ceased to be,
> From that deep, earth-hollowed spot,
> I can lift her up to me.

These words from Emma Lazarus's poem "Magnetism"[1] bring into being the queer genealogy I am searching for, where poetry can open new dialogue between past, present, and future, and challenge the workings of normative history. We must, however, "recognize the extent to which such genealogies are not vital, but rather, ghostly, impossible, interrupted," as Heather Love writes.[2] Lazarus's poem conjures the ghostly dimension of queer genealogy in a strikingly literal fashion, as her speaker is in dialogue with an *actual* ghost (who will return later in the chapter). If Love asks that we recognize the loss and absence inherent in genealogies connecting "real and imagined queer subjects," Lazarus's poem tells a story of queer desire past, made possible in her present by way of a spectral encounter. Following Lazarus's cue, the current chapter will take on the haunted and haunting aspects of queer genealogy, bringing together *apparitional lesbians* and *queer spectrality*. The *apparitional lesbian* is Terry Castle's term for the way the lesbian is cast in the role of ghost, at the same time that she is overlooked or "ghosted" out of existence in canonical literature: "Always somewhere else: in the shadows, in the margins, hidden from history, out of sight, out of mind, a wanderer in the dusk, a pale denizen of the night."[3] Castle traces the appearance of lesbian ghosts as a way to expose a history of lesbian presence, hoping at the same time to "recarnalize the ghostly lesbian body."[4] It should then be no surprise that the rare appearances of lesbian desire in early Jewish American and Yiddish poetry are conjured as forms of haunting and/or tied to ghosts. At the same time, this lesbian haunting is also part of the larger strategy of queerly disrupting (hetero)normative linear temporality and history traced throughout this book. Indeed, Carla Freccero offers queer spectrality as the perfect expression of this disruption, where haunting reminds us "that the past and the present are neither discrete nor sequential."[5] Looking at how voices from the past (whether ancestral or historical) appear as ghosts in poems by Jewish women, this chapter will put into practice the connection between spectrality, temporality, and queerness. Between haunting as a way to move between times (a movement we have been queerly exploring) and a way to embody otherwise forbidden (lesbian/queer) desire, this chapter will tell a Jewish lesbian ghost (hi)story, starring figures from Jewish history, women poets, and a cast of ghosts.

How does the ghost of lesbian desire in Yiddish reach us? Only just barely—and this is precisely what is at stake with haunting. Haunting is a way that lesbians get to survive through history—they are never fully there, but it also means they might still be, at least partially, here. Indeed, the lesbian herself may be lost, but lesbian desire still haunts the pages of Yiddish poetry.

אויף א באַלקאָן[6]

פֿון װײַטן זומער פֿליט צו מיר אַ הייס געלעכטער
פֿון צװיי קלײנע צאַרטע פֿרויען.
זיי בלעטערן אַ בילדערבוך.
זייערע הענט באַגעגענען זיך אין בענקשאַפֿט.
די װייכע אָקסלען זוכן זיך און צוקן.
איבער אַ דאָרשטיקער אָראַנזשן־רויטער לאַנדשאַפֿט
װעלבן זיך פֿאַרװױרט די העלע לײַבער.

איבער זיי טורעמט מעכטיק אַ מאַן
מיט שװערע גראַציע,
װי אַ פּרעכטיקע און איבעריקע דעקאָראַציע.

. . .

On a Balcony

    From a distant summer hot laughter floats toward me
    From two small and dainty women
    Leafing through a book.

> Their hands meet in longing.
> Soft shoulders searching quivering.
> Over a thirsty, orange-red landscape
> The bright bodies leap in confusion.
>
> A man towers over them
> With heavy grace,
> Like a grand superfluous decoration.[7]

This is a rare example of lesbian content in Yiddish literature,[8] from Anna Margolin, the same poet who wrote "Ikh bin geven a mol a yingling" ("I Was Once a Boy"). Besides undoing progressive and linear history in its movement between historical periods (Ancient Greece, Rome, and Early Christianity), "I Was Once a Boy" transcends boundaries of gender identity and sexual orientation, and offers distinct traces of queer practice in the homosocial spaces and homoerotic bonds it describes. It is thus as an example of queer temporality and queer content. The poem "On a Balcony" is far less swooping in its queer scope; it describes a single moment, an intimate, subtle interaction between two women. And yet, it holds in it an erotic charge that transcends its moment, where the echo of the women's interaction is amplified, first in the move between their hands and the "leap" of bodies, and then in the way this interaction reaches the speaker, and comes to be a poem. Making queer desire thematically seen and heard in and across time, the poem itself becomes a medium of queer haunting that reaches out to us, from *that* distant summer, and the now-distant poem.

The lesbian content of this poem is conjured in controlled poetic strategy. At the same time, it tells the story of the inability to control this content, which haunts the speaker, and therefore also the reader. If the poem begins by describing the auditory signal of two women's laughter, it quickly shifts to the realm of the visual, painting the picture of two women, who are themselves looking at a picture book. The poem gives a progressively more and more explicit description of the women's physical bodies. Though their movements are extremely subtle, the erotic charge gradually increases, at the same time that the reality of these bodies is gradually distanced. The initial description of the "small and dainty" women frames the desire (soon to be activated) very much in the realm of sameness. The positioning of lesbian desire as a connection based on sameness as opposed to a desire propelled by difference echoes the discussion regarding Goldberg's poem

"Dream of a Girl," from the previous chapter. Here the sameness is further constructed in the image of the meeting hands. Describing the hands collectively as "their[s]" refuses to distinguish which hand belongs to whom, which might be touching and which being touched, playing out this same-sex desire in the realm of undifferentiated symmetry. Through the synecdoche of the hands, the poet can articulate desire that would perhaps be too much to ascribe to the women themselves. The hands alone can freely meet each other in an explicit longing (*benkshaft*). The distance from the actual women continues with the mention of "soft shoulders." Dropping the possessive pronoun *their* and replacing it with the article *the*, this image transfers the agency of the "quivering searching" from the women to the independent shoulders. The third corporeal image is the most explicit one in the poem, that of "bright bodies leaping in confusion." Though the Yiddish verb is *arching* rather than *leaping*, the movement of the bodies toward each other is clear in both languages. Again, using the article *the* (*di* in Yiddish), instead of the possessive pronoun *their*, and placing the bodies after the spatial description (the "orange-red landscape") serves to link the different images, while accentuating the distance of the earlier metonymical descriptions of the women. This linking opens the closing couplet of the stanza to a double reading. Standing at the end of the stanza describing the women, it can either be read as a continuation of the women's physical interaction, their bodies intermingling, or as the image they are looking at in the picture book. Placing the detached bodies of the women reading the book, or of the women in the book (or men, as the "bright bodies" in question are actually not gendered), "over" ("*iber*") the landscape (whether the landscape is under the balcony or in the pictorial representation in the book) preemptively foreshadows the man towering over the reading women. But if the man acts as mere decorative background, as a *dekoratsye* hanging over (*iber*) the women, the women's bodies are portrayed interacting with the landscape they loom over, as their passion activates and erotically charges this "thirsty, orange-red landscape."

Clearly detracting from rather than adding to the scene, the man is hardly described as a desirable participant, and the idea of some kind of inadvertent erotic interaction with him (as with the thirsty landscape) seems foreclosed by the negativity with which he towers mightily (*turemt mekhtik*) over the women, overshadowing the brightness of their bodies. Despite the threatening potential this description evokes, it should be noted that he is being described from the speaker's vantage point, which is even more external than his own, while the women seem oblivious to both his presence and his potential threat. To the external speaker, he may not pose a threat, but he certainly serves as disruption, as we can gather from the description of him as superfluous (*iberik*) to the scene. His image is constructed through the apparent tension between his power and superfluousness, between grace and heaviness. The word used for grace, *gratsye*, is not the common Hebraic Yiddish term for grace, *kheyn*. *Gratsye* often serves in Yiddish as a derogatory, even misogynist slang term for a self-important pseudo-aristocratic "lady." Here the word seems to stand alone as an entity, a feminine noun with its own adjective rather than an adjective merely describing the man. The line break detaches the grace from the act of standing it describes, highlighting the preposition *mit* (*with*) and thereby asserting the independence of the grace.

Coming together with this external grace, the man is feminized. The idea of a man as decorative is also part of this feminization, reversing the misogynist cliché of women as decorative objects and women's creativity being associated with the decorative arts. This feminization of the male figure could be in line with other references in Margolin's poetry to Jewish men's particular form of masculinity, but the adjectives *heavy* and *towering* mark the oppressive potential encoded even in this effeminate male figure. Heavily towering, this figure continues Margolin's uses of the sculptural. Triangulated with the two women, another artistic resonance is born, as the man's *gratsye* intertextually evokes the Three Graces of Greek mythology, echoing the history of classical art Margolin critiques in her rhyming reference to the man as an *iberike dekoratsye*, a superfluous decoration. Rhyming *dekoratsye* and *gratsye* forms a closed couplet, further isolating the man in the first line of the stanza. Since these closing lines are the only perfect rhyme in the poem, they also enact their own decorativeness and their superfluousness to the poem. Consequently, the man is rendered superfluous to the intimacy among the women both poetically and thematically.

Still, the poem does not clearly map out all of the various positions of the figures that it contains. Even the title of the poem, "*Oyf a balkon*" ("On a Balcony") ambiguously positions the figures within the poem, an ambiguity that has significant function in how we read the poem's queer haunting. By making it equally likely that the women are the ones on a balcony, that the towering man is on that balcony (though it is enough for him to be standing behind them to have the height advantage), and that the speaker is the one witnessing the scene from the balcony, it is not clear who is watching whom. Beginning with the speaker positioned outside of the two women's interaction and closing with the towering man, this poem sets up a complex dynamic of voyeurism. The speaker is not part of the intimate, erotic, interaction. Instead, she has the panoramic point of view, which allows her to see what the women (might choose to) overlook—the man who "towers powerfully over them." In one interpretation of the poem, Avraham Novershtern asserts that the speaker is positioned in an equally superfluous position to the man, as an external voyeur. He argues that the speaker's subjective prism, through which "the image is filtered, actually receives limited space."[9] Novershtern sees this as a way to counter the potential sentimentality of the scene itself, allowing the poem to bring together "various elements whose purpose is to dull or weaken its portrayal of intense emotion." Whereas Novershtern counts the speaker's point of view as one of the stylistic elements that "weaken" the emotion in the scene, I argue that the necessity of emotional diffusion originates from the speaker herself, who proves to be anything but external. As the hot laughter "floats" or rather "flies" (*flit*) toward her, she is drawn into the scene, which she in turn narrates into being. The laughter comes not just from a spatial distance (between street and balcony) but also from a gap in time, as the memory of a "distant summer" reaches, writes Novershtern, "through temporal distance to touch the poet as well."[10] This might negate sentimentality (as Novershtern suggests), but it also removes the safe distance of the voyeur.

The women themselves are also engaged in a kind of voyeuristic indulgence, in the shared pleasure of "leafing through a picture book," though with the ensuing series of physical interactions it would seem that the aesthetic pleasure is secondary, indeed even a pretext for the physical pleasure and closeness that it enables. In this erotic economy the gaze is not what affords power, for neither the speaker nor the man possesses it. The objects of this gaze, the women, have full agency, becoming desiring subjects of each other. Closed to external intervention, they themselves haunt the speaker's memory or psyche, and make the past, "that distant summer," present. This closed scene is mediated for us, the readers, through poetic narration. What makes this intimate scene known to us, the readers, is then the craft of poetry, the "superfluous decoration," echoing the role the man plays in the poem. Through the poetic narration the readers become unwittingly complacent voyeurs as well, leafing through the book of poems as the women depicted in the poem leaf through the picture book. But we do not get to touch them, as the fantasy so often created by an objectifying gaze would have it; instead, just as the speaker becomes part of the scene whether she wants to or not, we have no choice but to be touched by them, as distant memory, as forgotten or unspoken desire. The queer touch of that distant summer and its hot (*heys*) interactions reverses the voyeuristic invasion.

I suggest we think of these women as queer specters, using haunting to describe the (nonconsensual) relation of scene and speaker. Following Freccero's queer model of spectrality, in this poem, "the past is in the present in the form of haunting," as the speaker enacts "the possibility of being haunted, even inhabited, by ghosts."[11] "Oyf a balkon" gives us two simultaneous models of queer spectrality. The first directly results from the translation of lesbian desire into a form of haunting, which makes haunting a symptom of queerness. In the second, haunting itself queers linear sequence, which makes queerness a symptom of haunting. Because normative sexuality (and specifically reproductive sexuality) underpins normative history, both models are in fact deeply related. Nowhere is the connection clearer than cases of intergenerational haunting, as we saw for example in the nightly visits in the poem "Froyen-lider" by Kadya Molodowsky, where long-dead women from the speaker's family come to her at night. If familial lineage represents the ultimate heterosexual sequence, intergenerational haunting disrupts the historicism of this chronological sequence "as it articulates alternatives to a historicism that represents sequential chronologies."[12] This form of intergenerational haunting can thus be seen to "refigure familial nucleated heteronormative temporalities."[13] Disrupting generational sequence, intergenerational haunting challenges the foundation of heteronormative kinship and temporality at once, using spectrality to queer the family and history alike.

Margolin herself offers an example of intergenerational haunting, in her poem "*Mayn shtam redt*" ("My Ancestors Speak").[14] The poem describes the speaker's ancestors: "Men in satin and velvet"; "Merchants from Leipzig and Danzig"; "A drunkard"; "A pair of converts in Kiev"; "Women bejewelled in diamonds like icons"; "Grand ladies in calico and linen"; and, finally, a few she is "ashamed of." If the speaker begins by setting the stage with this silent cast of characters from her *shtam*, her tribe, the end of the poem reverses the power dynamic, and they overpower her.

זיי אַלע, מײַן שטאַם,
בלוט פֿון מײַן בלוט
און פֿלאַם פֿון מײַן פֿלאַם,
טויט און לעבעדיק אויסגעמישט,
טרויעריק, גראָטעסק און גרויס
טראַמפּלען דורך מיר װי דורך אַ טונקל הויז.
טראַמפּלען מיט תּפֿילות און קללות און קלאָג,
טרייסלען מײַן האַרץ װי אַ קופּערנעם גלאָק,
עס װאַרפֿט זיך מײַן צונג,
איך דערקען ניט מײַן קול—
מײַן שטאַם רעדט.

All of them, my ancestors,
blood of my blood,
flame of my flame,
dead and living mixed together,
sad, grotesque, immense.
They trample through me as through a dark house.
Trampling with prayers, and curses, and wailing,
rattling my heart like a copper bell,
my tongue quivers,
I don't know my own voice—
My ancestors speak.[15]

This poem casts the encounter with the ancestors as a scene of possession, mixing living and dead, past and present. Invoking ties of blood and fire at first seems to set a scene of active conjuring, especially with the repetitive incantation: blood of my blood, flame of my flame. However, five lines down and yet still in the same sentence, it is clear that the speaker is passive, and indeed, possessed. The repetition of the verb *trample* poetically enacts the act of trampling—through the speaker and through the poem. The actual words of these ancestors are not narrated, but listed as three categories: prayers, curses, and wailing (or, complaints). And rather than hearing these appeals (or narrating them in the poem), the speaker narrates their mark, the visceral experience of this *dibbuk*, the quivering of her tongue, the loss of her own familiar voice. This intergenerational haunting resonates deeply with Molodowsky's uninvited and nonconsensual haunting in

"Froyen-lider." However, in Molodowsky's poem, the women of the past are granted their own script, an account of the suffering that made them haunt the speaker with their demands. And whereas the haunting silences Margolin's speaker, Molodowsky's speaker is able to have the last, defiant line.

Novershtern observes that Molodowsky "sketched her forbearers in traditional terms, thus laying the grounds for an intergenerational debate. The definitions here are quite clear, and the identity of the poet specific."[16] Novershtern contrasts this with Margolin's foreclosure of dialogue in "Mayn shtam redt": "[Margolin's] forebears do not appear before the poet when she wishes to illuminate her identity; on the contrary. They almost suffocate her from within. There cannot, on the whole, be any dialogue between generations."[17] But as we saw in the reading of Molodowsky's poem in chapter 1, and as we will continue to see in the reading that follows, the nature of the encounter is far from straightforward, and casting her forbearers in "traditional" terms might in fact serve the opposite goal from that which Novershtern suggests. As William Abrams writes as early as 1935, in *Signal*, the "*goldene keyt fun tsniesdike froyen-doyres*" ("the golden chain of modest generations of women") that the poet dreamed up "stand in her way today," weighing on her.[18] Speaking from his own ideological bent, Abrams is referring to the women of the past as deterring Molodowsky from "placing her feet safely in step with millions of armies" and keeping her from fully joining the Communist movement (for which *Signal* was an organ). Whether or not that is where Molodowsky would have gone were she detached from the golden-chain-of-modest-women Abrams describes, it is clear (in contrast with Novershtern's claim) that her speaker is not free from the *keyt*, the chain, and the dialogue staged between the women seems neither invited nor consensual. Indeed, in both published versions of the poem, the "autumn winds" ("*harbstike vintn*") chase or even hunt (*yogn nokh*) the speaker; in the first version these winds are the women's lives' "withered melodies" ("*farvelkte nigunim*"), and in the second version it is their "whimpering" ("*shtile farshtikte geveynen*"; the adjectives *silent* and *suffocated* are not included in the translation), leaving no more of an escape than Margolin's speaker had from her own ancestral voices. Over and against Abrams's ideological critique (chastising Molodowsky for her ties to the women of the past), as well as Novershtern's neat categorical division (which perceives Molodowsky at a safe distance from her ancestors), my reading joins the ambivalence emanating from both Molodowsky and Margolin, exploring the haunting past/past haunting as a mode of queer intergenerational encounter.

Moving from the speaker's own family to the wider stage of Jewish history, Molodowsky's poem "Dona Gratsye Mendes"[19] dramatizes an especially petrifying scene of haunting. Using the same framework of nightly visitation as in *"Froyenlider,"* this poem turns to a historical figure, Doña Gracia Mendes Nasi (c. 1510–69). Doña Gracia is a fascinating historical figure whose life spans spaces from Portugal to Constantinople, and is marked by repeated expulsions and hardships, as well as triumphs quite unusual for a Jewish woman of her time.[20] Despite her specific history, Doña Gracia's appearance in the poem is rather stereotypically ghostlike.

דער שטערן ברענט, ס'רוישט דורך מײַן שטוב אַ סאַמעטענע קליידונג,
אַן אויסגעשטרעקטע, בלייכע האַנט,
אַ רונג, אַ פֿלאַמיקער בריליאַנט,
אַ קול אין ציטער:

The star burns, a velvet dress rustles through my room,
An outstretched, pale hand,
A ring, a flaming diamond,
A trembling voice:

These fragmentary images of dress, hand, and voice, each detached from the other (and from any human form), are the only description we have of the self-identified "guest." She declares herself a wanderer, a *na ve'nad*, who spent her life hiding and protecting her God.

—Get used to night storms!
I am your guest now, remember it and use it,
I am still a wanderer, I am Doña Gracia Mendes.
A whole life long I kept and hid my God,
From land to land, from wandering to wandering.[21]

—זײַ צוגעוווינט צום נאַכטיקן געוויטער!
איך בין דײַן גאַסט אַצינד, געדענק עס און פֿאַרווענד עס,
כ'בין אַלץ נאָך נע-ונד, כ'בין דאָנאַ גראַציאַ מענדעס.
אַ לעבן לאַנג אַ באַהאַלטן און געהיט מײַן גאָט,
פֿון לאַנד צו לאַנד, פֿון נע-ונד צו נע-ונד.

This poetic account combines an apparitional exile, a ghost forced into eternal wandering, with Doña Gracia's biography, her own hiding and her wandering (she came from a family forced to hide their Jewishness during the inquisition in Portugal, and later in Antwerp and Venice, before finding safety in Constantinople). In addition, the poem invokes a long history of Jewish wandering and suffering, stating that "wherever plagued steps walked crooked and lame / the mark of Abraham remains eternal" (*"vu geplogte trit zaynen gelofn krum un lom / geblibn eybik iz der tseykhn fun Avrom"*). Abraham's mark, the ghost informs the speaker, is the ax. This is not the ax wielded by Abraham in the *akeyde*, the Binding of Isaac. Rather, the ghost clarifies that it is the ax that Abraham used to shatter all the idols in his father's home (according to rabbinic commentary on the Biblical narrative). The poem's ghost advocates a similar spirit of vengeance, invoking Doña Gracia's role in organizing a boycott of the port of Ancona in 1556. "Who says that hate isn't pretty?" (*"Ver zogt es dir az sine iz nisht sheyn?"*) she asks, insisting, "We used to be stronger once" (*"mir zaynen shtarkere geven a mol"*). Inviting a return to these days, the Doña Gracia of the poem is a ghostly fantasy of revenge, demanding the poet/speaker join her. Though the poem ends with quiet restored to the speaker's home, the closing image is a mark in the sky (*himl-flek*), the same sign the ghost of Doña Gracia claims will announce the enemy's downfall.

The poetic deployment of both the classic ghost story and the historical reality of Doña Gracia's life exposes the way haunting disrupts temporality, bringing people and events from the past into the present. However, it is not merely horrors past that are at play in Molodowsky's poem, but also the horrors of the poem's present moment. Published in 1946, in *Der meylekh Dovid aleyn iz geblibn* (*Only King David Remained*), Molodowsky's first book of poetry after the *Khurbn*, the call for vengeance at the close of the poem not only comes from ghosts past, but also speaks back to them with the heightened force of the present. Between the expulsion from Spain and the post-*Khurbn* world, Molodowsky stages a cross-historical queer haunting, which moves both forward and back.

This haunting, then, is reciprocal, expressing "a willingness both to be haunted and to become ghostly,"[22] as ghost and speaker become one: "For me there is no death, in death there is no quiet / so was I, so now are you." (*"Nishto keyn toyt far mir, nishto in toyt keyn ru . . . / azoy bin ikh geven, azoy bist itster du . . .*) The ghost denies the speaker the ability to remain separate from her. As

Freccero writes, "ghosts demand," and "the ghost's demand engenders a certain responsibility."[23] It is this responsibility we saw the speaker of "Froyen-lider" negotiating. Indeed, this poem shares many similarities with "Froyen-lider": in both poems an apparition of the dead visits the speaker, and the dead speak their own monologues. Like the foremothers protecting the bloodline across generations in "Froyen-lider," here Doña Gracia describes protecting her God across time, from "land to land." The poems also share the imagery of blood, cries, and even whips. However, if in "Froyen-lider" the ghosts' demands remain implicit (and even passive-aggressive) and the speaker can respond defiantly, and ultimately has the last word, here the ghost is the one who sets the final tone—in the *himl-flek*, a sign extending into the future. If queer spectrality brings the past into the present, in this account it also looks to the future, in the form of a promise (which is actually more of a threat). Reading from within the future anticipated by the poem's ghost queerly enacts the Jewish ghost (hi)story.

This (hi)story stretches queerly forward and back, undoing linear temporality and bringing together multiple histories simultaneously. If we follow the ghost of Doña Gracia back from Molodowsky's poem into Molodowsky's archive, a wider historical project is revealed, wherein Molodowsky dedicated a diverse range of writing to Doña Gracia's life. At the same time, following this trail queerly connects to multiple histories, and specifically to the poet Emma Lazarus. This connection is not entirely surprising, as the historical conditions of the expulsion from Portugal that shaped Doña Gracia's life are the same conditions that shaped the life of Emma Lazarus's ancestry. I want to position Lazarus within the historical span I've been considering, between the expulsion from Spain and postwar New York, between Doña Gracia and Molodowsky. Bringing to life a cast of historical figures, poets and ghosts, I will show how the lens of spectrality enables us to trace alternative lines of queer connection through intersecting histories, cross-temporal dialogue, and archival practice.

Besides the ghostly poem, Molodowsky dedicated a radio script, a biographical essay, and a play to Doña Gracia Nasi. The radio script, *Dray momentn in lebn fun Dona Gratsye Mendes Nasi* (Three Moments in the Life of Doña Gracia Mendes Nasi),[24] includes only two characters, Doña Gracia and a narrator. This script is far less elaborate than the script Molodowsky dedicated to Lazarus (discussed in chapter 2), which itself portrays historical haunting, where the dramatized Lazarus is visited by a portrait of George Eliot come to life, by a rabbi and by a nameless Jewish refugee, who each make their own ghostly visit. As mentioned above, a translation of this script is found in the YIVO archives of Zvee Scooler, in the same folder that holds an untranslated copy of the biographical sketch of Doña Gracia that Molodowsky wrote in Yiddish, bringing both women together.[25] The biographical sketch, "Dona Gratsye Mendes: Ir tifer gloybn un vunderlekh lebn" ("Doña Gracia Mendes: Her Deep Belief and Wondrous Life"), is part of Molodowsky's series on notable women (including Lazarus) published in the *Forverts* in the 1950s (which I discuss in chapter 5).[26] It narrates a specific dramatic moment of her history, when Doña Gracia rejected a marriage proposal from a non-Jewish baron, and opposed her sister Brianda's plan to send her niece to a monastery. The themes of the non-Jewish admirer and the tumultuous relationship between Doña Gracia and her sister also stand at the center of Molodowsky's play, *Nokhn got fun midber: Drame fun yidishn lebn in zekhtsntn yorhundert* (After the God of the Desert: Drama of Jewish Life in the Sixteenth Century).[27] In Molodowsky's play (and in the aforementioned sketch), Doña Gracia is described as acting out of her commitment to her (then-hidden) Jewish identity. This leads Brianda to denounce Doña Gracia to the Inquisition. The Sultan of Turkey intervenes, she is freed and the family goes to Turkey and openly professes their Jewishness. This history, and its portrayal in the play and the sketch, is closely echoed by (or, itself echoes) Emma Lazarus's play *A Dance to Death: A Historical Tragedy in Five Acts*[28] (which is a translation/poetic dramatization of Richard Reinhard's 1877 German prose narrative *Der Tanz zum Tode*). The connections between these texts pivot around themes of hidden Jewish identity, romantic connections between Jews and non-Jews, and a unique combination of familial drama with specific historical events.

The move across these various texts reveals that haunting takes place not only within certain texts (like the Doña Gracia poem or the Emma Lazarus script), but also between texts, and between times. Thus Lazarus can be both "ghost" and "ghosted," haunted by the past (of Doña Gracia) and haunting the future (of Molodowsky). In such cases haunting may not be in the familiar form of the ghost story, but in the way disparate historical times speak to and through each other. In this way Lazarus and Molodowsky haunt each other, as they are both haunted by the same history. This is evident especially in Lazarus's and Molodowsky's plays, which I am interested in especially because of the way the plots they portray serve to destabilize identity categories in ways that resonate with other definitions of the "queer" that haunts spectrality, where identities are formed (and concealed and revealed) in relation to specific (real and imagined) histories.

Molodowsky's focus on the familial drama in both the play and the radio script dedicated to Doña Gracia is striking considering the historical and geographical accuracy of their depictions, going back to a concrete time and place, a period of a few years spent in Venice and Ferreira, before moving to Constantinople. Lazarus's play *A Dance to Death* does not refer directly to Doña Gracia or to the historical drama of the expulsion (a history which often occupied Lazarus, as we saw, for example, in "By the Waters of Babylon" in chapter 2). Yet she too hinges her drama on a certain historical event (or at least claims to by naming the play a "Historical Tragedy"), while telling a very similar story to Molodowsky's. Both Lazarus and Molodowsky stage their plays on the eve of an impending disaster, focusing the drama around a case of hidden identity and romantic entanglement with a powerful non-Jewish official. Beyond the return to the sixteenth century, both plays also point back to an earlier Jewish source, the Book of Esther. In Molodowsky's Yiddish play, the reference is only implied. In Lazarus's play, two characters explicitly invoke the story. One of them is the non-Jewish Prince William who is wooing the Jewish Liebhaid.

> Did you not tell me scarce a month agone [says the prince
>   to Liebhaid],
> When I chanced in on you at feast and prayer,
> The holy time's bright legend? of the queen,
> Strong, beautiful, resolute, who denied her race
> To save her race, who cast upon the die
> Of her divine and simple loveliness,
> Her life, her soul,—and so redeemed her tribe.
> You are my Esther—but I, no second tyrant,
> Worship whom you adore, love whom you love![29]

Liebhaid, the Esther-figure, is the one who creates the parallel by telling the prince Esther's story. In a tragic reversal, however, instead of saving her people, Liebhaid is later revealed to be a Christian, but only after she is murdered in a pogrom.

This Biblical echo adds another temporal dimension to the already intricate queer cross-historical map my reading has been drawing. At the same time, it links this map to a foundational moment in queer theory, Eve Sedgwick's *Epistemology of the Closet*, where Sedgwick creates a detailed comparison between a gay coming-out and Esther's coming-out. Sedgwick uses this comparison to differentiate an idea of stable (Jewish) ethnicity from an unstable notion of gender and sexuality. Whereas gay coming-out destabilizes both concepts, "minority" and "gender," causing them to lose "a good deal of their categorizing (though certainly not of their performative) force," Esther's choice, according to Sedgwick, reflects "a firm Jewish choice of a minority politics based on a conservative re-inscription of gender roles."[30] However, within this disavowal of the potential of ethnic disruption, Sedgwick performs her own Jewish coming-out, as she describes herself dressed up as Esther, as part of the patriarchal instruction of submission directed at young Jewish girls, among which Eve-Esther suddenly becomes included.

> (Even today, Jewish little girls are educated in gender roles—fondness for being looked at, fearlessness in defense of "their people," non-solidarity with their sex—through masquerading as Queen Esther at Purim; I have a snapshot of myself at about five, barefoot in the pretty "Queen Esther" dress my grandmother made [white satin, gold spangles], making a careful eyes-down toe-pointed curtsey at [presumably] my father, who is manifest in the picture only as the flashgun that hurls my shadow, pillaring up tall and black, over the dwarfed sofa onto the wall behind me.)[31]

Naomi Seidman identifies this coming-out as "parenthetical,"[32] an identity only partially declared by remaining in parentheses: "Sedgwick simultaneously does and does not come out as Jewish and, less explicitly, she almost but doesn't quite come out as not-heterosexual. Whatever else you can say about this scene, it hardly involves a simple, 'non-disruptive' identity."[33] Parenthetical coming-out, then, still holds within it the force of disruption, despite its indeterminacy. Moreover, this racial and sexual indeterminacy ties back into queer spectrality. "Just as ghostliness designates an ambiguous state of being, both present and not, past and not, so too in these accounts racial mixture and sexual—including sexuality—stand in for, even as they mark the material place of, a critique of originary purity, simplicity and umixedness."[34] Queer spectrality, can therefore, add to our sensitivity to other modes of mixture, to moments of revelation and concealment, destabilizing both sexuality and ethnicity; specifically, I want to use this destabilization to return to Emma Lazarus, in order to suggest that queer spectrality ties together her nonlinear model of Jewish history with her complex portrayal of lesbian desire, bringing together the lesbian ghost and haunted history.

We have already seen an array of Lazarus's "Jewish themes" in the plays and poems discussed so far, whether Esther, Heinrich Heine (in "Venus of the Louvre") or the vast cast of figures from the Biblical Moses to Moses Mendelssohn (in the poem "By the Waters of Babylon"). But both in her life and in her posthumous career, the "Jewish question" is not a simple one. Coming from an assimilated background, Lazarus's relation to her Jewishness fluctuated throughout her life. After Lazarus's death, her sister Josephine attempted to minimize the role of Emma's Judaism. Subsequent literary scholarship, on the other hand, focused almost entirely on the Jewish aspect of her identity. At the same time, Lazarus has also left us with distinct clues to that other closet, expressing lesbian desire in multiple forms in her writing. How these two identities relate to each other is yet to be fully accounted for, yet already in 1951, Arthur Zeiger offered one theory for this link, suggesting that Lazarus's "displaced sexuality" may have been the force behind her conversion to what he calls "pro-Semitism,"[35] referring to her dedication to the cause of Jewish immigrants. Zeiger was the first to actively address the lesbian elements of Lazarus's poetry, in a dissertation that was never published in book form. While this claim cannot be substantiated, nor does it lead to particular poetic or political insight, it is nevertheless interesting to think about Lazarus's continued interest in Converso Jews (forced to convert and hide their identity) as parallel or even intersecting with the closet of sexuality. Moreover, staging both sexuality and ethnicity as constructed in the ambiguous interplay between concealment and revelation are, as we saw, not only analogous to queer spectrality, but rather deeply tied to it.

We saw these intricate connections in Leah Goldberg's poem "Dream of a Girl" (read in chapter 3), where lines of identity and desire were crossed in a scene of haunting. In that poem the speaker dreams herself into the figure of Jesus, in an erotically charged moment with Magdalene (specifying it is "Crivelli's Magdalena"). Rather than a moment of erotic rapture, the encounter is cast as nightmarishly haunting: "there was no way out of horror's dream / there was no escaping Magdalena." As we saw, Goldberg transposes the lesbian content she describes onto realms of otherness, of dream, of Christianity and of art. If my previous reading focused on Goldberg's use of Christianity, in the context of this chapter, we can point to the expression of lesbian desire through the lens of nonconsensual haunting as an additional psychological/literary mechanism for giving voice to desires that would otherwise be suppressed. But even when transposing the transgression outside of Judaism, and even in the fictionalized poetic form, the poet chooses to further distance the haunting by staging it in the realm of the dream.

Lazarus's poetry, on the other hand, will offer us a number of examples to counter Goldberg's lesbian horror. We will read "Magnetism" (the poem that opened this chapter) as a site of reciprocity both in terms of lesbian desire and queer spectrality. After that we will trace the same lesbian specter back through two dreams, which make space not for haunting horror, but for the desiring specter, the specter of desire.

Magnetism[36]

By the impulse of my will,
By the red flame in my blood,
By my nerves' electric thrill,
By the passion of my mood,
My concentrated desire,
My undying, desperate love,
I ignore Fate, I defy her,
Iron-hearted Death I move.
When the town lies numb with sleep,
Here, round-eyed I sit; my breath
Quickly stirred, my flesh a-creep,
And I force the gates of death.
I nor move nor speak—you'd deem
From my quiet face and hands,
I were tranced—but in her dream,
She responds, she understands.
I have power on what is not,
Or on what has ceased to be,
From that deep, earth-hollowed spot,
I can lift her up to me.
And, or ere I am aware
Through the closed and curtained door,
Comes my lady white and fair,

> And embraces me once more.
> Though the clay clings to her gown,
> Yet all heaven is in her eyes;
> Cool, kind fingers press mine eyes,
> To my soul her soul replies.
> But when breaks the common dawn,
> And the city wakes—behold!
> My shy phantom is withdrawn,
> And I shiver lone and cold.
> And I know when she has left,
> She is stronger far than I,
> And more subtly spun her weft,
> Than my human wizardry.
> Though I force her to my will,
> By the red flame in my blood,
> By my nerves' electric thrill,
> By the passion of my mood,
> Yet all day a ghost am I.
> Nerves unstrung, spent will, dull brain.
> I achieve, attain, but die,
> And she claims me hers again.

Lazarus's poem can thus be read as an instantiation of queer spectrality, where the queerness of haunting transgresses both normative sexual practice and normative temporal sequence. The poem stages a distinctly erotic encounter between a (presumably) female speaker and a (certainly) female addressee, who is also a ghost. I use the word *presumably* since there are no explicit gender markers for the speaker. And yet, the poem invites this reading. First, we tend to identify the first-person speaker of the poem with the poet unless we are directed otherwise by the poem itself (which here we are not). Additionally, the way the speaker and addressee seem to trade places in the poem could also imply they are both women. Finally, the spectral aspect of the poem actually serves to support the reading of the encounter as a lesbian one, considering that in nineteenth-century literature we are more likely to meet a lesbian ghost than an actual lesbian (to return to Castle's apparitional lesbian history). The ghost is, indeed, a proper nineteenth-century "lady." Despite her undead features and the grave clay clinging to her gown, she remains appealing, "white and fair," "with all heaven in her eyes." Their encounter lasts until consummation, when "to my soul her soul replies," but then the "shy phantom is withdrawn," leaving the speaker "lone and cold" (not unlike a corpse). If at first it seems that the speaker is the one in control, forcing "the gates of death," to conjure, "lift up," her "lady," and at the end the speaker reiterates it was she who forced the phantom to her will, she must also concede that despite her "human wizardry," "she is stronger far than I." By the final image, the speaker is the one who is a ghost ("all day ghost am I"), rather than a living human, and it becomes clear that the ghost she first conjured is the one who is actually in control: "I achieve, attain, but die, / And she claims me hers again." This ritual repetition of the scene highlights the way haunting undoes linear temporality. At the same time, blurring the lines between "she" and "I," ghost and ghosted, the poem also enacts queer spectrality's call "to live with ghosts (neither forgetting nor mourning) and to understand oneself as ghosted."[37] This call is fundamental to the breakdown of temporal distinctions haunting enacts.

If the "fair lady" from "Magnetism" comes at night, though without specifying whether the speaker is asleep or awake, this same figure has in fact haunted Lazarus's poetry from its very beginning, through dreams, which open a space of lesbian desire that steers away from any negative implications. Specifically, in one of her earliest poems, "Only a Dream," the "lady" from "Magnetism" appears as still a "maiden," and instead of being already resurrected from the dead, here Lazarus's speaker dreams of "a love that should last through life and death."

Only a Dream

A dream of glory and youth and faith,
And a love that should last through life and death.
A dream of a face with violet eyes,
And a smile of a tender, sweet surprise.
With a golden frame of wavy, soft hair,
Of a maiden at once both pure and fair.
A glorious dream while erst it did last
That illuminated so brightly all my past—
A dream that was lighted by Hope's bright gleam,
Through golden days,—but *only* a dream.

September 13th, 1864

Dated September 13, 1864, the poem was printed in a private edition of Lazarus's poems and translations meant for friends and family. This same edition was reprinted a year later for wider circulation.[38] "Only a Dream" did not appear in any of the versions of Lazarus's republished works, but luckily the Center for Jewish History in New York has preserved multiple copies of the private 1866 edition. The poem itself opens the question of survival; if a dream exists "only" "while erst it did last," the poem exists not only beyond the time of the dream but also beyond the time of the poet, charging the illuminating power of its vision over the past with an air of prophesy, making the future present. This is another example of the working of queer history's undoing of linear time's division of past and present. At the same time, the traces described in the poem, and the traces of the poem itself, allow us access to a history of queer desire, an intersection we see again in Lazarus's poetry when she returns to the dream, or rather, the dream returns to her, in a beautiful sonnet included in her 1886 manuscript:[39]

Assurance

Last night I slept, and when I woke her kiss
Still floated on my lips. For we had strayed
Together in my dream, through some dim glade,
Where the shy moonbeams scarce dared light our bliss.
The air was dank with dew, between the trees,
The hidden glow-worms kindled and were spent.
Cheek pressed to cheek, the cool, the hot night-breeze
Mingled our hair, our breath, and came and went,
As sporting with our passion. Low and deep
Spake in mine ear her voice: "And didst thou dream,
This could be buried? This could be sleep?
And love be thrall to death! Nay, whatso seem,
Have faith, dear heart; *this is the thing that is!*"
Thereon I woke, and on my lips her kiss.

This poem was not published in Lazarus's lifetime, and like the earlier dream poem, it was omitted from publishing (or republishing) for an entire century, yet Lazarus herself chose to include it in her self-compiled manuscript, on page 19, between another unpublished, dream-related poem, "Will o' the Wisp," and the more well-known sonnet "Echoes." The structuring of this poem and of the poem

"Only a Dream" is very similar, as they both open and close with the declaration that they are narrating a dream. And still, this later poem offers a new version of fulfillment, first of all within the dream itself, which allows for a much more explicit (if highly poetic) erotic encounter, and outside the dream, where the trace of the erotic encounter carries over into waking reality. We can read the opening as something of an alibi: "Last night I slept." This alibi is necessary, for were the speaker to omit this framing, the rest of the line would position her as waking with a very real kiss on her lips—for the line does not mention the dream setting where the encounter is staged. Moreover, the kiss is clearly removed, and not just by the sleeping, but also by the floating (rather than settling). Still, the kiss has left a trace, the tale of which is slowly revealed, though it is set up immediately as something potentially deviant: "For we had strayed." The enjambment plays a crucial role here, for we must wait until the end of the next line to understand the straying as spatial rather than moral. This space is first of all the space of the dream ("we strayed / Together in my dream"), and only later the natural space of the glade.

The lines that follow describe the natural setting of the glade, at the same time as they can be read as metonymies for the women's bodies: the air "dank with dew" is built on almost onomatopoeic alliteration, bringing to mind associations of female sexuality (specifically vaginal) and the hidden glowworms (which are not worms at all but rather female fireflies without wings, which kindle as part of a mating ritual) invoke clitoral imagery. We can perhaps compare this to the list compiled by Paula Bennett of clitoral imagery in Emily Dickinson's poems: "peas, pebbles, beads, berries, nuts, buds, crumbs, pearls, pellets, dews, gems, jewels, drops and ... bees—all central to Dickenson's writing."[40] Glowworms could join these, "small round and frequently hard objects," and even more so for exemplifying the process of arousal and satisfaction, being "kindled and spent." Reading the natural scenery and the women's bodies refracted through each other is further supported in the movement of the lines that follow, which alternate between nature and body, wind and breath, the women's cheeks and hair, touching and mingling. This particular sentence stretches across two and a half lines, creating fragmentary syntax (for example, leaving "the cool" detached both from the cheeks before it and the hot wind after it). This syntax mirrors the pace of the breath and wind, which "came and went / as sporting with our passion."

Finally, the voice of the other woman speaks, "low and deep," and again because of the enjambment we do not know what is "low and deep" until the next line. "Her voice" stands synecdochically apart, like the speaker's ear, and both women's cheeks and hair, all isolated from the bodies as a whole. The words uttered by the woman begin midconversation, with the word *and* implying a context to which we are not privy. She recruits the trope of the dream almost accusingly, telling the speaker it would be delusional to think "this could be buried," "could be sleep." Such repression, she says, would let "love be thrall to death," in effect choosing death over love, or choosing the death of *this* love. She goes on to clarify, if we (or the speaker) had any doubt, that come what may (or: "whatso seem"), she should have faith, for: *"this is the thing that is!"* Joining this assurance of one woman to the other, we the readers receive our own reassurance, as the final line returns us to the moment of waking, but this time, the kiss has landed on her lips.

Dan Vogel, the first to publish the poem in 1980, after nearly one hundred years of omission, insists there is no reason to read this is as a lesbian dream.[41] However, the poem and its lesbian potential has played a role in Lazarus scholarship, starting with Zeiger's aforementioned dissertation. Whereas Zeiger writes that "it would be difficult to interpret it as anything but a lesbian fantasy,"[42] those who refute the lesbian reading make the valid claim that there is no reason to identify the speaker's gender with that of the poet[43] (as is indeed too often the case with readings of lyric poetry by women, as I mentioned earlier). On careful examination of the poem, we can agree that there are no explicit gender markers associated with this speaker that would lead us to identify the speaker one way or the other. Instead, what is clear is that the poem fits well with other conventions of the sonnet—which often include an erotic gaze at a woman, an exalted status of the beloved, and some kind of unresolvable tension, as this sonnet does.[44] This generic adherence might appear to undermine the lesbian potential of the poem (making it "just like any other sonnet"), but another reading shows that the form itself serves to underscore the lesbian potential of this poem rather than undoing it.

Indeed, the sonnet's conventions, writes Lisa Moore, make the sonnet form readily available for lesbian poetry: "Not only the authorship and the subject matter of individual sonnets but also the form itself all have the capacity to reflect and express the desire of one woman for another."[45] She goes on to trace a lesbian genealogy of the sonnet, rooting Petrarch's development of the sonnet in his imitation of Catullus, imitator (and translator) of Sappho. Moore also ties the later revival of the sonnet to the female traditions of Charlotte Smith (the great influence on Wordsworth's sonnet writing), and to the more explicitly lesbian Anna Seward. Seward's 1780 "Sonnet xxxiii" is in fact sharply echoed in both of Lazarus's lesbian dream poems, as is evident from its opening lines: "Last night her Form the hours of slumber bless'd / Whose eyes illumin'd all my youthful years."[46] The irregular rhyme scheme of "Assurance" (ABBA CDCD EFEF AA) also continues Charlotte Smith's highly irregular rhymes, tying Lazarus directly to the tradition Moore is naming as lesbian. Indeed, much of "Assurance" fits Moore's analysis, in voice, in the erotic imagery, and in the setup of the dream, all of which announce there is a "straying" here. The way the erotic interaction is built through the landscape is so central a practice that Moore dedicated a whole book to it: *Sister Arts: The Erotics of Lesbian Landscapes*.[47]

On the other hand, "Assurance" refuses one of the sonnet's central conventions, that of the *volta*, which serves as a rhetorical turn or even a reversal in the poem's narrative. Instead of such a turn, once we reach the ending of "Assurance," the situation the sonnet began with, waking with a kiss, has only been reinforced, with a closing rhyme to match its opening (kiss-bliss-is-kiss). If male poets relied on the sonnet's "potentially revelatory turns," Amy Christine Billone tells us that revelation "is precisely what nineteenth-century women poets refuse to dramatize."[48] We can see this refusal on the structural level of Lazarus's sonnet (where the end reinforces the beginning), and even more so in her choice to leave this poem, nearly alone of all the poems in the manuscript, undated. Esther Schor reads this as evidence that Lazarus is "eager to prevent posterity from reading this poem against the days of her life,"[49] denying us the tools of historical investigation and verification. This is very much in line with Billone's assertion that "in many ways, nineteenth-century women's sonnets construct elaborate disguises which, rather than spotlighting biographical selves, as critics often assume to be the case, instead camouflage, obscure, and withhold them." However, Billone continues, "It would be a mistake, I think, to cover our eyes to every biographical light that shines through."[50]

Following this warning, we cannot underestimate the significance of Lazarus's choice to include the poem in her collection, in what Schor terms "a single act of courage, a decision to break through yet one more type of decorum—one that occurred especially to seemly, aristocratic spinsters."[51] In this complicated fashion, "Assurance" leaves us with competing measures of revelation and disguise. Lazarus includes it in her oeuvre as a historical trace, at the same time that she erases its historical markers (the same markers of time and place she is so careful to give in her other poems). Even the refusal of the revelation that I described as the poem's cyclical form contributes to this duality, mixing the waking and the dream. While doing away with any epistemological or ideological conflict that might be posed by reinforcing the dream's validity, the sonnet insists that it is both *"only* a dream" (to quote from her earlier poem) and that it *"is the thing that is."*

There is no answer for the question of Lazarus's sexuality, nor is her sexuality that which stands here in question. Instead, "Assurance" offers us its own model of lesbian history, where, in the fashion of queer spectrality, the lesbian is neither entirely present nor absent, neither present nor past. She tells us an "open secret." The phenomenon of the "open secret," writes D. A. Miller, "does not, as one might think, bring about the collapse of those binarisms [private/public, inside/outside, subject/object] and their ideological effects, but rather attests to their fantasmatic recovery."[52] Indeed, it is this collapse between Lazarus's concealment and her invitation that makes her dream haunt us to this day, touching across and against history. This is the same collapse of binarisms we found in both Molodowsky and Margolin's failed negotiations of self and "tribe," past and present. In the following chapters we will turn to the more recent history of Jewish lesbian-identified writers of the 1970s. For these writers, the Yiddish women writers of the current chapter become haunting ghosts. Focusing on Adrienne Rich and Irena Klepfisz will allow us, following Moore, "to read backwards from a more established figure in lesbian history to influences we may not otherwise perceive as belonging in the archives of lesbian culture."[53] This backward reading is part of a specifically lesbian historical recovery project that I will go on to explore. But as the readings in this chapter have shown, lesbian identity is not what stands as the basis of lesbian history, as its absence proves just as haunting as its presence. Between absence and presence, ghosting and being ghosted, this history moves queerly across time.

FIVE COMMUNITY ACROSS DISCONTINUITY

This chapter was meant to move from lesbian ghosts to real live lesbians, but during its initial writing, one of its central figures, Jewish lesbian poet Adrienne Rich, passed away. How to write her death, to come to terms with the already imaginary but now necessarily impossible task of talking to her, became an added challenge my own writing needed to take on. "What do we want from each other / after we have told our stories," asks Audre Lorde, lamenting that "there are no honest poems about dead women," as her poem is titled.[1] Rich quotes these lines in the introduction to *Of Woman Born*'s tenth anniversary edition, asking how to move beyond "the individualistic telling with no place to go" to "a collective movement to empower women."[2] Heeding Rich's call, as I interpret it, to politicize, historicize, and theorize, I dedicate this chapter to her, in an effort to write about her generation with the honesty she demanded when writing about her own foremothers, the "exceptional / even deviant" heroines who drew their "long skirts across the nineteenth century." Facing them head on, Rich asks,

> how can I give you
> > all your due
> > > take courage from your courage
> honor your exact
> > legacy as it is
> recognizing
> > as well
> > > that it is not enough?[3]

Continuing Rich's questions, this chapter confronts multiple moments across Jewish women's literary history; Yiddish women writers circa 1928, Jewish lesbians circa 1982, and 2018, my own (queer) time. The year 1928 was major for women's writing in general,[4] and lesbian writing in particular.[5] That same year, *Yidishe dikhterins*, the first anthology of Yiddish women's writing, was published.[6] In 1982, between the feminist sex wars and the Lebanon War, *Nice Jewish Girls*, the first Jewish lesbian anthology, came out.[7] This was also the year I was born. Twenty-eight years later, I came together with the editor of and many contributors to the anthology at the conference "In Amerika They Call Us Dykes: 1970s Lesbian Lives," and presented my work on Jewish lesbians and the Yiddish women's poetry they helped introduce to me. Looking at these multiple moments as sites of contiguity and contemporaneity (noncontemporaneous or otherwise), and of discontinuity, conflict, and complication, I will argue for queer modes of cross-temporal community building.

"Were all things equal," writes Blanche Cook, "1928 might be remembered as a banner year for lesbian publishing."[8] She then goes on to explain how things are not equal at all, as many lesbian lives and texts "have until so recently been forced out of history, ripped from our collective memory."[9] Thus, for example, Emma Lazarus's explicitly lesbian poem "Assurance," written in the 1880s, was not published until the 1980s. Cook asserts that "like the historical denial of women's history generally, the historical denial of the vast range of women-loving-women has not been an accident."[10] It is in this denial that Jewish lesbian poet Adrienne Rich anchors her analysis in "Compulsory Heterosexuality and Lesbian Existence," offering her own account of the consequences of erasure and its impact on women's collectivity.

> The destruction of records and memorabilia and letters documenting the realities of lesbian existence must be taken very seriously as a means of keeping heterosexuality compulsory for women, since what has been kept from our knowledge is joy, sensuality, courage, and community, as well as guilt, self-betrayal, and pain.[11]

Or phrased poetically in "Transcendental Etude," the final poem of Rich's 1978 *Dream of a Common Language*,

> Birth stripped our birthright from us,
> tore us from a woman, from women, from ourselves
> so early on
> and the whole chorus throbbing at our ears
> like midges, told us nothing, nothing
> of origins, nothing we needed
> to know, nothing that could re-member us.[12]

Both pieces connect the erasure of female and lesbian knowledge and history to the dominance of particular identities (enforcing heterosexuality) and to the foreclosure of community. Rich's poem ties this historical erasure to the fundamental psychoanalytic notions of female lack, only to discount the power of both; "but in fact we were always like this," writes Rich right before the lines quoted above, "rootless, dismembered: knowing it makes the difference." "Like this" is a state of lack, being "rootless, dismembered," echoing the psychoanalytic female condition. Teresa De Lauretis cites Rich's poem as a site "where the fantasy of dispossession is most explicitly linked to the subject's loss of the female body in the mother, in herself and in the other woman."[13] Over and against the fantasy of dispossession, I read the recognition that "we were always like this" as a way of denying not the female body ("lack" of penis included), but castration itself; this didn't "happen" to us, "we were always like this." Castration is then no threat, and Rich counters the phallocentric understanding of females as "dismembered." Rather than reading "this" (lack) in relation to the biology or psychoanalytic models of an individual, Rich invites us to read her text as part of the very struggle against denial and erasure, a reclaiming of history, recasting the Oedipal drama as a collective call. Following this reading, the later wish to "re-member" (in the final line quoted) is not the near literal reparation of an original castration, focusing on a male "member," but instead a way of connecting as members to a female collectivity, repairing the rupture created when birth "tore us from women." It is a return to a lost collectivity. The model of community that emerges is, therefore, one that exists both across time and within time, making memory and history necessarily communally based and community-generating projects.

Striving for such community, the feminist and lesbian movements of the late 1970s and early 1980s placed significant emphasis on women's history. In the Jewish case, this is particularly evident in projects like the 1986 *Tribe of Dina* that "revealed Jewish women's participation in Jewish life,"[14] offering a diverse portrait of contemporary Jewish feminist reality, while dedicating significant weight to historical writing. While *The Tribe of Dina* was not titled a lesbian anthology, it was originally published as a special issue of the journal *Sinister Wisdom*, "A Multicultural Lesbian Literary & Art Journal." This is the oldest surviving lesbian literary journal, launched in 1976 and edited in the early 1980s by Adrienne Rich and her long-term partner, Michelle Cliff. Irena Klepfisz and Melanie Kaye/Kantrowitz, the editors of *The Tribe of Dina*, explicitly connect the beginning of their project to *Nice Jewish Girls*, the first Jewish lesbian anthology, published just a few years earlier. *Nice Jewish Girls* broke barriers of silence and erasure, and served as an important platform for articulating the challenges entailed in Jewish lesbian identities. Following in its footsteps, *The Tribe of Dina* was able to offer more contemporary breadth while giving voice to women of the past, thus becoming one of the first occasions on which translations of primary texts by Yiddish women writers were published, including texts by Kadya Molodowsky, Anna Margolin, and Fradel Shtok.[15]

Certainly, by the 1980s there were a number of other English-language anthologies of Yiddish writing, some of which included women, but as scholar and translator Kathryn Hellerstein bemoans, the number of women included was by no means representative of their actual participation, leaving English readers unaware of how rich women's cultural production in Yiddish has been.[16] And though for Yiddish readers the treasures of women's writing were available through diverse publications, first and foremost Ezra Korman's 1928 anthology *Yidishe dikhterins*, they were neither widely known nor accessible. Hellerstein, for example, describes being a graduate student of Yiddish literature in the 1980s and having no knowledge of women's writing, and details her process of discovering this history.[17] Twenty-some years later my own experience was not dissimilar, illuminating the combination of hurdles facing projects such as my own; the challenges women faced when trying to enter Jewish history; the challenge of discovering women's history in the face of its discontinuous transmission; the challenge of identifying the lesbian over and against her historical erasure; the challenge in overcoming the persistent marginalization of both women and Yiddish in Jewish and Israeli culture.[18] In order to overcome these challenges and become *Found Treasures*, as one relatively recent translation anthology is titled, most (Yiddish and/or lesbian) women's texts had to wait many years, and many are still waiting, expectantly.

Contrasting the trajectories of lesbian history and Jewish history, Rich writes, "lesbian existence has been lived (unlike, say, Jewish or Catholic existence) without access to any knowledge of a tradition, a continuity, a social underpinning."[19] Jewish women had to struggle for inclusion in Jewish tradition and history. And continuing this dynamic, Rich's turn to the Jewish past entailed a complex coming-to-terms with her own history and identity. As she reveals in her famous 1982 essay, "Split at the Root," and in numerous other works, Rich's own access to Jewish tradition was more interrupted than continuous. What she inherited from both her father, whom she describes as an assimilated Jew, and her mother, a southern Protestant, was a sense of shame about her Jewishness. The essay makes clear how fraught her path to Jewish identity was: writing about it feels like a "dangerous act filled with guilt and shame."[20] Besides societal shame over being Jewish and/or gay, Rich and many of the women writing in *Nice Jewish Girls* (where the essay first appeared) describe not having access to all of the resources of Jewish culture as a source of shame, frustration, and anger. Despite the frustration Rich and other Jewish lesbians of the 1970s felt at being cut off from Jewish texts past and present, we might see this shared marginalization as an experience connecting them directly to their Jewish foremothers, who were in general more directly marginalized from Jewish history and Jewish learning.

"The Yiddish cultural legacy, *di goldene keyt*, which had been passed on to me was strictly male," protests Irena Klepfisz, writing as part of the emergent lesbian movement in the 1970s–'80s. But Klepfisz desperately wanted to find out "*vos di froyen hobn getrakht un geshribn*, what the women had thought and written."[21] Klepfisz then goes "searching for *di bikher un sforim* from which Molodowsky's page might have been torn." Klepfisz explains that feminist identity politics, "with its implicit multiculturalism pushed many of us to strengthen our ties to our cultural origin and to search for our specific women's history, our cultural foremothers and role models."[22] For Klepfisz this is a meeting of feminism and a Jewish perspective, and is part of her "beginning to think from a Jewish feminist perspective, helping make visible a woman's link in the chain of Jewish history."[23] For "it would be presumptuous of any of us to act as if nothing came before us,"[24] writes Klepfisz, calling for Jewish writing in English that looks back to the Yiddish texts of the nineteenth and twentieth centuries, making Yiddish women writers a "significant reference point in our writing,"[25] as Klepfisz herself does. And looking back, we see that even Kadya Molodowsky, one of the pioneers of Yiddish women's literature, herself made women of the past "a significant point of reference." Molodowsky's turn to the past and her special interest in the notable women who came before her is manifested in the extensive series of women's biographies she wrote under the name Rivke Zilberg, published in the New York Yiddish newspaper *Forverts* in the 1950s.[26] There she writes about world-famous women, such as Sappho and Harriet Beecher Stowe, Jewish women such as Emma Lazarus, Glikl of Hameln, and Henrietta Szold, as well as wives and mothers of famous Jewish men.[27] While researching this series in the archives of YIVO, the Institute for Jewish Research in New York, I was surprised to discover a strikingly similar series written by the Yiddish journalist Esther Luria, in the women's pages of the *Forverts*, in addition to essays she published in *Tsukunft* and *Glaykhhayt* from 1914 to 1920.[28] Luria, born in Warsaw in 1887, was far less successful than Molodowsky, and is said to have died "alone and in poverty" in New York in the 1920s.[29] While Molodowsky's selection of women is very close to Luria's, the essays themselves bear little resemblance to each other, and Molodowsky likely had no knowledge of Luria's work. For example, Molodowsky's essay on Sappho, published in the *Forverts* on August 28, 1955, bears no resemblance to Luria's essay on Sappho, published in the *Tsukunft*, vol. 25, 1920.[30] This unknowing repetition serves as an apt model for the perils of women's history and its many fissures and voids. Rather than telling a story of loss, however, when reading these projects together, repetition becomes echo, queerly creating connections and community across history.

Before Molodowsky began dedicating her industrious efforts to women's history, she rebelled in one of her earliest published essays "Bagegenishn" ("Encounters"),[31] against the separate category of women's writing. Molodowsky describes the challenges, possibly insurmountable, of building a contemporary community of Yiddish women writers. In contrast to Klepfisz's and Rich's desire and search for such a community, Molodowsky is responding to disparaging literary critiques that categorically lump "women's poetry" into one category, or even onto one page. Molodowsky insists that the poets themselves do not believe in (*haltn nisht fun*) such a grouping, nor do their poems. "They," the poems, "stand with their backs to one another and often don't even meet/bump into each other, they want to avoid each other." Molodowsky brilliantly continues by way of parody, bringing to life the encounters poets have when their poems share a single page, "*eyn zaytl*," being quite literally confined together in various journals under the "characterless rubric of *froyen-dikhtung* [women's poetry]." Weaving together images and quotes from their poems she animates each poet, just to show how little they have in common with one another. While Miriam Ulinover (1890–1944) speaks of God and Jerusalem, Esther Shumiatcher (1899–1985) invokes Allah and crucifixes. Rokhl Korn (1898–1982) walks barefoot, and Anna Margolin wears a mask. Molodowsky herself meets Khane Levin (1900–69), who is holding a "Lenin in one hand and a revolver in the other," whereas Molodowsky stands surrounded by names from an old prayer book. When Levin notices this "enemy relic" (*fayntlikhe relikvye*), as she terms the prayer book that Molodowsky is holding, she points the revolver at her, causing the cloud of names floating around her to disperse "and a white paper trail" to stretch between them.[32]

The target of Molodowsky's critique was actually one of Molodowsky's avid supporters, the Yiddish writer and literary critic Melech Ravitch (1893–1976). In his review of Ezra Korman's anthology *Yidishe dikhterins*, Ravitch similarly animates women's poems, presenting them as a chorus of women, each speaking louder than the next, trying to "out-sing" (*iberzingen*) the others.[33] Ravitch deems Molodowsky the actual *firshtin* (princess) of the entire anthology, saying Korman could easily have tripled the space he gave her (which already consists of nine pages, when many writers only have one), letting her speak longer in this *froyen-asife* (women's gathering). This inaugural "gathering" of Yiddish women's writing, *Yidishe dikhterins*, is the only Yiddish anthology of women's writing published to date, and holds poems from more than seventy Yiddish women poets ranging from 1586 to 1928.[34]

The sheer weight of the book is astounding, defiantly declaring *mir zaynen do*, we are here. Indeed, my own initial surprise at the existence of Yiddish women's poetry seems especially misplaced when encountering the breadth of Korman's anthology. And yet, like so many other Yiddish books, like so much of women's history, it was not passed down to me as an integral part of my cultural legacy. Similarly, the history the anthology brings forth is itself a rescue project, as Korman himself "claimed that this '*froyen-literatur*' had been buried in the dust of archival libraries, inaccessible to the reading public and also even to literary researchers and historians," as Hellerstein writes.[35] Like the case of the parallel works of Luria and Molodowsky, here too, women's history is repeatedly lost and found. Moreover, Korman is not only excavating materials of the past, but also making available a wide range of contemporary (or recently past) materials that Jewish dispersion made inaccessible, for example, works separated by the geographical distance of South Africa or Australia, or by the political distance of the Soviet Union. Both aspects of the encounter offered by the anthology, the encounter across time and the encounter across space, create community across discontinuity. This anthology, then, is in and of itself another version of a boundary-transgressing "queer tribe."

Perhaps the most haunting aspect of the work is the inclusion of small photographed portraits of writers pasted within the hundreds of pages, which lend this large volume the feel of a handmade scrapbook or family album, making it all the more precious, fragile, and ultimately fleeting.[36] Echoing this personalized touch, *The Tribe of Dina* also includes portraits of its contributors, from Anna Margolin to Irena Klepfisz. Some are photographed in context, like a very young Sarah

Schulman, posing in front of the New York City skyscape, or the family-style portraits included under the rubric "The Women in Our Family," ranging in date between Kadya Molodowsky and Yiddish translator Ruth Whitman. These photographs serve, like those in Korman's anthology, to build a sense of familiarity and even familial kinship with the writers, while visually marking a temporal difference between the writers and today's reader. Even if the authors themselves were to return to the book, certainly their own distance from the time in which they were portrayed must be one of the first things they encounter. The photos thus mark the passage of time as much as they bring the past closer to the reader, in an unmediated visual presence.

Korman himself roots his anthologizing strategy in his historical time: since the new modernist *froyen-dikhtung*/women's poetry is only at its beginning stages and not at yet at its "zenith," he explains, he will refrain from judgments and generalizations, though these will certainly come.[37] Realizing Korman's prediction, Hellerstein's long-awaited study, *A Question of Tradition: Women Poets in Yiddish, 1586–1987*, "picks up where Korman left off. More than eighty years after his anthology appeared, with the benefit of subsequent scholarship in Yiddish and gender studies, we are now in a position to read these poets qualitatively and analytically," she writes.[38] A central aspect of this work involves activating the wide historical span Korman offers, by reading modern poems for their premodern, and specifically religious, resonance, while recognizing the unique strategies of both modern and premodern poets. This indeed was Korman's own stated intention: he explains that his juxtaposition of old and new enables us to see, in his words, both the *yerushedikayt*, the value of the legacy of "our modern women-poets," as well as *di vayte nesiye* ([their] far journey), on the path divined and traveled by those before them.[39]

The question of connection between the premodern and the modern (or the question of *tradition*, as Hellerstein has it) is far from straightforward. In fact, the project of literary genealogy, whether Korman's, Hellerstein's or my own, is rather based in the ability to, and the necessity of, actively searching for *usable pasts*[40] and making new connections across difference. For example, Hellerstein claims that including premodern poets is part of Korman's attempt to "resolve the contradiction between his desire to ground modern Yiddish poetry in premodern traditions and his stated belief in the *lack of a direct connection* between the two bodies of work. In other words, Korman was creating a tradition that he believed did not really exist."[41] Similarly, Avraham Novershtern, scholar of

Yiddish literature (and my first teacher) suggests that rather than discovering a "tradition" of Yiddish women's poetry, Korman creates the *illusion* of such a "tradition."[42] This illusion is, according to Novershtern, the anthology's most concrete influence (*hashpa'ah muḥashit*). Novershtern deems the lineage Korman establishes to be a "false scope" (*prisah medumah*), claiming that in practice only four of the seventy poets actually belong to the category "old Yiddish literature" (ending in the eighteenth century), and only two are from the nineteenth century.[43] He goes on to argue that Yiddish women poets never attempted to create their own literary tradition. First, he writes, "it is hard to point out a woman's poem in Yiddish that has an explicit dialogue with another woman's poem in Yiddish";[44] women poets generally turn to a male addressee (overturning the convention of Yiddish literature's female audience);[45] women poets do not refer to the female traditions that preceded them, the tradition of the *tkhines* (supplication prayers); rather, women poets draw on the *taytsh-khumesh* (the literal translation of the Bible), and the *tsene-rene*, the rendition of the Bible written for women but not by them;[46] and finally, women poets do not use the women's voices available through Yiddish folklore.[47]

Novershtern is particularly concerned with Korman's focus on numbers of women writers, and he suggests that his criterion for selection favored quantity over quality, which not only skews the image of women's writing, but also misleads later readers. It appears that the worst consequence of this "illusion" is the feminist study of Yiddish it enables, against which Novershtern is staging his intervention, naming among others Norma Fain Pratt, Kathryn Hellerstein, and Anita Norich. Reducing the work of feminist scholarship to a focus on "the feminine essence" (*hahavayah hanashit*), Novershtern binds this scholarship to the early ghettoizing of Yiddish women's writing, showing that the category of "women's writing" is the product of a literary criticism controlled entirely by men. Speaking to the political and academic concerns of feminist scholars, who would most likely rather not be viewed as the heirs of a misogynistic tradition of literary criticism, Novershtern goes on to recruit Molodowsky and other Yiddish women's own rejection of their grouping. This analysis aims to "expose" feminist scholarship as a double betrayal of women's writing, by aligning it retroactively with the women's critics and against the women's wishes.

Ironically, these feminist scholars are not just the objects of Novershtern's critique, but also presumably, his target audience, since his study appeared in a special issue of the Israeli journal *Bikoret ufarshanut* (*Criticism & Interpretation*) dedicated to women's writing. Overall, it would seem that what Novershtern is most disturbed by is the very desire that there be a tradition of women writing, whether expressed in the 1920s, in the 1970s, or today. Answering this critique in her aforementioned study, *A Question of Tradition*, Hellerstein undoes many of Novershtern's generalizations, armed with some thirty years of meticulous archival and literary scholarship. *A Question of Tradition* proves that a gendered lens does not limit our reading to one common denominator, but rather reveals the many ways in which women had to vie with Jewish tradition, making it their own. As much as he rails against the idea of women's tradition, up until the publication of Hellerstein's book, Novershtern's essay was not only one of the most comprehensive pieces of scholarship on women's poetry, it was also one of the only works to offer an overview of literary criticism about women's Yiddish writing, including feminist criticism. Therefore, Novershtern himself made an invaluable contribution to the legacy of Yiddish women writers and the writing about them, inadvertently producing another offshoot of the "imagined tradition," which he criticizes,[48] actively creating his own version of a cross-temporal queer community, which he therefore joins.

The desire for a cross-temporal community of women has certainly fueled much of the work on Yiddish women's writing, and the investment in an "imagined tradition" reflects both the desire for tradition and the fact that at times it can only be constituted by the imagination. Indeed, the limited availability of histories often led women to generate imaginary and fictional versions of the lives of both famous and anonymous women, as Bonnie Zimmerman notes specifically regarding lesbian authors: "Whether the image is created by Stephen Gordon, Beebo Brinker, or mythic Amazons, the reconstruction of past history is constant."[49] Because even archival research and translation projects offered only partial access to the past, leaving many narratives lost and inaccessible, many women chose to imagine and re-create images of that past that was not passed down to them. "I looked around and saw that so many of my generation's activists were Jewish dykes, and I felt like we couldn't have sprung full-grown from our moment in time—we must have had some kind of origin," writes Elana Dykewomon, who went on to write *Beyond the Pale*, which recasts the classic Jewish tale of life in Eastern Europe and the immigration to America as a lesbian bildungsroman.[50]

I myself was seized by a similar impulse when first conducting research at Żydowski Instytut Historyczny (ZIH), the Jewish Historical Institute in

Warsaw—an impulse to invent a lesbian Yiddish poet to stand in for the history I desired/the history of my desire. Imagine my surprise when I discovered one already existed, as I first discovered the work of Irena Klepfisz, who is not only an editor and scholar, but also a Yiddish-writing lesbian poet. I encountered her work not in an archive, but at a Jewish feminist conference at Mills College in California in 2006, where Klepfisz read the bilingual poem "*Der Soyne*/The Enemy: An Interview in Gaza,"[51] in which a Palestinian child's encounter with an Israeli soldier is narrated in the first person in Yiddish and then in English. This poem, to which I return in the final section of this book, offers a striking attempt to use Yiddish to "enfold within this language our contemporary lives and crises."[52] At the same time, other parts of Klepfisz's oeuvre use English and bilingual English-Yiddish poetics to imagine and create voices from the Jewish past.

But above all, Klepfisz seems driven by a desire for community, as she repeatedly wishes for a context within which her poems would grow "*tsuzamen mit di lider fun andere froyen* (together with the poems of other women)."[53] Klepfisz's desire for contact and community offers an opposite vision to that of Molodowsky's "Bagegenishn," discussed earlier in this chapter. Molodowsky has "context" of community, on the page and to a certain extent in her life, and can thus resent it, and rebel against it by depicting women's poems turning their backs on each other, even as they share a single page. For Klepfisz it is the lack of actual community that generates the vision of community in her writing. In creating a similar image that detaches poems from their poets, Molodowsky and Klepfisz both position dialogue as impossible. In Molodowsky's case we understand this as a product of actual differences between the poets, differences even more pronounced than their texts reveal, so that while the poems may be printed on one page, the poets have good reason to resist being grouped together. In Klepfisz's case we are led to believe that there are no poets with whom she can share a context, and the most that could even be desired is the company of other poems. For as much as Klepfisz yearns to establish "a dialogue *mit der yidisher fargangenhayt*, with the Yiddish/Jewish past, a dialogue that would have to include women,"[54] she consistently positions herself alone in the present, relegating Yiddish poets to the past. And while it is true that the heyday of Yiddish poetry passed long before she started writing, true that the Khurbn (the Nazi extermination project) serves as an unbridgeable rupture on all counts, true that since then Yiddish has been on the decline, it is also a fact that there were women writing Yiddish contemporaneously with Klepfisz's beginning as an English poet, and even when she began writing bilingual Yiddish-English poetry in the 1980s.[55] Klepfisz bears no witness to any interaction with these poets, nor does she even make note of their existence, although many of them were living and working in the very same city at the time; in effect, she turns her back on them as she looks backward for them.[56]

The community within which Klepfisz was active was the lesbian movement, which was gaining force socially, politically, and culturally. As a writer whose lesbian identity became public relatively early (with the publication of the journal *Conditions*),[57] it is perhaps not surprising, considering the homophobia in Jewish communities (Yiddish-speaking and otherwise) and in society at large, that Klepfisz felt more comfortable in conversation with poetry past than present poets. Indeed, if we think back to the image of Adrienne Rich and Kadya Molodowsky reading together in 1969, we are reminded that Rich could only share this stage before coming out, and not after. On the other hand, after coming out, Rich and Klepfisz were the ones to share many a stage and many a page, as active Jewish lesbian writers and activists. They both wrote for and edited the lesbian journal *Conditions*, contributed to the anthology *Nice Jewish Girls*, and perhaps my favorite, they were part of the group *Di Vilde Khayes* (the Wild Animals). This radical Jewish lesbian group came together in 1982 in order to speak out against Israel's actions in Lebanon and lesbian anti-Semitism at once.[58] Still, Klepfisz and Rich wound up in very different positions, certainly in terms of literary fame and the material security that can come with it. They each offer a very different story about Jewish lesbian life and literature in terms of their disparate Jewish backgrounds and the different roles they ultimately took in the women's movement and in the sphere of American poetry.

Adrienne Rich published continually from the 1950s to her death, and has long been a widely known and highly appreciated English-language poet. Irena Klepfisz is known in much narrower circles, and the focus has too often been on her Khurbn poetry and her role as the daughter of Michał Klepfisz, regarded as a hero of the Warsaw Ghetto Uprising who died protecting his better-known comrade, Marek Edelman. Klepfisz used this measure of acceptance to voice her own radical politics. For example, at the 2006 talk she gave at Mills College, she described how, invited to read poetry at the fiftieth anniversary of the uprising, she chose to read the poem "*Der Soyne*/The Enemy: An Interview in Gaza" about the Israeli occupation of Palestine. She also described causing great discomfort at the National Yiddish Book Center, repeating the word *lezbianke* as she read her poem "*Etlekhe verter oyf mame-loshn*/A few Words in the Mother Tongue."[59]

Whereas Rich had to struggle to access her Jewish heritage, alongside her struggle to reclaim the stories of women's history, Klepfisz studied Yiddish with Max Weinreich (one the most important figures in Yiddish Studies in the twentieth century), and although she was an active researcher and translator, as she became more visible in the lesbian movement in the late 1970s, she became less welcome in the institutional world of Yiddish.[60] Rich gained literary fame in English and translated Yiddish poetry before coming out as a lesbian. Whereas working with Yiddish stands out as an exception in Rich's English-language career, Klepfisz's career drew closer and closer to Yiddish, culminating (for now) in a series of bilingual Yiddish-English poems, collected in *A Few Words in the Mother Tongue* (1990).[61] Klepfisz spent many years silent in the field of poetry, in effect joining the Yiddish women writers she translates and writes about. Happily, this silence has very recently been broken.[62] Klepfisz is now finally receiving the public appreciation her work certainly merits, as she was awarded the Adrienne Cooper Dreaming in Yiddish award in 2016.

Considering the trajectories of Klepfisz's and Rich's lives and careers, it becomes clear that there are present reasons for their turn to the past. Turning to the past to forge community serves as a way to overcome the challenge of forging communities in the present. Understanding the politics of the early lesbian present (which is now past), and specifically the history of homophobia, can itself explain the early Jewish lesbian turn to the past (similarly, it could be suggested that anti-Semitism can explain the Yiddish writers' turn to the non-Jewish past). Allowing them to identify with a foremother who could not reject them, this turn also offered them an alternative to engaging with their contemporaries, who might reject them if given the chance. And it is not only straight society that can potentially reject these lesbian writers, for the lesbian movement itself was (and is) a site of active internal struggle. The 1970s lesbian ideal of "sisterhood" and the desire that "all women" be grouped in a "common cause," not only rhetorically but also politically proved to elide important differences between women, problematizing politics of collaboration and representation. Cross-temporal community is then a way to avoid challenges faced by the lesbian writers both internally and externally. It is no coincidence, then, that so far I have been exploring alternative queer conversations through imagination, recuperation, and translation;

no coincidence that these are the avenues Margolin and Molodowsky, Klepfisz and Rich have chosen over actual encounter. Returning to Molodowsky's image of poems turning their backs on each other and Klepfisz looking backward while turning her back on her potential contemporaries, it becomes clear that contemporary "sisterhood" is indeed a challenge. I learned this on my flesh from my own experience of intergenerational encounter with (some) 1970s lesbians, which brought out aggression (in myself and in others) I would never have expected.

The 2010 CUNY Center for Lesbian and Gay Studies conference "In Amerika They Call Us Dykes: 1970s Lesbian Lives" was meant to recognize the "momentous decade," calling on "experience, memory, and scholarship to represent as fully as possible the broad and wide experience of lesbians during the 1970s," as their website proclaimed.[63] The 1970s, I quickly discovered, were not merely the historical moment studied by the conference, but rather they were indeed present. Experiencing the simultaneity of my own time and the time of 1970s lesbians, many of whom are alive (and kicking!), demanded a new mode of understanding the very history of the movement, as well as the movement of history, exposing "what the language of feminist 'waves' and queer 'generations' sometimes effaces: mutually disruptive energy of moments that are not yet past and yet are not entirely present either,"[64] as I described the encounter between Rich and Molodowsky. Mirroring their encounter, I too shared a New York stage with my elders, discussing Jewish lesbian literature with the women who pioneered in the field, such as Evelyn Torton Beck[65] and Elana Dykewomon. Instead of an imaginary noncontemporaneous contemporaneity (as I discussed via Anna Margolin and Emma Lazarus in chapter 1), I was faced with what Bonnie Morris, another panel member, defined as an awkward era of shift between lesbian generations.[66] Morris (who identifies as "part of a bridge generation. A child in the radical 1960s and a teen in the feminist 1970s"[67]) describes the challenge of this simultaneous existence, and of the process of "making it into history": "Although various woman-identified, lesbian separatist platforms and events that characterized a self-proclaimed dyke subculture throughout the 1970s–'90s still exist, they aren't yet popular subjects of historical inquiry. Instead, these remaining activists and institutions have become popular subjects of criticism and contempt."[68] Morris's recent book *The Disappearing L: Erasure of Lesbian Spaces and Culture*, aims to battle the disappearance of the lesbian from contemporary queer politics and from the writing of history. She writes: "Right now, it's imperative that we find better ways for the vanishing ideas, sites, and inherited *stuff* of late 20th-century lesbian culture to be valued, preserved, and known by future generations."[69]

The CUNY conference offered a valuable site for the production, consolidation, and celebration of this historical knowledge, and indeed that is what drew me and other young scholars and activists born after the '70s were over. However, many of the encounters proved charged and indeed painful. "I found myself in the wreckage of social movements," writes Kaitlin Noss, a conference participant describing the reactions of (some) older lesbians to the panel she participated in.[70] "Several women had stormed out of the room, each declaring loudly that such academic language was antifeminist and that the younger generation was apolitical and once yelling, 'Nonconsensual phallus!' when an image of a dildo was presented in a slide."[71] This particular panel crystallized conflicts that caused tensions throughout the conference: some older women resented the very use of the word *queer*, and (wrongly) equated the resistance to the term *lesbian*, posed by many queers, with resistance to the term *feminist*. Some were extremely resistant to the academic language used by some of the younger queers. Finally, there were accusations that the "queers" were apolitical. These conflicts were strikingly Freudian, my desperate desire to subvert that dynamic notwithstanding. I have my own straight mother to rebel against (and embrace), I thought to myself. These women of the earlier lesbian movement were not a "mother figure" I wanted or needed to reject. Significantly, many of them are not mothers at all, and if they are, it is often itself in rebellion of reproductive heteronormativity rather than as a concession to its dictates. Cross-generationally, we share the same position in the Freudian family drama, against the "patriarchal father." Therefore, we are not only potential allies, but potential lovers outside a logic of incest and heterosexual propriety. When I tried to suggest this at the panel described by Noss, I was, however, shot down by another audience member who responded to my suggestion of erotic potentiality by shouting, "*Who cares?*" Queering the family model, then, cannot offer an easy way out of the "generational trap"[72] of aggression I was attempting to deconstruct, as I learned firsthand, falling through the generational gap into the trap of *straight*-up struggle.

I was especially taken aback by the vehemence of these sentiments, considering that to me they each represented a point of connection rather than conflict; it was the older generations' bold gender-nonconforming lives and bodies that enabled the undermining of the gender binary that is so crucial to the queer movement; it was the groundbreaking work of early dyke scholars like Esther Newton and Lillian Faderman (both conference participants) that enabled the inclusion of queers in academia, and that has served as the basis for much queer thinking and writing; it is on the basis of the lesbian-feminist analysis of intersecting oppressions that so many queer-driven fights for social justice are now being staged. These lines of connection are what Linda Garber calls "the nuanced genealogy of lesbian and queer theories."[73] Acknowledging this genealogy, I hoped to replace confrontational identity politics with a dialogue that might bridge the generational gap "which is not one."[74] And indeed, during the conference days I found many sisters in struggle, despite differences in age and opinion. Evelyn Torton Beck and I danced joyously at the conference closing party. Joan Gibbs, lesbian woman of color, longtime activist, lawyer, and editor, spoke about addressing the racism and classism of the movement in the '70s, and about her current work on intersectional oppressions beyond the movement, as she works for immigration rights. Barbara Hammer, one of the first out lesbian filmmakers, proudly embraced the word *queer* in a room full of women expressing suspicion and even rage against it.

And then, there were the queerest moments of all, when the lesbian past was indistinguishable from my queer present. As I brewed my own tea during the opening reception, I thought, "How lesbian of me," and that was finally okay—in this space, *lesbian* could not be a derogatory term. Watching home videos from the '70s in one of the panels, the affinity was even more obvious—plaid shirts, big plastic glasses, the spitting image of many a contemporary California queer. This physical similarity beautifully echoed Eve Sedgwick's essay "White Glasses,"[75] where Sedgwick finds herself indistinguishable from gay scholar-activist Michael Lynch because they are wearing the same white glasses. In the glasses she bought to look like his, Sedgwick *looks* and *sees* like a gay man. Offering another way of thinking of the external affinity between 1970s lesbians and contemporary queers, Elizabeth Freeman deploys the term "temporal drag," with all the associations that the word *drag* has, not just with cross-gendered performance, but with "retrogression, delay, and the pull of the past upon the present."[76] As much as embodying the past pulls the present backward, it also pulls the past forward, confronting the present with it, pushing it through the present into the future. Freeman writes that in many discussions of the relationship between the lesbian and the queer, "it often seems as if the lesbian feminist is cast as the big drag, drawing politics inexorably back to essentialized bodies, normative visions of women's sexuality, and single-issue identity politics." Refusing this generational rejection, Freeman opens a new possibility "for those of us for whom queer politics and theory involve not disavowing our relationship to particular (feminist) histories even as we move away from identity politics."[77] But much as I was eager to point out the lesbian genealogy of my queer present, those whom I was naming as "foremothers" had a thing or two to say about me, and it wasn't always pretty.

My goal in the conference, and in these lines, was to highlight the connections and configure an active evolution of 1970s lesbian politics into contemporary queer politics, a genealogical account that uses the past to explain the present (and vice versa). "Identification with an ancestor," writes Nealon, reveals "how history works, what it looks like, what possibilities it has offered in the past, and what those possibilities suggest about our ineffable present tense."[78] But seeing as the past is not quite gone, it should come as no surprise that the lesbian ancestors of the 1970s hold their own account of the present, resisting their very relegation to the past. That is why, as Rich admits in the poem "Granddaughter," it is "easier to invent a script for each of you, / myself still at the center, / than to write words in which you might have found / yourselves."[79] I don't have to dream or invent a past, even if I would have preferred to do so. Taking on dead Yiddish women poets is no doubt easier for the 1970s and for me alike, easier than opening up an intergenerational dialogue. But the 1970s generation granted contemporary queers a history to build on. At the same time, I recognize that, as Rich writes in her introduction to Klepfisz's poetry, "[to] inherit an uninterrupted and recognized culture is a privilege,"[80] one she herself did not have, either in Jewish or in lesbian terms. If earlier in this book my concern was how women writers might overcome their exclusion from history, this current chapter has dealt with the challenge of having a history—especially a history persisting into the present. For my generation is in a unique position, insofar as we have lesbian-identified forerunners, whose achievements we can study and celebrate, as opposed to all of the earlier, repressed stories patriarchal history did not pass on. I want to acknowledge with gratitude the great privilege of having a lesbian history, and more than that, to recognize how my own way into the more distant past is itself mediated through these earlier lesbian projects. What Rich and her generation left behind, then, was finally something I could, and must use.

> Everything we write
> will be used against us
> or against those we love.
> These are the terms,
> take them or leave them.
> Poetry never stood a chance
> of standing outside history.[81]

In these lines Rich sets up her own legacy, allowing for the fact that it must undergo changes. If these lines echo the Miranda Warning given by the police to their arrestees, "Anything you say can and will be used against you," Rich's poem moves from the spoken to the written, from the second-person singular to the first-person plural, from "anything" to "everything." Most importantly, Rich omits the conditional "can" and uses only the definite "will be used," revealing the certainty of change. She thereby removes the aspect of threat (to herself and to other writers), taking control at the same time that she relinquishes it by submitting to being used. Linda Garber takes on this idea of Rich's poetry being "used," and even, "used against her" by "lesbian feminist supporters and queer detractors,"[82] and, I add, by lesbian detractors and queer supporters. A danger on all fronts indeed, but in Garber's sophisticated move, Rich is read out of her time, enabling her to stand not just as lesbian feminist poet, but as proto-queer theorist. Garber recognizes the queerness already inherent in concepts like the "lesbian continuum," in defining a fluid identity over and against heteropatriarchy. Equally important, she reads Rich *in* time, tracing the development in Rich's own position, as she came to better understand difference among women (for example), showing the effects of living and changing within history. My own writing is similarly positioned in changing times, as was made painfully clear with Rich's passing. She was eighty-two, three years older than Kadya Molodowsky was in the photograph they shared not long before Molodowsky's own death. If challenges in the present lead Jewish lesbian writers to look to the past for continuity and community, they also fulfill the expectancy of texts past, helping them overcome their own historical challenges, coming together as queer communities across time.

SIX TRANSLATING GENERATIONS
Irena Klepfisz

This final chapter turns to the work of lesbian poet Irena Klepfisz, writing bilingual Yiddish-English poetry in New York starting in the 1970s, in order to offer a model of queer translation. Turning to Yiddish, Klepfisz joins a subversive trend in lesbian poetic practice by disturbing the ultimate dominance English usually holds, while subverting the workings of heteronormative language and lineage; using Yiddish is a political—not a naturalized—means of cultural transmission. It involves looking to Jewish women of the past and preserving for the future a past that should have been forgotten, because it pertained to women, and because it was in Yiddish. Yet, through acts of queer translation, the past is not simply preserved as is, but rather is politically transformed, as is the present. Over and against the conflicts explored in the previous chapter, Klepfisz's work brings a new poetics into being. This poetics undoes the border (and the potential conflict) between present and past, by refiguring the workings of English and Yiddish, and the relationship between them. So far we have encountered Klepfisz's work as a contributor to *Nice Jewish Girls*, expressing the complex identity of Jewish and lesbian, as editor of *The Tribe of Dina*, creating a space for feminist Jewish writing and translation, and as a scholar writing about Yiddish women's writing and specifically Molodowsky's poetry. Turning now to her bilingual poetry, we will see her politics and scholarship put to poetic practice, in the poem "*Di tsung*/The tongue," which moves between English and Yiddish on the primal level of sounds, vowels, and bodily gestures; the poem "Fradel Shtok," which narrates the transition from Yiddish to English; and the poem "*Etlekhe verter oyf mame-loshn*/A few words in the mother tongue," which moves between the two languages to create original bilingual Jewish lesbian poetry. Read together, these poems queer both translation and transmission, offering translation as a mode of queer transmission.

Narrating and enacting movement between languages, these poems create a liminal space, expressed in content and form alike. This space is both here and not here, past and present, Yiddish and English. For example, she writes in the poem "*Di rayze aheym*/The journey home,"[1]

Do
here
ot do
right here
muz zi lebn
she must live.

As the spaces between the words on the page and the languages of the poem indicate, "home" and "here" are not simple places to pinpoint. This poem is part of a cycle with the same title, "Di rayze aheym/The journey home," which Maeera Schreiber calls "one of Klepfisz's most sustained efforts to reside in language."[2] Klepfisz herself brings Czesław Miłosz's statement that "language is the only homeland" as an epigraph to the poem "Fradel Shtok." However, as we shall see, two of the poems we will read, "Di tsung/The tongue" and "Fradel Shtok," both narrate and poetically embody the difficulty of residing between two languages. The final poem I read in the chapter, "Etlekhe verter oyf mame-loshn/A few words in the mother tongue," can be seen to resolve the tension between the languages, by repurposing them both into a new poetic tongue.

In "*Di tsung*/The tongue,"[3] which is also part of the cycle "*Di rayze aheym/ The journey home*," Klepfisz physicalizes the struggle for speech and for memory, stripping the movement between Yiddish and English to a nearly preverbal state.

8. *Di tsung*/The tongue

Zi shvaygt.

Di verter feln ir
she lacks the words
and all that she can force

is sound
unformed sound:

a
der klang
          the sound

o
dos vort
          the word

u
di tsung
          the tongue

o
dos loshn
          the language

e
di trern
          the tears.

The poem's title begins by using "*Di tsung*/The tongue" as body-part; later in the poem Klepfisz uses the Hebraic word "*loshn*," which brings with it the meaning of tongue as language, as in English. The words Klepfisz chooses also move us from the meaning of tongue as body part to tongue as language, from unformed sound into meaning, in not one, but two languages, first in Yiddish and then in English. Offering a "sound," or more specifically, a vowel, which could either be English or Yiddish, Klepfisz then brings full Yiddish words to illustrate the sounds she lists: not *a* as in apple, but rather *o* as in *vort*. As they accumulate, the reader not only learns a lesson in Yiddish pronunciation, but gains the basic vocabulary, in both Yiddish and English, for poetic proficiency—the sound, the word, the tongue, the language, the tears—returning to the speaker the words she lacks for writing/speaking, and to the reader what she lacks for understanding a Yiddish poem.

    But it is not just a Yiddish narrative the poet restores. She also points us back through Jewish history, to Psalm 137, where the psalmist, after bemoaning the impossibility of song, makes a vow to memory, positioning enforced silence as a punishment for forgetting: "Should I forget you, Jerusalem, may my right hand wither. May my tongue cleave to my palate if I do not recall you" (Psalm 137:

5–6, translation by Robert Alter).⁴ Klepfisz's poem seems to speak out of this enforced silence, as her tongue must relearn speech. In the psalm, forgetfulness and silence work hand in hand both as threat and as punishment—if I forget thee, the tongue that sings and the hand that writes will no longer function; as long as I remember you I will keep writing and singing. This imperative to remember Jerusalem is the imperative to be conscious of the reality of exile. Rather than the impossibility of song, the psalm positions the awareness of exile as the condition of poetry itself. In Klepfisz's poem, it is not Jerusalem that is forgotten, but speech itself. In the poem opening the cycle from which "*Di tsung*/The tongue" comes, Klepfisz states this explicitly. Referring to the psalm even more directly, she writes,

> And our tongues have become
> dry the wilderness has
> dried out our tongues and
> we have forgotten speech.⁵

In "How to Tame a Wild Tongue," a section of her bilingual work *Borderlands/La Frontera*, Chicana lesbian author Gloria Anzaldúa quotes these very lines, after describing the shock at hearing, for the first time, the feminine plural "*nostras*" and realizing how "we are robbed of our female being by the masculine plural. Language is a male discourse."⁶ She follows this realization by quoting Klepfisz's lament.⁷ The bilingual poetics of Klepfisz and Anzaldúa are indeed in a fascinating dialogue with each other, here and elsewhere, both in mutual references and in their shared use of English alongside Yiddish/Spanish.⁸ In fact, Klepfisz directly credits Anzaldúa and other Chicana writers with the inspiration to create bilingually. However, for the purpose of our current discussion, I want to dwell only on what is perhaps the most significant difference between them: that Anzaldúa is using a language still widely spoken and growing (with its own set of contemporary political challenges, to be sure), whereas Klepfisz is using a language that speaks (to) the Jewish past, at least in terms of the reality she herself depicts. For indeed, there is a large ultra-Orthodox Yiddish-speaking community living not far from where Klepfisz is writing in New York, and yet this community is not the audience of secular poetry, especially not radical lesbian poetry. Klepfisz can therefore be seen to be transgressing not only borders of space (like Anzaldúa), but also borders of time. Turning to Yiddish, Klepfisz takes up not the sacred Hebrew tongue in which the Psalm was written, but the tongue of Jewish Diaspora. What she narrates in it is not the history she is commanded to remember, but what she (and we) were meant to forget. This forgetting is tied not only to Yiddish history, but is, as Anzaldúa asserts, intimately tied to women's history and lesbian history.

Recovering and inventing women's histories is an essential part of lesbian poetics and politics, a task Klepfisz undertakes in her poem "Fradel Shtok." [9] In the poem, Klepfisz takes on the voice of a specific Yiddish writer, the poet Shtok. Klepfisz then speaks for her as one would for a fictional character, at the same time insisting on her actual existence by supplying an epigraph that is a biography, grounding Shtok as an historical figure.

> Yiddish writer. B. 1890 in Skale, Galicia. Emigrated to New York in 1907. Became known when she introduced the sonnet form into Yiddish poetry. Author of *Erzeylungen* (Stories) in 1919, a collection in Yiddish. Switched to English and published *For Musicians Only* in 1927. Institutionalized and died in a sanitarium around 1930.[10]

In just a few lines, this extremely condensed version of an entire life supplies the information needed to understand the poem, at the center of which stands the linguistic struggle between Yiddish and English. This struggle is present even in the simple description "Emigrated to New York," which focuses on the act of leaving (emigration) rather than on the arrival (immigration). Naming Shtok a "Yiddish writer" despite her eventual "switch" to English implies the failure of this transition, linking it to her subsequent insanity and hospitalization. While recent research has shown that in fact Shtok did not die in an asylum and continued publishing until 1942,[11] the connection Klepfisz draws echoes other narratives of the conflict between gender and creativity experienced by women writers,[12] epitomized in Yiddish by the work of Celia Dropkin.[13] Dropkin's short story "Di tentserin" ("The Dancer") describes a woman's descent into madness as linked to her failed dream of becoming a dancer,[14] offering a model for the myth of Shtok's demise. Another myth the biographical epigraph invokes is that Shtok was the one who introduced the sonnet form into Yiddish. While this is not actually true,[15] it is indeed very likely that Shtok wrote her own sonnets without having before her eyes any Yiddish model to follow. In that sense her sonnets do prove innovations in Yiddish form and content alike. Similarly, Klepfisz uses Shtok to bring a Yiddish voice into English-language poetry, in an innovative form. For the poem not only narrates the struggle of transition between Yiddish and English, it embodies and expresses this struggle with a set of unique poetic devices.

> They make it sound easy: some disjointed
> sentences   a few allusions   to
> mankind.   But for me   it was not
> so simple   more like   trying
> to cover the distance   from here
> to the corner   or between two sounds.
>
> Think of it: *heym*   and   *home*   the meaning
> the same   of course   exactly
> but the shift   in vowel   was the ocean
> in which I drowned.
>
> I tried. I did   try.
> First held with Yiddish   but you
> know   it's hard. you write   *gas*
> and   *street*   echoes back
> No resonance.   And—let's face it—
> memory falters.
> You try to keep track of the difference
> like *got* and *god*   or *hoyz* and *house*
> but they blur   and you start using
> *alley*   when you mean *gesele*   or *avenue*
> when it's a *bulevar*.
>
> And before you know it
> you're on   some alien path
> standing   before a brick house
> the doorframe   slightly familiar.
> Still   you can't place it
> exactly. Passers-by   stop.
> Concerned   they speak   but you've
> heard   all this   before   the vowels

shifting   up and down   the subtle
change   in the guttural sounds
and now   it's nothing more
nothing   more   than   babble.
And so   you accept it.
You're lost.   This time   you really
don't know   where you are.

Land or sea   the house floats before you.
Perhaps you once sat   at that window
and it was home   and looked out
on that *street* or *gesele*.   Perhaps
it was a dead end   perhaps a short cut.
Perhaps not.
A movement by the door.   They stand there
beckoning   mouths open and close:
Come in! Come in!   I understood   it was
a welcome.   *A dank! A dank!*
I said   till I heard the lock
snap   behind me.

One of the first elements that stand out in this poem is the gaps within the lines between words and between languages, which seem to map out the physical strain of the distance between English and Yiddish. Even though "they make it sound easy," Klepfisz's poem physically holds the struggle of language transition, which it narrates by way of mixing English and Yiddish, and creating a form that perfectly reflects the narrated content. This allows the speaker/poet (the real and the imagined) to prove *"she knew from trying."* She goes on to describe what this attempt entailed, making her predicament explicit. Her *holding with Yiddish*—a calque translation for the Yiddish idiom "*haltn mit*"—is like attempting to cling to driftwood to avoid drowning, though this might have worked against her, as "the shift in vowel was the ocean" in which she drowned. Turning to the addressee, she then tries to seek sympathy while justifying herself, "but you / know it's hard." However, the enjambment after the turn "but you" resonates accusingly, implying "I tried, but you got in my way." Still, the following line allows the addressee not to bear the blame but to join the struggle. The addressee is the one who "knows" it is hard, the one whose language later also slips: "and you start using / *alley* when you mean *gesele*." Together with the speaker, the addressee is asked to "face it," the faltering of memory. In this idiomatic English expression, speaker and addressee, as well as the two poets, Klepfisz and Shtok, admit not just the struggle to learn English, but the challenge of remembering Yiddish. This joint realization, or even confession, stands as a concise two-word line, as opposed to the longer, still-struggling lines that precede it, itself threatening to falter, falling off the end of the stanza.

While the formal devices—enjambments, calque translation, shifts in tone—alongside the mixed use of Yiddish and English, create a poem that is distinctly of Klepfisz's time rather than the time of the poet who is her subject, at the same time, this poem corresponds richly with the original time of Yiddish women's poetry. For example, the visceral struggle Klepfisz attributes to the transition between languages (the same struggle we saw in the cycle "*Di rayze aheym*/The journey home") echoes Margolin's depiction of the struggle between the ancestral voices and that of her speaker in the poem "*Mayn shtam redt*" (My Ancestors Speak).[16]

[זיי] טראַמפּלען דורך מיר ווי דורך אַ טונקל הויז.
טראַמפּלען מיט תּפֿילות און קללות און קלאָג,
טרייסלען מײַן האַרץ ווי אַ קופּערנעם גלאָק,
עס װאַרפֿט זיך מײַן צונג,
איך דערקען ניט מײַן קול—
מײַן שטאַם רעדט.

They trample through me as through a dark house.
Trampling with prayers, and curses, and wailing,
rattling my heart like a copper bell,
my tongue quivers,
I don't know my own voice—
My ancestors speak.[17]

The most striking similarity between the two poems is the image of a house, to which Margolin's speaker compares herself. If in Margolin's case the experience is of being a home that is invaded, a "dark house" being trampled through, Klepfisz's poem ends when the speaker is lured into a house, and then locked in it. Klepfisz's house has a "doorframe slightly familiar. / Still you can't place it / exactly," which renders it foreign and familiar at once, and makes the home *unheimlich*, literally, in German, un-home-like. The uncanny moment echoes the description of the voice of Margolin's speaker, which she herself cannot recognize (*ikh derken nit mayn kol*). In addition, this doorframe might seem familiar, as it invokes a poem by Adrienne Rich, "The Fact of a Doorframe," and the collection that bears the same name.[18] Speaking for Shtok, Klepfisz is in a sense also speaking back to Margolin and across to Rich, while thematizing the very difficulty of this speech and the interrupted and disjunctive connections it generates.

The histories Klepfisz recovers and the poetic mode she uses to rework them form a mode of queer translation, between figures, languages and times. While Margolin and Shtok had very different literary personas and life stories,[19] we can see them both refracted through Klepfisz's poem, as Klepfisz tells her own story, to them and through them, narrating the reverse struggle she herself has with Yiddish. Using Shtok's voice, Klepfisz is at once defining her own poetic self (of which linguistic struggles are but one aspect), as well as "rescuing" from "drowning" a Yiddish poet at risk of being forgotten. Yet she takes this still another step further, not just "discovering" Yiddish women writers, but becoming one, thereby placing herself in the very lineage she is creating. To this end she undertakes a double move in which she must discover and invent both her female writing predecessors as well as herself in the figure of "Yiddish poetess," as she would have been called in the 1920s. This is akin to the move male writers were undertaking earlier in the twentieth century, such as Sholem Aleichem's self-fashioning as the grandson of Yiddish literature by naming S. Y. Abramovitsh the *zeyde*/grandfather.[20] Indeed, as Tynyanov wrote, "In the struggle with his father, the grandson turns out to resemble his grandfather."[21] Anita Norich terms this "a stroke of mythmaking genius by Sholem Aleichem, who understood that a respectable literature must have a history and forefathers."[22] This "peculiar genealogy," writes Norich, "obliterates not only the maternal line, but the authority of the father as well."[23] Obliterating the authority of the direct past and favoring instead a more distant and thereby less threatening past is a move very fitting in that it avoids the direct intergenerational conflict explored in the previous chapter. It is interesting to note that the distance of '70s lesbians from the Yiddish women poets falls somewhere between mothers and grandmothers, much like the distance between myself and the women of the 1970s. Moreover, the fact that both many

'70s lesbians and many Yiddish women writers challenged reproductive heteronormativity (whether in politics or in practice), opens the structure of lineage to queer construction and invention.

Over and against the patrilineal myth, Klepfisz's genealogical project illuminates the matrilineal line Norich cites Sholem Aleichem as obliterating. However, leading back to Shtok, this matrilineage does not tell a triumphant story of identity formation that can accord authority, even as it serves as part of identity politics. Instead, the story that emerges for both Klepfisz and the writers she recovers is one of struggle and the instability of language and of identity at once. The turn to the past, and the way that past is portrayed is, therefore, not identity affirming; rather, it comes to terms with the "complicated and meaningful ways that identity is continually compromised, imperiled, one might even say *embarrassed* by identification," as Diana Fuss warns any identity politics should.[24] For even if "identifications are the origin of some of our most powerful, enduring, and deeply felt pleasures, they are also the source of considerable emotional turmoil, capable of unsettling or unmooring the precarious grounding of our everyday identities."[25] The destabilizing power of identification with Yiddish women writers is epitomized in Klepfisz's move to identify herself *as* a Yiddish woman writer, most notably in the poem "*Etlekhe verter oyf mame-loshn*/A few words in the mother tongue."[26]

"*Etlekhe verter oyf mame-loshn*/A few words in the mother tongue" uses the bilingual form to undermine dominant patriarchal discourse in English and Yiddish at once. Though the poem culminates in Yiddish, it uses a vocabulary the poem itself has actually equipped the English reader to understand. At the same time, it instructs the reader just how much she has lost and stands to lose through language, not just on the front of the disappearance of Yiddish, but on the level of the daily struggle over meaning and naming so central to feminist politics.

> *Etlekhe verter oyf mame-loshn/*
> A few words in the mother tongue
> עטלעכע ווערטער אויף מאַמע-לשון
>
> *lemoshl*: for example
>
> *di kurve* the whore
> a woman who acknowledges her passions

di yidene   the Jewess   the Jewish woman
ignorant   overbearing
let's face it: every woman is one

di yente   the gossip   the busybody
who knows what's what
and is never caught off guard

di lezbianke   the one with
a roommate   though we never used
the word

dos vaybl   the wife
or the little woman

***

in der heym   at home
where she does everything to keep
yidishkayt alive

yidishkayt a way of being
Jewish   always arguable

in mark   where she buys
di kartofl un khalah
(yes, potatoes and challah)

di kartofl   the material counter-
part of *yidishkayt*

mit tsibeles   with onions
that bring *trern tsu di oygn*
tears to her eyes   when she sees
how little it all is
veyniker un veyniker
less and less

di khalah   braided
vi ir hor far der khasene
like her hair before the wedding
when she was *aza sheyn meydl*
such a pretty girl

di lange shvartse hor
the long black hair
di lange shvartse hor

***

a froy kholmt   a woman
dreams *ir ort oyf der velt*
her place in this world
un zi hot moyre   and she is afraid
so afraid of the words

kurve
yidene
yente
lezbianke
vaybl

zi kholmt   she dreams
un zi hot moyre   and she is afraid
ir ort
di velt
di heym
der mark

a meydl kholmt
a kurve kholmt
a yidene kholmt
a yente kholmt
a lezbianke kholmt

a vaybl kholmt
di kartofl
di khalah

yidishkayt

zi kholmt
di hor
di lange shvartse hor

zi kholmt
zi kholmt
zi kholmt

In this poem, Klepfisz activates the Yiddish language, its past context and its present relevance. Imitating a dictionary or the glossary in a language-learning primer, Klepfisz pairs Yiddish words with what appears to be their English translation. The opening example, "*lemoshl*" translated accurately as "for example" indicates such a straightforward exchange. The next pair, the word "*kurve*" and the English translation "whore," might seem to follow suit; however, the explanatory sentence that follows, "a woman who acknowledges her passions," is of course anything but the expected elucidation of "whore" in either Yiddish or English-speaking circles. Rather than simply inculcating us into the "secrets" of the Yiddish she uses, the secondary, subversive interpretation of the words Klepfisz provides instruct the reader that there is no neutral translation, and that certain words are translated into silence and erasure. She thereby exposes the mechanism by which dominant discourse dictates norms of language and behavior. These are the norms that define what a *sheyn meydl* is (a pretty girl, as I used to hear from my grandparents, always with a wistful tone, bemoaning how short my hair is, how masculine my clothing).

These same norms demand that *lezbianke*, a word seldom, if ever, used in Yiddish,[27] must remain unspoken even in its English version, lesbian, erasing it through the closeted and/or homophobic euphemism "roommate." Adding the qualification "though we never used the word," Klepfisz highlights both the presence and the unspeakability of the lesbian dwelling in the term "roommate," and in the Yiddish word *lezbianke*, which may be explicit, but is equally unused. Moreover, by letting the woman in the poem "acknowledge her passion" in English, and be a *lezbianke* in Yiddish, Klepfisz avoids an assimilationist progress narrative in which we move from an oppressive traditional world (in Yiddish) to a modern liberated world in English. Alternating between languages and registers, letting them take turns being both oppressive and expressive, Klepfisz resists a simplistic dichotomy in which English represents the progressive discourse over and against the dark Jewish past, or one that would make Yiddish radical by force of being a queer reclaimed language resisting mainstream English language culture.

Reading the poem, we follow Klepfisz like children in the traditional Jewish *kheyder* (schoolroom), who recited the sacred language of the Hebrew Bible and followed it by a Yiddish translation called *taytsh*. *Kheyder taytsh* language, mechanical language drills and even the dictionary do not invoke sought-after educational opportunities, but rather instruction without understanding, as well as the exclusion of women from such study practices in traditional Jewish society. Klepfisz's poem can indeed be seen as parodying such modes of language instruction and cultural transmission (or lack thereof), referring perhaps most directly to the popular genre of mock Yiddish-English dictionaries, which well outnumber legitimate Yiddish dictionaries since World War II, as Jeffery Shandler describes.[28] These comic texts are formatted like dictionaries, but rather than giving equivalent glosses or actually translating Yiddish terms into English, they offer comically "bogus definitions."[29] Klepfisz's bilingual poetics, on the other hand, pose a challenge to translation itself, and to language more broadly, as she repurposes and changes Yiddish and English alike.

Moving gradually from the conflict with the dominant discourse, represented as tensions between English and Yiddish, into the world of women represented *through*, and later solely *in* Yiddish, the poem ends in the meeting place of material *yidishkayt* and the Yiddish dream. In this dream, were we to translate it ourselves, "a woman dreams a woman." But if we continue with the enjambment to the next line, the rest of the translation, as Klepfisz slowly supplies it, reveals that it is a woman dreaming "her place in this world." This dream teeters on the brink of nightmare, bringing to life the words the woman most fears. But as the poem moves into the realm of Yiddish and leaves the English behind, it allows the "other," the Yiddish, the feminine, the lesbian, the past, to overtake the present, in a queer haunting that echoes Molodowsky's nocturnal visits and Margolin's possession.

In her essay "*Khaloymes*/Dreams in Progress: Culture, Politics and Jewish Identity,"[30] Klepfisz recasts the unnamed dreaming woman of "*Etlekhe verter oyf mame-loshn* / A few words in the mother tongue" as Kadya Molodowsky in her

"Froyen-lider": "still when Kadia dreamed, she knew and remembered what she dreamed of."[31] And Klepfisz dreams too, but her "dreams as a Jew and a poet are murkier and not easily remembered," she writes, for her distance from the women in her family is "more marked."[32] But since, as Carolyn Dinshaw writes, "our hermeneutic connection with the past includes—in fact is based on—distance,"[33] it is arguably Klepfisz's distance from the women in her family and from the poets she is in search of that enables her to use Yiddish to construct a conversation with and about them, in dreams and in writing. And even farther detached than Klepfisz stands Rich's "dream of a common language": "the true nature of poetry. The drive / to connect. The dream of a common language."[34] Klepfisz picks up this dream and constructs a poetic version of it in a language that is not "common" at all.

If Yiddish was historically a "common language" because of being "subordinate to Hebrew, viewed traditionally as the language of 'women, children, and ignorant men,'" belonging to the street, as Maeera Shreiber writes,[35] by the time Klepfisz is writing in the 1980s, Yiddish is no longer common at all. It is certainly not common to the women of the lesbian movement, and is not even shared between Klepfisz and Rich; indeed, Yiddish is a central point of difference between Rich and Klepfisz, the former translating Yiddish into English early in her career, the latter transitioning from being an English writer to a bilingual poet as her career progressed. In both cases Yiddish was something that marked their difference from their lesbian comrades, while at the same time joining the particular trend of Chicana lesbians such Gloria Anzaldúa, as we saw above.

Klepfisz's dream, whether its language is common or not, reclaims "some of the improvisatory methods for which 'dreaming' is a placeholder, turning them into queered protocols of historical research, and even into queer historiography."[36] Elizabeth Freeman suggests such dreaming as a mode in which queer historians might work, often from outside the discipline of history. Indeed, Klepfisz herself has been to a certain extent marginalized from history both by writing in Yiddish and by declaring her lesbian identity. But in her dream, the dream she invites us to dream with her, Klepfisz allows Yiddish to voice her poetic and political concerns, using the English/Yiddish encounter to undermine dominant norms in both languages, creating a new language, a new mode of conversation, a queer historiography, a dream of women's history.

If Klepfisz's poem "*Etlekhe verter oyf mame-loshn* / A few words in the mother tongue" brings to life Kadya Molodowsky as the dreaming woman, Kadya

Moldowsky's "Froyen-lider" brings to life the women who came before her. But these encounters are not only poetic dreams, as we saw in the 1969 photograph of Kadya Molodowsky and Adrienne Rich, which brought these two different poets and languages to one stage. The image in the photograph recasts the encounter of the speaker in "Froyen-lider" and her grandmothers, for in it Molodowsky is the one who can be taken for a *bobe*, a grandmother. But she did not have children or grandchildren, not in a biological sense that would make her a "kosher grandmother," nor metaphorically, for she does not have a direct lineage of Yiddish readers who can follow her. Published in her early thirties, the "Froyen-lider" cycle in its entirety offers a complex engagement with childbearing and barrenness, as Kathryn Hellerstein has discussed.[37] The poem "Mayne kinder"[38] (My Children), published after Molodowsky turned fifty, "expresses directly the consequences of a poet's choice between creativity and reproductivity," as Hellerstein writes.[39] In this poem, instead of spectral foremothers, the speaker is haunted by her unborn children, who ask why she kept from them the "living world" ("*lebedike velt*").

Without biological descendants, Molodowsky is made a *bobe* by the presence of the young Rich at her side. For Rich grandmaternity came through the biological children she so honestly wrote about in *Of Woman Born*. For Klepfisz, not reproducing was a choice she describes in one of her bravest essays, "Women without Children,"[40] written when such a decision would need to be made (it was first published in 1977, when she was thirty-six). There she admits that "the emptiness of the past, the vagueness of the future, leave me fearful, hesitant about my decision not to have a child," positioning the question of reproduction in the framework of temporal continuity. In a much later essay, published in 1997, Klepfisz reformulates her own position in this continuity, as she prepares to enter *bobe*-hood. Joining her mother's generation, she is "transformed into a true *bobe*, the next generation's past,"[41] thereby joining Molodowsky's generation as well. Klepfisz thus conceives of herself as a *hemshekh*, a continuation, but not one focusing on what she will leave behind, but rather on what came before her. For Klepfisz, as for Molodowsky before her, children are clearly not the end of the line. Indeed, as we have seen, one of the things these women writers in the 1920s and in the '70s had in common is that they did not necessarily traditionally reproduce. Therefore, like Molodowsky, Klepfisz's idea of continuity is created by turning to her foremothers, and not by looking forward to the future. Klepfisz thus defines herself as "a dependent Jew,"

> dependent on Mama Lo's generation to provide me with a sense of *hemshekh*/continuity. They've been the visible *goldene keyt*/the golden chain to which I've wanted to hook the link I've been forging through my life and my work. With them gone, where am I supposed to hang myself?[42]

Klepfisz's harrowing word choice, asking where she might "hang" herself, exposes the vulnerability of her position. But turning backward she finds a solution, not just to the potential finitude of lesbian lineage, but to the impending finitude of Yiddish. For indeed this backward gaze is particularly pregnant when we consider the future of Yiddish—not just as a language ripe for *bobe*-hood from its early associations with "maternity or grandmaternity,"[43] but also as a language devoid of a (secular) reproductive heteronormative future. To continue the line of Yiddish or the lesbian lineage both demand a transgression of reproductive heteronormative transmission. This transmission is not uninterrupted; on the contrary, as Rich writes in "Transcendental Étude,"

> No one who survives to speak
> new language, has avoided this:
> the cutting-away of an old force that held her
> rooted to an old ground[44]

Resisting "the cutting-away," I root my own queer language in the "old ground" of 1970s lesbians, and in the older ground of Yiddish. By learning the language itself, I am no longer dependent on the translations of Rich and Klepfisz, for I have direct access to the words of the *bobes*. But arriving at the *bobes* through the mediation of the 1970s continues the queer model I am in search of. I continue the 1970s desire for foremothers, as well as their struggle with them. Out of the two alternative modalities of genealogy that Molodowsky set up in the two versions of her poem, that of words and that of blood, I glean a genealogy constructed on the very tension between text and blood, continuity and distance. When Klepfisz references Molodowsky's poem, she replaces the image of the "missing line" torn from the book with an "illegible line,"[45] thereby implanting the possibility of reclamation that the missing line of the original poem forecloses. For what is illegible is nonetheless written and present, and what must change is our ability to read it. The 1970s made Yiddish women's past legible to me, made lesbian life legible to me. Defiantly talking back to the 1970s and to the 1920s, gratefully talking back through them, I want to make myself legible, even if I am not the future these women of the past expected. Allowing myself to make use of women('s) past, I must also account for the resistance this use might (no, will!) incur, a resistance to being deemed "past." For indeed, this resistance is the very basis of the nonlinear antiteleological mode this work advocates.

CODA
Queering the Present of Jewish Literary History

"It is unwise during periods of stress / or change to formulate new theories," writes Irena Klepfisz,[1] and wise as her warning is, this book grew from the conviction that the stressful times in which we live, where authoritarian regimes are gaining power worldwide, making struggles for justice (political, economic, environmental, or otherwise) seem more doomed than ever, urgently demand new theories, as well as new practice. Starting where I am, as a queer female Jewish citizen of the State currently called Israel, I have taken on a small part of this task by rethinking literary lineage through Yiddish (as part of a multilingual Jewish literary past), through women's writing, and through queer theory. For the politics of language and the complex realities represented in literature can prove to be a site of producing new visions of the past, bringing about alternative future possibilities so vital for our present.

It is a similar impulse to respond to our current moment that led Dan Miron to move *Toward a New Jewish Literary Thinking*, as his recent magnum opus, *From Continuity to Contiguity*, is subtitled.[2] Embracing Jewish literature not as a "normal national literature," Miron argues for the advantages of the "total abnormalcy of the Jewish literary complex."[3] Miron's "new literary thinking" outlines a threefold effort for a reconfiguration of the Jewish literary complex: realigning Hebrew with Yiddish as *a*, rather than *the*, Jewish language; finding new ways of identifying literature in non-Jewish languages as "Jewish literature"; and making room in Hebrew for non-Jewish narratives. Implied in these three moves are the shortcomings of much of Hebrew literary scholarship, Miron's included.[4] Implemented together, they would amount to a radical undoing of the nationalistic model of Hebrew literature that has long dominated Hebrew literary scholarship. And yet, by returning to one final poem by Irena Klepfisz, I want to show where Miron's theory falls short, despite its persuasive rhetoric, as it fails to undertake the undoing it promises, and ultimately conserves existing theories and structures of power. Over and against this conservative move, Klepfisz's poem "*Der Soyne*/The Enemy: An Interview in Gaza" gives voice to the Yiddish, the Jewish American (specifically the female and lesbian that Klepfisz is identified with), and the non-Jewish (specifically the Arab non-Jew) within Jewish literature. The poem acts simultaneously as a realization of Miron's literary complex, and as a counter to it. Putting political and literary theory into queer poetic practice, the poem offers an example of juxtaposition and undoing that activates bodies in context, combining Yiddish and English to write about the Arabic/Hebrew context of Palestine/Israel.

Der Soyne/The Enemy: An Interview in Gaza[5]

i.

I live here with my family.
The Jews come. I throw rocks.
I yell out: *Heil Hitler!*
My friend is shot with a rubber bullet.
They take him to the hospital. He will
live but he's a cripple.
My Mother weeps: When will it end?
Me? I'm happy school is closed.
Who needs to study?
I like to see them hide
behind the walls. Down with the Jews!
Long live Palestine!

ii.

Ikh voyn do mit der mishpokhe.
Di yidn kumen. Ikh varf shteyner.
Ikh shray: Heil Hitler!
A fraynd vert geshosn mit a gumner koyl.
Men nemt im in shpitol. Er vet
lebn ober er vet zayn a kalike.
Di mame veynt: ven vet es zikh endikn?

> *Ikh? Ikh bin tsefridn az di shul iz farmakht.*
> *Vos darf ikh lernen?*
> *'Sgefelt mir ven zey bahaltn zikh*
> *unter di vent. Nider mit di yidn!*
> *Zol lebn palestine!*

Written at the end of the 1980s, during the first intifada, the poem narrates the realities of the Occupation from a Palestinian youth's perspective. The Occupation is presented as an ongoing reality, highlighted by the poem's adherence to a strict present tense. This grammatical structure is part of the conversational tone of the poem, and yet clearly reflects intentional poetic and political construction. The result is a repetitive time in which there is no distinction between singular and recurring events, between the friend being shot and the throwing of stones. The only glimpse of the future occurs in the friend's prognosis: "He will / live but he's a cripple." While the promise of life is rendered future ("will"), the crippling wounds return the poem to the present ("he's a cripple," rather than: "he *will* live but *will* be a cripple"). The mother's lament, "when will it end? / *ven vet es zikh endikn?*" is similarly emptied of future hope by the implied continuation of her present weeping, and the speaker's question, "Who needs to study?" offers the final foreclosure of future hope.

While the poem offers no horizon after the Occupation, in its linguistic choices and extratextual references it brings a complicated historical background into play. According to Klepfisz's own account, the poem was an experiment "to see how a language associated with Jewish powerlessness sounded in the mouth of someone who was oppressed by Jewish power."[6] Speaking in Yiddish, the Palestinian youth speaks the voice of the Jewish past, and specifically the voice of Jews before they had gained national power. At the same time, the speaker's salute to Hitler, the pleasure he expresses at seeing the "Jews" hide behind/under the walls, like bugs rather than a powerful aggressor, and his lack of distinction between Jews and Israelis, all align him with anti-Semitic discourse spoken by those in power against the Jews. While the threat "Down with the Jews!" holds limited power spoken by a stone-throwing child, especially in the face of Jews with power, the fact that it is spoken in Yiddish invokes a history of very real Jewish persecution that cannot be ignored.

Unlike other bilingual poems in which Klepfisz moves back and forth between English and Yiddish, as we have seen in the previous chapter, this poem is constructed in two separate sections (numbered i and ii). Non-Yiddish speakers, presumably the majority of the readers, are rendered dependent on the English section. The fact that the English comes before the Yiddish might make the Yiddish appear superfluous. Still, the fact that Klepfisz offers the Yiddish text in legible English transcription rather than in the Hebrew/Yiddish alphabet (here and in all of her bilingual poetry), encourages the reader to pursue the Yiddish reading even without the promise of understanding it. This pursuit comes with small rewards of legibility, in the form of words and phrases that are familiar across languages, such as *"palestine,"* and possibly also *"yidn"* and *"mishpokhe"* (especially in a Jewish context). The only words of the Yiddish version an English speaker would certainly understand without the English version are the words "Heil Hitler." In both the English and the Yiddish the call is left in German spelling, appearing in italics in English and breaking the italic pattern in Yiddish. This untranslated mirroring is the very clue that instructs the reader that the English and the Yiddish text are one and the same. It is this phrase that proves the Yiddish to be anything but superfluous, for it is only by way of the Yiddish that the Nazi salute, and the poem as a whole, can become Jewish self-critique, or alternately, non-Jewish critique anchored in the Jewish experience.

In its bilingual Yiddish/English form, this poem masks the two languages of its actual context, Hebrew and Arabic. The poem's title makes both absent languages present; Modern Hebrew is echoed in the word Klepfisz uses for "enemy," choosing the word *soyne*, which comes from Hebraic origins, rather than its synonym of Germanic origins, *faynd*. The word *soyne* bears additional ambiguity, as it holds both the title of the "enemy" (as the English makes clear) as well as the act of hating (more rooted in the Hebrew context, where the *soyne* could be both the hated one and the one who hates). In any case, it is unclear who is being called the "enemy"—the Israeli soldier, or the Palestinian who is being "interviewed" in the poem. Calling the poem "an interview" invokes the Arabic in which the interview would most likely have been conducted, the language the Palestinian youth would actually be speaking. As opposed to the bilingual repetition of the poem as a whole, the title translates the term *soyne* into English but does not offer a Yiddish parallel for the subtitle "An Interview in Gaza." In fact, the Yiddish version would be strikingly similar (in sound if not in spelling): *"An intervyu in aza."* The word for *interview* is a Yiddishized version of the English word, whereas the word for *Gaza* would be the biblical word now used in Modern Hebrew, *Aza*.

These multilingual echoes do not render the languages interchangeable—just the opposite. Imagine for example an extension of Klepfisz's own poetic experiment, replacing her English verse with a Hebrew one. In such a version, both halves, the Hebrew and the Yiddish, the Palestinian would be speaking a Jewish language, but if the latter is what Klepfisz calls "the language associated with Jewish powerlessness," the former is the current language of Jewish power in the Israeli/Palestinian context.[7] If putting Yiddish in the mouth of a Palestinian is a mere thought experiment on Klepfisz's part, it would surely be truer to reality to convey the Palestinian child's words in Hebrew, for at least when the poem was written, there was still traffic between Gaza and Israel, and Palestinians young and old had potential access to Israelis and to Hebrew, mostly by being employed as a cheap labor force. In the current state of siege (imposed since Israel officially declared Gaza a "hostile entity" in September 2007, when Hamas was elected as the ruling party), young Palestinians are far less likely to speak any Hebrew beyond basic military commands. Beyond the vocabulary learned through interactions with the Israeli military, the main way for Palestinians to become fluent was, and continues to be, incarceration in Israeli prisons.[8] For the Palestinian youth to speak Hebrew in the poem would therefore invoke the very real conditions of current language politics and state violence.

In this hypothetical translation experiment, the Yiddish that follows the Hebrew is reinscribed in the language politics that have shaped it, as another victim of Israeli state policies. Therefore, arming the Palestinian youth with Yiddish not only connects the Palestinians to a history of Jewish powerlessness, it also speaks to (or rather, speaks the) internally repressed sides of the Israeli past and the Israeli psyche. Certainly this may seem more obvious in an Ashkenazi context, but it is my contention that the massive "success" of Israeli *Sho'ah* (the Hebrew word most widely used for the Khurbn) education, which has rendered the trauma a collective one, has also given Yiddish a newly sanctified cultural role that touches the wider Jewish population.[9] In the case of the poem, then, the use of Yiddish can therefore be read as invoking the particular Zionist language politics that played an active role not only the near demise of Yiddish, but in the silencing of many other languages, and can thus also be read as a stand-in for other oppressed Jewish languages and cultures, including the Arab-Jewish culture. Continuing this line of thought, and the poetic experiment, if we imagine a parallel poem narrating the role of the Israeli soldier in Arabic, this would bring forth a reality that is not imaginary at all, for many Jewish homes did in fact speak

Arabic. Additionally, there are Israeli soldiers who are Arabic-speaking, of Druze and Bedouin minorities, further complicating divisions of identity and power as they play out in the Israeli context.[10] Creating this analogy—not identity—between Yiddish and Arabic (alongside the other languages subjected to Hebrew's dominance) in their historically specific position in relation to hegemonic language and power, and specifically in their relation to Hebrew, this reading should make clear how the bilingual form and its multilingual echoes activate the intricately violent interactions among the languages and their contexts, past and present.

The poem's multilingualism can be seen as enacting Miron's vision of multiplicity. However, its juxtaposition of languages (both present and absent) brings to light the power dynamics within which they are embedded, thereby undermining the possibility of fluidity Miron imagines. In his vision, Jewish literature is configured as a "vast, disorderly, and somewhat diffuse" complex "characterized by dualities, parallelisms, occasional intersections, marginal overlapping, hybrids, similarities within dissimilarities, mobility, changeability, occasional emergence of patterns and their eventual disappearance, randomness, and when approximating a semblance of significant order, by contiguities."[11] This "vast complex" reads strikingly like the beginnings of queer theory from the early 1990s. Compare it to Judith Butler's 1990 definition of gender in *Gender Trouble*: "a complexity whose totality is permanently deferred, never fully what it is at any given juncture in time," calling for a coalition that "will be an open assemblage that permits of multiple convergences and divergences without obedience to a normative telos of definitional closure."[12] The rhetorical similarities between the two visions are striking, and even exciting, yet it is precisely their likeness that demands that we account for the very tangible differences between them.

Both Miron and Butler are arguing against a binary system, what Chana Kronfeld diagnosed as "the entrenched critical practice of bipolar thinking."[13] Butler's impetus is to expose the binary regulation of sexuality, which separates male from female and assumes continuity between sex/gender, sexual practice and desire, showing how this regulation "suppresses the subversive multiplicity of a sexuality that disrupts heterosexual, reproductive, and medicojuridical hegemonies."[14] In Miron's complex, on the other hand, there seems to be simply no need for binaries: "once we make the Jewish literary complex as a whole our subject of study," he writes, "we can safely put aside the major/minor, as well as many other binary oppositions; for what really counts is the dynamics of the complex as dictated by the movement of diverse entities within it, the brands of contiguity these entities formed when coming in touch with each other."[15] What Miron does not account for are the different forces at play in deploying various binaries; if certain binaries might be perceived as equal (and thus interchangeable), this is certainly not the case for "major" and "minor," not to mention other binaries like "national" and "diasporic," "normal" and "abnormal," or even "continuity" and "discontinuity," which all come with clear hierarchies. In fact, in an earlier text, Miron reveals his own investment in the hierarchies themselves: "without hierarchy, not only the evaluation but also the sheer historical description of a literature cannot be practiced in the framework of a genuine historical pursuit."[16] But hierarchies, like the binaries they are based on, are anything but descriptive; rather, they are prescribed by the power dynamics that produce both their reality, and the description of that reality. Doing away with the binaries too easily allows Miron to erase systemic power dynamics, the hierarchy that the binaries both reflect and construct.

"Separating things into categories and assigning them a role and even a status is not at issue here. But border control is," writes Anita Norich.[17] Indeed, the literary complex, even in its most fluid vision, must be characterized by a set of internal and external borders, policed not by those outside the borders, but rather by those who hold the power within. Without accounting for the very material ways in which Jewish language (and) politics have played out, Miron runs the risk of hitting the same pitfall Butler herself had to vie with: what to do about the body and how to account for material reality. Butler rigorously grapples with this challenge, starting with her 1993 *Bodies That Matter*,[18] finding new ways to account "for what bodies 'are'"[19] or are not, how they can, or cannot, be talked about. Over time, queer theory has in fact become more attentive to the body. Even fluid visions such as Carolyn Dinshaw's noncontemporaneous contemporaneity return to and rely on the body: "What it feels like to be a body in time, or in multiple times, or out of time, is a *queer* history—whatever else it may be."[20] Echoing earlier theoretical foundations, Miron does not account for the important developments the past twenty years have afforded (whether in queer theory or in Jewish literary scholarship), nor does he reflect on his own earlier views.

Miron's discounting of material differences is made all the more evident in his specific turn to corporeal metaphors. The title of the Hebrew version of Miron's *From Continuity to Contiguity: Toward a New Jewish Literary Thinking—Harpayah letsorekh negi'ah*,[21] which translates approximately as "releasing in order to touch"—sets up a theoretical mode of touch that both the Hebrew and English versions of his study rely on. Likening elements in the literary complex to bodies (and more specifically, to bodies involved in a sexual interaction), Miron fantasizes about "a touching, which does not involve overlapping or penetration," "a kind of light or diminished contact." [22] There is much to be said for this delicate mode of touch, which was indeed embraced by the 1970s equation of penetration and patriarchy propagated by both lesbians and feminists. But whereas those women politicized the most private touch, Miron's resistance to penetration can be read as depoliticizing, and—together with his antibinary move—discounting the material realities through and within which languages and literatures, as well as their speakers, touch each other, often not lightly at all.

Nowhere is this more evident than in Klepfisz's poem, which uses language, history, and poetry to tell a story of power and its perils, highlighted by queer multiplicity rather than veiled by it. Moreover, it exposes what Miron's theory most acutely lacks, and that is all those voices outside the traditional monolithic hegemonic canon of Ashkenazi male Jewish writing, who remain as silenced in his new theory as they were in so many theories past. In the Hebrew version Miron does invoke "marginal influences"—"the underground world of cultural-literary-linguistic possibilities suppressed and kept out for reasons of ethnic, gender and political difference."[23] He recognizes how the work emerging from this "underground world" over the past fifty years continues to reshape major literatures. Indeed, it is the potential influence these marginal works hold that seems to be the very drive for his new theory, the sign of the "period of stress" he is writing in. But the fact that Miron's new theoretical model does not actually attend to any of the "others"—women, queers and non-Jewish writers of Jewish literature—exposes the inevitably conservative nature of his project, attempting to reinscribe power rather than redistribute it.[24] Preemptively defending the center from what is, according to Miron's own account, the inevitable rise of the margins, he can use the "others" to build a theory, but they are still refused a voice.

The key to this omission lays at the closing of this massive tome. It is here that the political context of Miron's intervention is revealed to be not "Jewish" but rather, Israeli: "the continuation of the Occupation and the conflict threaten Israel's cultural health as much as it undermines its political, social, and ethical viability."[25] What is at stake, then, for Miron, is not the Yiddish suppressed in the past or the Arabic-speaking voices oppressed in the present, but what effect these (language) politics ultimately have on Jewish Israeli Hebrew culture, whose position Miron seems intent on preserving. This intention is manifested in the gap between his theory's rhetoric and its practice, wishing the Arab voice into Hebrew and repositioning Yiddish and Hebrew together, side by side alongside other majoritarian European languages, without accounting for the damages of history and the raging horrors of the present. What would a new Jewish literary complex look like if it did account for the realities of marginalization past and present? How could it undermine the reified divisions of "center" and "margin" instead of reaffirming them? Following Miron, Butler, and Klepfisz, this book closes by asking what it would take to truly destabilize the binary system, reimagine history and redistribute power.

These questions are not merely rhetorical, and have been asked in the context of Jewish literature by scholars across decades and continents. One bastion of this investigation is "the Berkeley school of thought" (*Askolat Berkeley*, as termed by Miron himself).[26] Over the past twenty years, the work of Chana Kronfeld and many of her students has been in search of an understanding of Jewish literature through its margins rather than through its center, creating comparative projects that bring new histories to light, while problematizing any attempt to essentialize either "center" or "margins."[27] Most recently, Lital Levy and Allison Schachter have taken on the discourse of world literature to challenge both the monolingual legacy of Jewish literature (namely the legacy dictated by Zionist literary history), as well as world literature's own reliance on divisions of major and minor.[28] Like Klepfisz's poem, their intervention is materially multilingual, tracing languages and their contexts across boundaries of time and space. Here too, what emerges is not a fluid complex but a concrete map of surprising exchanges that undermines theories of world literature and Jewish literature alike. They call for Jewish literature to internalize a truly comparative and transnational ethos, so that it might offer an alternative to the dominant center-periphery paradigm, as their own intervention does.[29]

Beyond undoing models of center verses periphery (or margin), queer theory offers an understanding of "the context of an entire cultural network of normative definitions, definitions themselves equally unstable but responding to different sets of contiguities and often at a different rate."[30] Eve Sedgwick's definition here, deploying "contiguity" to describe the workings of (normative and normalizing) powers rather than to erase them (again over and against Miron), opens for us the potential synthesis of the fluid antibinary model (where Miron and queer theory intersect) and the material realities of disparate times and contexts. Sedgwick elucidates the power of the very contradiction of material history and antibinary thinking, where "a deconstructive understanding of these binarisms makes it possible to identify them as sites that are peculiarly densely charged with lasting potentials for powerful manipulation—through precisely the mechanisms of self-contradictory definition or, more succinctly, the double bind."[31] Heeding this complex mapping, I join queer theory's impulse to subvert regulatory systems rather than protect them, not by erasing lived realities, but by attending to them, exposing the stakes involved in doing this queer history of Jewish literature today.

If throughout this work I used queerness as a strategy to undo divisions of past and present, to touch the past and to turn away from the future, I want to close by enlisting a queerness that brings a different future into being. This mode of queerness, following José Esteban Muñoz, "is essentially about the rejection of a here and now and an insistence on potentiality or concrete possibility for another world."[32] I am particularly invested in Muñoz's ideas of this queer connection to the future because it offers a theory that is "attentive to the past for the purpose of critiquing the present."[33] Similarly, Irena Klepfisz's juxtaposition of Yiddish and English, past and present, asks how our conceptions of the past are serving us today. Her linguistic experiment (and my own) employs a queer method to recognize the way power shifts in specific moments, rendering us all the more interconnected, all the more accountable for how we use our power and our history, demonstrating the material differences that make both bodies and languages untranslatable. For it is the Yiddish in Klepfisz's poem that exposes the interconnectedness of the Jew and Palestinian, as each is positioned in relation to Zionist history and the larger currents of the twentieth century. Linking Jewish and Palestinian powerlessness through the contemporary context of Jewish military power, Klepfisz complicates the glorification of Jewish powerlessness associated with the nostalgic image of the past.

Using Yiddish at such a time of relative Jewish powerlessness to critique the male-dominated centers of Western culture, Anna Margolin's 1929 poem, "*Ikh bin geven a mol a yingling*" ("I Was Once a Boy"), which I discussed in chapter 2, resonates deeply with Klepfisz's "*Der Soyne*/The Enemy: An Interview in Gaza." Both poems blur otherwise rigid distinctions between victim and victor, insider and outsider, speaking the voice of a non-Jewish male youth. Instead of the Palestinian boy of Klepfisz's "*Der Soyne*," Margolin's poem speaks the voice of a *yingling* (boy in Germanized Yiddish) in the context of Greco-Roman antiquity. Besides sharing this narrative perspective, as well as a focus on male friendship (and its homoerotic potential), both poems play on the irony of shifting powers and perspectives. Each of the speakers voices an irreverent yet anachronistic challenge to power, powers that be, powers past, or powers to come. Klepfisz's youth seems oblivious to the historical weight of the call "Heil Hitler," and indeed within the history he is living in, Hitler has already lost. Margolin's speaker joins the Romans mocking the early Christians, even while it is clear that Margolin's own historical moment is shaped by Christian hegemony. Margolin's poem narrates the inevitable fall of certain powers (namely the Greek and then Roman empires), while ironically foreshadowing the rise of Christianity and ominously hinting at the destructive powers yet to come with the rise of Nazism. Klepfisz's poem echoes this understanding of the cyclical nature of history and the dangers it holds for victim and victor alike, in a context Margolin's poem could not have anticipated. In this new context, following both the Khurbn and the establishment of the State of Israel, Klepfisz strategically draws on Yiddish language and history to critique Jewish abuse of power. This move both mirrors and inverts Margolin's deployment of Yiddish; writing in a Yiddish-speaking context, Margolin places Yiddish in the mouth of ruling powers past, whereas Klepfisz, writing in the face of Yiddish's decline, puts it in the mouth of those subjected to Jewish ruling powers. Both create a Yiddish present/history that never was, in order to critique what *is*.

What Klepfisz's poem allows us to see is not pretty, and indeed, as she herself recounts, it caused at least one academic-poet to refuse to be on a panel with her. This same academic-poet was a fan of her Khurbn-related bilingual work, but drew a rigid line between what Yiddish could and couldn't do. According to Klepfisz, what he resisted was using Yiddish to embrace the present, aiming instead to use Yiddish as "fantasy, nostalgia, escapism, an attempt to turn back the clock. Yiddish as denial."[34] Over and against this denial, Klepfisz aims to use Yiddish to "enfold within this language our contemporary lives and crises,"[35] much like it did when it was being used by Margolin and the other poets this book has discussed.

Resisting both Yiddish as denial (of present and past complexity) and the denial of the loss of Yiddish (in fighting for its future survival), what I want to offer is another option, embracing "spaces and modes of unknowing, failing, and forgetting as part of an alternative feminist project."[36] This is what Halberstam calls "the queer art of failure."[37] Rather than reinscribing Yiddish as an option for the present, I acknowledge its past reality, and the future it could have offered, but didn't. Returning to Yerushalmi's recognition "that not everything of value that existed before a break was either salvaged or metamorphosed, but was lost," I remember also that "some of what fell by the wayside can become, through our retrieval, meaningful to us."[38] This retrieval is a response to crisis and loss, the crisis of the present, the losses in the past, and already foreseeable losses in the future, such as those Margolin's poem preemptively hints at. The act of retrieval demands that we actively enlist what fell by the wayside (in the past) and what is being pushed to the wayside (in the present) to reimagine what might be possible in the future. Juxtaposing Yerushalmi's "retrieval" and Halberstam's queer failure, what emerges are "alternative political imaginaries" that embody "the suite of 'other choices' that attend every political, economic and aesthetic crisis and their resolutions,"[39] even when resolution is nowhere in sight.

By treating Yiddish as an alternative past and an alternative passed, one avenue of Jewish history that did not come to fruition, it becomes a queer tool for the present. The value of bringing it into our current conversation by going back to its time of expectancy lies in understanding the present we are living in as but one of the many futures that Jewish history could have had. And it is opening that past potentiality that can make room for complexities that the present would have us obscure. Here I find a past I never knew existed, and through it alternative futures emerge—those futures that did not come to pass. This is not the past passed down to me through my Israeli education, which systematically marginalized both Yiddish and women (not to mention women writing Yiddish) and entirely erased the history and possibility of queerness. Turning to these alternative histories, and alternative, queer, approaches to history, I am in search of ways to actively enlist the past to alter the present. Whether focusing on Israel/Palestine, or on the Jewish diaspora, my study of Jewish literature aims to recover and to generate "other possibilities, the other potential outcomes, the non-linear and non-inevitable trajectories that fan out from any given event and lead to unpredictable futures."[40] Instead of progressive narratives of emergence, I use the past of Jewish women and Jewish literature to imagine a queer time that challenges the dominant narratives of the inevitable course of history. Rather than fighting for a national heteronormative future viability that leaves much of the Jewish past and present behind at the expense of actively oppressing many others, I turn backward in search of a queer history, in queer expectation of radical change now.

NOTES

INTRODUCTION: WHAT TO EXPECT WHEN YOU'RE NOT EXPECTING

1. Translation mine. Yocheved Bat-Miriam's poem reproduced here from *Shirim* (Tel Aviv: Sifriyat Po'alim, 1972), 29. Additional versions published in *Meraḥok* (Tel Aviv: Hebrew Writers' Association, 1932), 137–38 and *Maḥatsit mul maḥatsit: Kol hashirim* (Tel Aviv: Hakibuts Hame'uḥad, 2014), 71–72. A discussion of the different versions is to follow.

2. Christopher S. Nealon, *Foundlings: Lesbian and Gay Historical Emotion before Stonewall*. (Durham: Duke University Press, 2001), 67.

3. Lee Edelman, *No Future: Queer Theory and the Death Drive* (Durham: Duke University Press, 2004), 29.

4. For more information see Wendy Zierler, "Yokheved Bat-Miriam (Zhelezhniak)," in *Jewish Women: A Comprehensive Historical Encyclopedia*, Jewish Women's Archive, March 1, 2009. https://jwa.org/encyclopedia/article/bat-miriam-yokheved, and Wendy Zierler, *And Rachel Stole the Idols: The Emergence of Modern Hebrew Women's Writing* (Detroit: Wayne State University Press, 2004).

5. On the significance of this move see Ilana Pardes, "Yocheved Bat-Miriam: The Poetic Strength of a Matronym," in *Gender and Text in Modern Hebrew and Yiddish Literature*, ed. Naomi B. Sokoloff, Anne Lapidus Lerner, and Anita Norich (New York: The Jewish Theological Seminary of America, 1992), 39–63. Pardes also offers a beautiful translation of Bat-Miriam's 1939 poem "Miriam," about the Biblical prophetess.

6. Naomi Seidman, *A Marriage Made in Heaven: The Sexual Politics of Hebrew and Yiddish* (Berkeley: University of California Press, 1997), 117.

7. Nealon, *Foundlings*, 23.

8. Ruth Kartun-Blum, "Imi, Yokheved Bat-Miriam: Re'ayon im Dr. Mariassa Bat-Miriam Katzenelson," *Sadan* 2 (1996): 153–63.

9. Heather Love, *Feeling Backward: Loss and the Politics of Queer History* (Cambridge: Harvard University Press, 2007), 2.

10. Ibid., 147.

11. For an analysis of the political role of poetic address in the context of Hebrew and German poetry, see Maya Barzilai and Katra Byram, "The Challenge of Lyric Address in War Poems by Yitzhak Laor and Ingeborg Bachmann," *The Yearbook of Comparative and General Literature* 53 (2007): 155–68.

12. See Ruth Kartun-Blum's essay in the new edition of Bat-Miriam's collected poetry, "Vegadol minir'eh halo-nir'eh: Al shirat Yokheved Bat-Miriam," in *Maḥatsit mul maḥatsit*, 481–521, as well as her monograph, which is the only book-length study devoted to Bat-Miriam: *Bamerḥak hane'elam: Iyunim beshirat Yokheved Bat-Miriam* (Ramat Gan: Sifriyat Makor, 1977).

13. As evidenced by the title of Ruth Kartun-Blum's essay, which states that "there is more unseen than seen" ("Vegadol minir'eh halo-nir'eh").

14. Dan Miron, "KesheYokheved Bat-Miriam kiblah al atsmah et din hakni'ah," *Haaretz*, October 13, 2014, https://www.haaretz.co.il/literature/study/1.2455476.

15. Rachel Bluvshteyn, "*Ivria*," *Davar*, 6, no. 5 (November 14, 1930).

16. Translation mine.

17. My translation can hardly convey the richness of the original lines, not just in their sound pattern, but also as they build on Biblical repetition (*tikbolet*) between the first two lines.

18. Carolyn Dinshaw, *Getting Medieval: Sexualities and Communities, Pre- and Postmodern* (Durham, NC: Duke University Press, 1999), 41.

19. José Esteban Muñoz, *Cruising Utopia: The Then and There of Queer Futurity* (New York: New York University Press, 2009), 1.

20. Dan Miron, *Imahot meyasdot, aḥayot ḥorgot: Al shtey hatḥalot bashirah ha'EretsYisra'elit hamodernit* (Tel Aviv: Hakibuts Hame'uḥad, 1991).

21. See the chapter "Multilingualism" in Benjamin Harshav's *The Polyphony of Jewish Culture* (Stanford: Stanford University Press, 2007), 23–40. For a reading of Jewish multilingualism through the lens of Jews in Palestine see Liora Halprin, *Babel in Zion: Jews, Nationalism, and Language Diversity in Palestine, 1920–1948* (New Haven: Yale University Press, 2014). On the case of Jews writing in Arabic see Ammiel Alcalay's *After Jews and Arabs: Remaking Levantine Culture* (Minneapolis: University of Minnesota Press, 1993); Gil Hochberg, *In Spite of Partition: Jews, Arabs, and the Limits of Separatist Imagination* (Princeton: Princeton University Press, 2007); and Lital Levy, *Poetic Trespass: Writing between Hebrew and Arabic in Israel and Palestine* (Princeton: Princeton University Press,

2014). For a study of Ladino and Yiddish press see Sarah Abrevaya Stein, *Making Jews Modern: The Yiddish and Ladino Press in the Russian and Ottoman Empires* (Bloomington: Indiana University Press, 2003), and for a study of Sephardic poetry see Monique Balbuena, *Homeless Tongues: Poetry and Languages of the Sephardic Diaspora* (Stanford: Stanford University Press, 2016).

22. Dan Miron, *From Continuity to Contiguity: Toward a New Jewish Literary Thinking* (Stanford: Stanford University Press, 2010), 38.

23. Ibid., 191.

24. Much important feminist work has been done to consider gender as a factor in Jewish history. See, for example, Paula Hyman, *Gender and Assimilation in Modern Jewish History: The Roles and Representations of Women* (Seattle: University of Washington Press, 1995), and Marion A. Kaplan and Deborah Dash Moore, *Gender and Jewish History* (Bloomington: Indiana University Press, 2011).

25. For an extensive account of Jewish women's education, see Iris Parush, *Reading Jewish Women: Marginality and Modernization in Nineteenth-Century Eastern European Jewish Society* (Waltham: Brandeis University Press, 2004).

26. Over the past twenty years there has been an emergence of critical works (and specifically anthologies) that have illuminated the history of women's writing in Hebrew and Yiddish. My own critical introduction was largely through Sokoloff, Lerner, and Norich, eds., *Gender and Text*. See also Parush, *Reading Jewish Women*; Judith R. Baskin, ed., *Women of the Word: Jewish Women and Jewish Writing* (Detroit: Wayne State University Press, 1994); Carole Bailin, *To Reveal Our Hearts: Jewish Women Writers in Tsarist Russia* (Cincinnati: Hebrew Union College Press, 2000); Zierler, *And Rachel Stole the Idols*; Tova Cohen and Shmuel Feiner, *Kol almah ivriyah: Kitvey nashim maskiliot bame'ah hat'sha'-esreh* (Tel-Aviv: Hakibuts Hame'uḥad, 2006); and Tova Cohen, "Portrait of the 'Maskilah' as a Young Woman," *Nashim* 15 (2008): 9–29.

27. See Sandra M. Gilbert and Susan Gubar, *The Madwoman in the Attic: The Woman Writer and the Nineteenth-Century Literary Imagination* (New Haven: Yale University Press, 1984).

28. Recent research has revealed notable exceptions. See Chava Turniansky's work on Glikl of Hameln and on women in Old Yiddish literature and the work of Chava Weissler and Devra Kay on women's early modern prayer in Yiddish. Still, the existence of these texts did not necessarily offer women a continuous history to rely on, as they were not consistently preserved and transmitted.

29. For example, the case of Dvora Baron. See Sheila Jelen, *Intimations of Difference: Dvora Baron in the Modern Hebrew Renaissance* (Syracuse: Syracuse University Press, 2007).

30. If the Biblical imperative to "be fertile and increase, fill the earth and master it" (Genesis 1:28) was originally directed at men and women alike, over time it applied to, and impacted, men and women differently. For an historical discussion see the chapter "Be Fruitful and Multiply," in Ronit Irshai, *Fertility and Jewish Law: Feminist Perspectives on Orthodox Responsa Literature*, trans. Joel A. Linsider (Waltham, MA: Brandeis University Press, 2012), 25–52, as well as Rochelle L. Millen, *Women, Birth, and Death in Jewish Law and Practice* (Waltham, MA: Brandeis University Press, 2004).

31. Judith Butler, *Gender Trouble: Feminism and the Subversion of Identity* (New York: Routledge, 1999), 179.

32. Brook Thomas, *The New Historicism and Other Old-Fashioned Topics* (Princeton: Princeton University Press, 1991), 33.

33. Ibid., 41.

34. David Myers, *Resisting History: Historicism and Its Discontents in German-Jewish Thought* (Princeton: Princeton University Press, 2003), 5. Myers's model is linked to Eric Hobsbawm's "invented traditions," which "so far as possible, use history as a legitimator of action and cement of group cohesion." "Introduction: Inventing Tradition," in *The Invention of Tradition*, ed. Eric Hobsbawm and Terence Ranger (Cambridge: Cambridge University Press, 2012), 12.

35. To echo the powerful title of Yael Chaver's book *What Must Be Forgotten: The Survival of Yiddish in Zionist Palestine* (Syracuse: Syracuse University Press, 2004).

36. On the history of the term *queer* see Siobhan B. Somerville, "Queer," in *Keywords for American Cultural Studies*, ed. Bruce Burgett and Glenn Hendler, New York University Press, accessed October 27, 2017, http://keywords.nyupress.org/american-cultural-studies/essay/queer/.

37. See *Lesbiyot: Israeli Lesbians Talk about Sexuality, Feminism, Judaism and Their Lives*, ed. Tracy Moore (London: Cassell, 1995). Even though this book was not published until the 1990s, its American and Israeli contributors are the activists and writers of the 1970s to 1980s.

38. Blanche W. Cook, "'Women Alone Stir My Imagination': Lesbianism and the Cultural Tradition." *Signs* 4, no. 4 (Summer 1979): 736.

39. Miron, *From Continuity to Contiguity*, 275. See "Coda" below for a detailed engagement with the implications of Miron's literary intervention.

40. Irena Klepfisz, "Periods of Stress," in her *Periods of Stress* (New York: Out & Out Books, 1975), 20.

41. H. N. Bialik, "Ḥevley lashon" (1905), in *Kol kitvey H. N. Bialik* (Tel Aviv: Dvir, 1965), 197–201.

42. For example by Benjamin Harshav in his book *Language in a Time of Revolution* (Berkeley: University of California Press, 1993).

ONE. QUEER LINES: ADRIENNE RICH AND KADYA MOLODOWSKY

1. The poem and the translation come from *Paper Bridges: Selected Poems of Kadya Molodowsky*, translated, introduced and edited by Kathryn Hellerstein (Detroit: Wayne State University Press, 1999). Hellerstein's work on Molodowsky, and on Yiddish women's writing in general, has been essential for the development of this book.

2. See Einat Amitay's rigorously researched blog post, "Mi himtsi' et Kadya Molodovski be'ivrit?" (Who Invented Kadya Molodowsky in Hebrew?), *Yoman masa leḥeker 100 shnot tarbut leyeladim bakibutsim*, May 2, 2011, http://tarbut-yela dim.blogspot.ca/2011/05/blog-post.html.

3. The most extensive biography of Molodowsky is found in Hellerstein's introduction to *Paper Bridges*, and in her entry on Molodowsky in *Jewish Women: A Comprehensive Historical Encyclopedia*, Jewish Women's Archive, March 20, 2009, https://jwa.org/encyclopedia/article/molodowsky-kadya.

4. Amir Shomroni attributes her return to the United States to the Israeli State's rejection of Yiddish (Amir Shomroni, " 'In Yisroel un tsurik: Al nesibot akiratam me'Artsot Habrit leYisrael veazivatam beḥazarah shel Kadya Molodowsky veSimḥah Lev le'or haperek ha'aharon shel zikhronoteiha ha'otobiografiim 'Mayn elterzeydns yerushe,' shelo pursam veshenimtsa ganuz be'arkhiyonah beYIVO beNyu York," unpublished).

5. On the significance of blood in Jewish tradition, see David Biale, *Blood and Belief: The Circulation of a Symbol between Jews and Christians* (Berkeley: University of California Press, 2007).

6. Kathryn Hellerstein, " 'A Word for My Blood': A Reading of Kadya Molodowsky's 'Froyen-lider' (Vilna 1927)," *AJS Review* 13, nos. 1–2 (1988), 47–79.

7. The rest of Hellerstein's work continues with this important project, alongside the many other works on Yiddish women's poetry on which this book relies, namely the work of Irena Klepfisz, Sheva Zucker, Anita Norich, Janet

Hadda, Barbara Mann, Naomi Brenner, Yael Chaver, Norma Fain Pratt, and others.

8. Hellerstein, "'A Word for My Blood,'" 72.

9. Ibid.

10. Hellerstein also offers a detailed bibliography for this discussion, ibid., 49n6.

11. Ibid., 49.

12. *A Treasury of Yiddish Poetry*, eds. Irving Howe and Eliezer Greenberg (New York: Holt, Rinehart and Winston, 1969).

13. This is evident in the translations themselves, as well as in "A Note on the Translation," which Hellerstein included in *Paper Bridges*, 61–66.

14. Kathryn Hellerstein, "Translating as a Feminist: Reconceiving Anna Margolin," *Prooftexts* 20, nos. 1–2 (2000): 191–208.

15. Ezra Korman, *Yidishe Dikhterins: Antologye* (Chicago: L. M. Shtayn, 1928).

16. For other readings considering the complex multiplicity of the poem, cf. Sheva Zucker, "Kadye Molodowsky's 'Froyen-Lider' ('Women's Songs')" *Yiddish* 9, no. 2 (1994): 44–52 and Hellerstein, "'A Word for My Blood.'"

17. (Vilna: B. Kletskin, 1927).

18. Kathryn Hellerstein, who has researched Molodowsky extensively, did not find earlier versions than the ones we are reading here (private communication).

19. The first stanza is the same in both Yiddish versions. Beneath it, the Yiddish version on the right is from Kadya Molodowsky's *Khezhvndike nekht*, 11. The Yiddish version on the left is from Korman's *Yidishe dikhterins*, 190. Adrienne Rich's translation appears in *A Treasury of Yiddish Poetry*, 284, and Kathryn Hellerstein's translation appears in *Paper Bridges*, 69.

20. On the image of blood in the entire "*Froyen-lider*" cycle see Hellerstein, "'A Word for My Blood.'"

21. Note that the difference between *missing* and *torn* is in the translation only and does not reflect a difference in the Yiddish originals. In the two Yiddish versions, the difference in the final word lies only in the punctuation, in the difference between the full stop and the question mark.

22. She discusses her access to Jewish education most extensively in "Split at the Root: An Essay on Jewish Identity," originally published in *Nice Jewish Girls*, ed. Evelyn Torton Beck (Watertown: Persephone Press, 1982), 67–88.

23. Kathy Rugoff, "Sappho on Mount Sinai: Adrienne Rich's Dialogue with Her Father," in *Multicultural Literatures through Feminist/Poststructuralist Lenses*, ed. Barbara Frey Waxman (Knoxville: University of Tennessee Press, 1993), 9.

24. Ibid., 19.

25. Seidman, *A Marriage Made in Heaven*, 9. Seidman quotes famous Yiddish literary critic Sh. Niger: "Yiddish literature may well be unique among the literatures of the world in its having, until very recently, addressed itself to a female rather than male audience [...] Jewish women were not only the readers and consumers of Yiddish books, they were also often the ones who encouraged the writers to write in Yiddish—to write, in fact, especially for them" (15). Thus, "while both men and women spoke and read Yiddish," Seidman writes, "the 'femininity' of Yiddish is a widely acknowledged cultural myth" (27), as suggested by Niger's statement. Naturally, however, behind this myth lies a complex reality, within which mostly men could thematize and mobilize the trope of writing or not writing in Yiddish, whereas women were often actively kept away from Hebrew.

26. Kathryn Hellerstein, e-mail message to the author, December 4, 2011.

27. Lori Chamberlain, "Gender and the Metaphorics of Translation, *Signs* 13, no. 3 (Spring, 1988): 461.

28. Chana Kronfeld, *The Full Severity of Compassion: The Poetry of Yehuda Amichai* (Stanford: Stanford University Press, 2015), 209.

29. Tejaswini Niranjana, *Siting Translation: History, Post-Structuralism, and the Colonial Context* (Berkeley: University of California Press, 1992), 2.

30. Anita Norich, "A Response from Anita Norich," *Prooftexts* 20, nos. 1–2 (Winter/Spring 2000): 213.

31. Ibid.

32. Ibid.

33. Hellerstein, "Translating as a Feminist," 192.

34. Ibid., 197.

35. Barbara Johnson, *Mother Tongues: Sexuality, Trials, Motherhood, Translation* (Cambridge MA: Harvard University Press, 2003), 16.

36. Judith Butler, "Imitation and Gender Insubordination," in *The Lesbian and Gay Studies Reader*, eds. Henry Abelove, Michèle Aina Barale, and David M. Halperin (New York: Routledge, 1993), 313.

37. Ibid.

38. Naomi Seidman, *Faithful Renderings: Jewish-Christian Difference and the Politics of Translation* (Chicago: University of Chicago Press, 2006), 38.

39. Ibid.

40. Jack Halberstam, *In a Queer Time and Place: Transgender Bodies, Subcultural Lives* (New York: New York University Press, 2005). Halberstam actually moves

between identifying as lesbian and identifying as trans, while others have gone, and continue to move, in so many directions, placing "trans" not as a destination, but as a movement "between."

41. "Granddaughter," in: Adrienne Rich, *A Wild Patience Has Taken Me This Far: Poems, 1978–1981* (New York: Norton, 1981), 37.

42. "For memory," ibid., 20.

43. Yosef Hayim Yerushalmi, *Zakhor: Jewish History and Jewish Memory* (Seattle: University of Washington Press, 1982), 110.

44. Kime Scott, *Refiguring Modernism,* Volume 1: *The Women of 1928*, xvi.

45. Chana Kronfeld, *On the Margins of Modernism: Decentering Literary Dynamics* (Berkeley: University of California Press, 1996), 63. I will elaborate on this model in chapter 5.

46. Ludwig Wittgenstein, *Philosophical Investigations* (West Sussex: Wiley-Blackwell, 2009), 64.

47. Kronfeld, *On the Margins of Modernism*, 64.

48. Michael Gluzman, "The Exclusion of Women from Hebrew Literary History," in *Prooftexts* 11, no. 3 (1991): 264.

49. Gilbert, Sandra M., and Susan Gubar, "The Infection of the Sentence: The Woman Writer and the Anxiety of Authorship." *The Madwoman in the Attic*, 45–92.

50. Adrienne Rich, "Introduction to the Poetry of Irena Klepfisz," in *A Few Words in the Mother Tongue: Poems Selected and New (1971–1990)* (Portland: Eighth Mountain Press, 1990), 13.

51. Yerushalmi, *Zakhor*, 4.

52. Carolyn Dinshaw, "Temporalities," in *Middle English*, Oxford Twenty-First Century Approaches to Literature, vol. 1, ed. Paul Strohm (Oxford: Oxford University Press, 2007), 109.

53. Ibid., 115.

54. Ibid., 122.

55. Ibid.

56. *A Treasury of Yiddish Poetry*, eds. Howe and Greenberg.

57. Hollander is absent from the version of the picture in Klepfisz's essay where I first encountered the image. In Klepfisz's version the photo evidently underwent separatist cropping to include only the women. Klepfisz, "Di mames, dos loshn/ The mothers, the language: Feminism, Yidishkayt, and the Politics of Memory." *Bridges* 4, no. 1 (Winter/Spring 1994): 36.

58. We know this from Rich's autobiographical writings, and Hollander states as much explicitly in a 1985 interview with Edwin Honig, *The Poet's Other Voice* (Cambridge: University of Massachusetts Press, 1985), 23–42.

59. Hollander did make a significant contribution to the history of Jewish women's poetry, as the editor of Emma Lazarus's *Selected Poems* (New York: Library of America, 2005).

60. I am referring to recent controversy on the limits of free speech regarding Israel/Palestine in the Bay Area Jewish community, which resulted in Rich being invited to read at the San Francisco JCC in 2006, right after the JCC canceled an event connected to Jewish Voice for Peace (JVP), an organization on whose board Rich served. She bravely spoke to this at her reading: "Since the birth of Israel as a Jewish state, a narrow orthodoxy regarding Jews and Israel has claimed itself as the official Jewish position in America. Any monologue, marginalizing dissent, is like a kind of intellectual house arrest, and there is a kind of hopelessness in that condition." I am grateful to my dear friend, colleague, and comrade Sarah Anne Minkin for sharing with me Rich's remarks (which she received in advance from Rich).

61. Carolyn Dinshaw, "Temporalities," 122.

TWO. VANISHED HELLAS AND HEBRAIC PAIN: EMMA LAZARUS AND ANNA MARGOLIN

1. Emma Lazarus, "Echoes," in *The Poems of Emma Lazarus*, vol. 1 (Boston and New York: Houghton, Mifflin and Company, 1889), 201.
2. Dinshaw, "Temporalities," 115.
3. Dinshaw, *Getting Medieval*, 36.
4. Emphasis mine.
5. Ralph Waldo Emerson, *Essays* (Boston: J. Munroe, 1841), 129.
6. Besides many chapters and pamphlets dedicated to her life, there are at least three full-length monographs: Dan Vogel's 1980 *Emma Lazarus* (Boston: Twayne Publishers, 1980), Bette Roth Young's *Emma Lazarus in Her World: Life and Letters* (Philadelphia: Jewish Publication Society, 1995), and most recently Esther Schor, *Emma Lazarus* (New York: Schocken, 2006).
7. Lazarus, *The Poems of Emma Lazarus*, vol. 1, 202.
8. Emma Lazarus, "By the Waters of Babylon: Little Poems in Prose," *Century Illustrated Monthly Magazine* 33 (March 1887): 801–3.
9. Michael Weingrad, "Jewish Identity and Poetic Form in 'By the Waters of Babylon,'" *Jewish Social Studies* 9, no. 3 (Spring–Summer 2003): 107–20.

10. Lazarus, "By the Waters of Babylon," 5: 7.

11. Ibid., 7:4.

12. Kramer, Aaron. "The Link Between Heinrich Heine and Emma Lazarus." *The Burning Bush: Poems and Other Writings (1940–1980)*, ed. Thomas Yoseloff (New York: Cornwall Books, 1983), 215.

13. Emma Lazarus, *Poems and Ballads of Heinrich Heine* (New York: Hurst & Co, 1881).

14. Emma Lazarus, "The Poet Heine," *Century Illustrated Monthly Magazine* 29 (December 1884), 210–17.

15. Lazarus, *The Poems of Emma Lazarus*, vol. 1, 203. Emphasis in the original.

16. According to Heine's own account in his afterword to *Romanzero* (discussed in Paul Reitter, "Heinrich Heine and the Discourse of Mythology," in *A Companion to the Works of Heinrich Heine*, ed. Roger F. Cook [New York: Camden House, 2002], 201), one of his last excursions in Paris (before an eight-year confinement) in May 1848 was a pilgrimage to bid farewell to his idols at the Louvre, where he found himself weeping prostrate at the feet of Venus de Milo, who looked down on him sympathetically and inconsolably at once, as though to say, "Can't you see I have no arms and therefore cannot help you?" Paul Reitter suggests that the fact that Venus (and the sensuous mythological tradition more broadly) vanished from Heine's poetry after this is due in part to Heine's return to Judaism (202).

17. For readings of Margolin's poetics and biography see Norma Fain Pratt, "Anna Margolin's Lider: A Study in Women's History, Autobiography, and Poetry," *Studies in American Jewish Literature* 3 (1982): 11–25; Sheva Zucker, "Ana Margolin un di poezye fun dem geshpoltenem ikh," *YIVO bleter* 47 (February 1991): 173–98; and Shirley Kumove, "Drunk from the Bitter Truth: The Life, Times and Poetry of Anna Margolin," in *From Memory to Transformation: Jewish Women's Voices*, eds. Sarah Silberstein Schwartz and Margie Wolfe (Toronto: Second Story Press, 1998), 35–48. For readings of "*Ikh bin geven a mol a yingling*" see Barbara Mann, "Picturing the Poetry of Anna Margolin," *MLQ: Modern Language Quarterly* 63, no. 4 (2002): 501–36 and Avraham Novershtern, "'Who Would Have Believed That a Bronze Statue Can Weep': The Poetry of Anna Margolin," *Prooftexts* 10, no. 3 (1990): 435–67.

18. Her fondness for pen names renders this statement tentative rather than definitive.

19. Anna Margolin, *Lider* (New York: Oriom Press, 1929), 5.

20. Translated by Kathryn Hellerstein, in *Jewish American Literature: A Norton Anthology*, ed. Jules Chametzky (New York: Norton, 2001), 265.

21. The pronoun *they*, which is often used in English to refer to a person without specifying their gender, is increasingly also being used by individuals wishing to challenge the gender binary.

22. For a historical analysis of the construction of Jewish masculinity, see Daniel Boyarin, *Unheroic Conduct: The Rise of Heterosexuality and the Invention of the Jewish Man* (Berkeley: University of California Press, 1997).

23. For further reading on the particular nature of Yiddish as both a fused and open language, see Benjamin Harshav, *The Meaning of Yiddish* (Berkeley: University of California Press, 1990). For additional accounts of the history of Yiddish in general, see *The Field of Yiddish: Studies in Yiddish Language, Folklore, and Literature*, ed. Uriel Weinreich et al. (New York: Linguistic Circle of New York, 1954–1993) and Joshua A. Fishman, *Yiddish: Turning to Life* (Amsterdam: John Benjamins, 1991).

24. For example, some texts use pseudo-Germanized Yiddish (*Daytshmerish*) in order to "borrow" the higher status associated with German high culture, as was common in the early Enlightenment period and in some later literature; alternatively, overemphasizing the *loshn-koydesh* component can serve as a way to make Yiddish utterly incomprehensible to non-Jews, for example, in the famous phrase "*der orl iz meyvn kol-dover*" ("the non-Jew understands everything"—so don't use standard Yiddish in his presence). In this sentence, the vocabulary is nearly exclusively made up of *loshn-koydesh* words, with the exception of *iz*, a form of the Germanic verb *zayn*. The same meaning could be expressed using Germanic vocabulary, but this *loshn-koydesh*–heavy formulation is designed to exclude a non-Jewish listener.

25. Notable here is also the phonetic spelling of *nazaret*, chosen over the Hebraic spelling, which would be pronounced *notseres*, and would not rhyme.

26. Mann, "Picturing the Poetry of Anna Margolin," 512.

27. In Ruth Whitman's translation in *An Anthology of Modern Yiddish Poetry* (New York: October House, 1966), 133.

28. In Marcia Falk's translation in *The Penguin Book of Modern Yiddish Verse*, Irving Howe, Ruth Wisse, and Khone Shmeruk, eds. (New York: Viking, 1987), 218–19.

29. Judith Butler, *Gender Trouble*, 179.

30. Ibid., 179.

31. Mann, "Picturing the Poetry of Anna Margolin," 511.

32. Ibid. Mann is referring to Falk's translation in *The Penguin Book of Modern Yiddish Verse*.

33. In fact, the image of the torso in Margolin's poem directly echoes Rainer Maria Rilke's "Archaic Torso of Apollo." Rilke's poem reminds the readers of what "Never will we know," be it Apollo's "fabulous head" or "glowing loins," referring to the role that the marble fragment of a statue plays in our access to the past (or lack thereof) (see *Rilke: Selected Poems*, ed. and trans. C. F. MacIntyre [Berkeley: University of California Press, 2001], 92–93). The turn to Rilke also connects Margolin's poem to Hebrew via the epoch-making poem by Shaul Tchernichowsky, "Before the Statue of Apollo," written in 1899. Staging a scene of veneration and prostration before a youthful foreign god (and his artistic representation), the poem culminates as Apollo is bound in tefillin (phylacteries). Shaul Tchernichovsky, *Shirim* (Jerusalem and Tel Aviv: Schocken, 1957), 74.

34. See Midrash Eikhah Rabbah 1:50 for one version of the story.

35. Mann, "Picturing the Poetry of Anna Margolin," 501.

36. Ibid., 505.

37. That said, the image of the marble torso has added significance in Margolin's poetic vocabulary, most notably in the poem that was used as her epitaph, with which I close this chapter.

38. *Jewish American Literature: A Norton Anthology*, 265n3.

39. Ariel Bloch and Chana Bloch, *The Song of Songs: A New Translation* (Berkeley: University of California Press, 1995), 175.

40. The term used here for high spirits, *hoykhmutikn fridn*, could perhaps better be translated as "arrogant satisfaction." The nonfused German nature of the term makes it possible to read echoes of fascist anti-Semitism in these lines published in 1929.

41. For accounts of the dramatic tale of the sculpture's purchase and identification, see Christine Mitchell Havelock, *The Aphrodite of Knidos and Her Successors: A Historical Review of the Female Nude in Greek Art* (Michigan: University of Michigan Press, 2007) and Gregory Curtis, *Disarmed: The Story of the Venus de Milo* (New York: Vintage Books, 2003).

42. Novershtern, "'Who Would Have Believed That a Bronze Statue Can Weep,'" 467.

43. Quoted in *The Poems of Emma Lazarus*, vol. 1, 36.

44. Kadia Molodowsky Collection, RG 703, Box 7, Folder 102, YIVO Archives, YIVO Institute for Jewish Research, New York, NY.

45. It was possibly written for (and maybe even produced by) the Jewish Theological Seminary's program "The Eternal Light." Alternately, it could have been written/produced for the General Foods Jewish home show on WATV channel 13, as a play Molodowsky wrote about Doña Gratsya has this written on its cover, along with the year 1956. The connections between the figures of Lazarus, Doña Gratsya, and Molodowsky are rich and intricate. I return to them in chapter 4.

46. Molodowsky Collection, RG 703, Box 7, Folder 102, YIVO Archives; Zvee Scooler Collection, RG 1262, Box 50, Folder 515, YIVO Archives.

47. Lazarus, *The Poems of Emma Lazarus*, vol. 1, 202.

48. I will return to this brand of female (in)action in the next chapter's reading of Leah Goldberg.

49. The poem originally appeared in *Yiddish*, June 10, 1932. It is reprinted in *Anna Margolin: Lider*, ed. Avraham Novershtern (Jerusalem: Magnes, 1991), 136. Translation by Barbara Mann, in "Picturing the Poetry of Anna Margolin," 504.

50. Reuven Ayzland, *Fun undzer friling: Literarishe zikhroynes un portretn* (New York: Inzl, 1954), 130. I relied on Ayzland's literary portrait of Margolin for many of her biographical details.

51. For a reading of this poem and its significance as it appears on Margolin's gravestone, see Naomi Brenner, "Slippery Selves: Rachel Bluvstein and Anna Margolin in Poetry and in Public," *Nashim: A Journal of Jewish Women's Studies & Gender Issues* 19, no. 19 (2010): 100–33.

52. Yerushalmi, *Zakhor*, 101.

THREE. WAITING IN VAIN: LEAH GOLDBERG AND ANNA MARGOLIN

1. From the poem "Epochs," Lazarus, *The Poems of Emma Lazarus*, vol. 1, 44–45.

2. Audre Lorde, "A Litany for Survival," *The Black Unicorn* (New York: Norton, 1995), 31.

3. Barbara Mann, "Of Madonnas and Magdalenes: Reading Mary in Modernist Hebrew and Yiddish Women's Poetry," in *Leket: Yidishe shtudyes haynt, Jiddistik heute, Yiddish Studies Today*, eds. Marion Aptroot, Efrat Gal-Ed, Roland

Gruschka, and Simon Neuberg (Düsseldorf: Düsseldorf University Press, 2012), 49–68.

4. On this topic in Hebrew Statehood Generation poetry see Hamutal Tsamir, *Beshem hanof: Le'umiut, migdar vesubyektiviyut bashirah hayisra'elit bishnot haḥamishim vehashishim* (In the Name of the Landscape: Nationalism, Gender, and Subjectivity in 1950s and 1960s Israeli Poetry) (Tel Aviv: Keter, 2006).

5. See Parush, *Reading Jewish Women*.

6. The prose writer Dvora Baron (1887–1956) is a notable exception to this rule.

7. Some examples: Rokhl Korn (1898–1982) and Anda Pinkerfeld (1902–1981) both began writing in Polish. Korn switched to Yiddish and Pinkerfeld switched to Hebrew. Celia Dropkin (1887–1956) switched from Russian to Yiddish and Rachel Bluvshteyn (1890–1931) switched from Russian to Hebrew.

8. See Samuel Niger and Jacob Shatzky, *Leksikon fun der nayer yidisher literatur* (New York: Alveltlekher Yidisher Kultur-Kongres [1956], 1981).

9. Though the school was independent, it was founded under the principles of the *Tarbut* school movement, a network of secular, Hebrew-language schools, which were established and operated mainly in interwar Poland. For further information on the Jewish education networks in Poland between the two World Wars, see Miriam Eisenstein, *Jewish Schools in Poland, 1919–39: Their Philosophy and Development* (New York: King's Crown Press, 1950).

10. The same group Yocheved Bat-Miriam, the poet whose work I discuss in the introduction, belonged to as well.

11. Leah Goldberg, *Yomaney Leah Goldberg,* eds. Rachel Aharoni and Aryeh Aharoni (Bnei Brak: Sifriyat Po'alim, 2005).

12. Ibid., 67.

13. Leah Goldberg, "*Ḥalom na'arah*" ("Dream of a Girl"), in *Ketavim* (Merḥavyah: Sifriyat Po'alim, 1972), 71. The poem was first published in 1931, and then was included in her first collection, *Taba'ot ashan* (Smoke Rings), in 1934. Translation mine.

14. Actually, the singular should be *ḥalom balahot* and the plural *ḥalomot balahah*, but the title of *ḥalom na'arah* seems to be echoing a combination of plural and singular, *ḥalom balahah*.

15. I am grateful to Galit Hasan-Rokem for this linguistic insight. Yosefa Raz and Rachel Wamsley also gave valuable feedback on all of the Goldberg translations. Rachel Wamsley and I worked collaboratively on Goldberg and Margolin in

2006, and some of our joint efforts are reflected in this chapter. Even earlier than that, it was Tamar Hess who sparked my obsession with this poem and the others discussed in this chapter.

16. Goldberg, *Ketavim*, 28.

17. For a discussion of the tensions between positioning lesbian desire as a story of sameness versus a desire propelled by difference, see Teresa De Lauretis, *The Practice of Love: Lesbian Sexuality and Perverse Desire* (Bloomington: Indiana University Press, 1994).

18. Of course, the context of early Christianity is also a Jewish context, as Daniel Boyarin has argued, showing the artificiality of the "border-markers" set to distinguish the former from the latter (see Daniel Boyarin, *Border Lines: The Partition of Judeo-Christianity* [Philadelphia: University of Pennsylvania Press, 2004]). Goldberg's turn to early Christianity, on the other hand, is still rooted very much in transgressing said "border-markers."

19. Goldberg, *Ketavim*, 38.

20. Goldberg, *Ketavim*, 69.

21. Leah Goldberg, Yfaat Weiss, and Giddon Ticotsky. *Ne'arot ivriyot: Mikhtevey Le'ah Goldberg min haprovintsiah, 1923–1935* (Bnei Brak: Sifriyat Po'alim, 2009), 262.

22. Ibid.

23. In fact these two imperatives are not altogether distinct from each other, as Elana Bloomfield writes: "Many Zionists found religious narratives of women's fertility to be particularly important in constructing the rhetoric and imagery of their modern nationalism." See Elana Bloomfield, "Conceiving Motherhood: The Jewish Female Body in Israeli Reproductive Practices," *Intersections* 10, no. 2 (2009): 238.

24. This poem was first published in 1933 and was included a year later in her first collection, together with the other poems read in this chapter. Goldberg, *Ketavim*, 39.

25. Translation mine. Among the many challenging decisions, the need to sacrifice the tight rhyme scheme of the Hebrew original was perhaps the most difficult.

26. The Christian resonance of *crossing* is entirely absent from the Hebrew. Instead, the Hebrew invokes maternity through the idiom given for *crossing*, *em drakhim*, built from the combination of *mother* and *roads*. I chose *crossing* rather

than *crossroads* since I use the latter to translate *parahsat drakhim* in the opening and closing stanzas.

27. The "other" is gendered female, and could also be translated as "another woman."

28. Uri Tsvi Grinberg's writing, both in Hebrew and in Yiddish, can serve as a notable example. One of his poems, "Uri Tsvi farn tseylem INRI" (Uri Zvi Before the Cross INRI) is even typographically set up in the form of a cross (*Albatros* 2 [Warsaw, 1922]: 3).

29. Matthew Hoffman, *From Rebel to Rabbi: Reclaiming Jesus and the Making of Modern Jewish Culture* (Stanford: Stanford University Press, 2007).

30. Ibid., 2–3.

31. This is distinct from the role Emma Lazarus gave "Jewish Jesus" in her poetry. According to Wolosky: "Throughout her later poetry, Lazarus persistently makes Christ the central figure for Jewish history itself. In doing so, she draws on the newly contemporary and still controversial studies of the historical Jesus in his Jewish context. [. . .] Lazarus, moreover, goes beyond reclaiming Jesus as Jew and actor in Jewish history. She makes Christ her defining figure of Jewish identity, with the Jews, as an historical people, themselves the body of Christ." Shira Wolosky, "An American-Jewish Typology: Emma Lazarus and the Figure of Christ," *Prooftexts* 16, no. 2 (May 1996), 119.

32. I borrow the term *cross-identification* from Daniel Boyarin, who applies it both cross-temporally and across genders in his thrilling portrait of Bertha Pappenheim, "Retelling the Story of O.; Or, Bertha Pappenheim, My Hero," in *Unheroic Conduct*, 313–59.

33. The word Goldberg uses for *desolate* (in the last line of the second stanza), *shomemot*, is also tied to barrenness, joining the word *worn* (*balot*) to bolster the nonreproductive reading.

34. See discussion in introduction of the present book.

35. Carla Freccero, *Queer/Early/Modern* (Durham: Duke University Press Books, 2006), 104.

36. Ibid.

37. Michael André Bernstein, *Foregone Conclusions: Against Apocalyptic History* (Berkeley: University of California Press, 1994).

38. Love, *Feeling Backward*, 93.

39. Love, *Feeling Backward*, 147.

40. Ibid.

41. Kronfeld, *On the Margins of Modernism*, 17.

42. Avraham Ben-Yitshak, *Kol hashirim*, ed. Hannan Hever (Tel-Aviv: Hakibuts Hame'uhad, 1992), 20.

43. The various versions we have of the poem date from 1925 to 1928. See Kronfeld, *On the Margins of Modernism*, 239n23).

44. Avraham Ben-Yitshak, *Kol hashirim*.

45. Hannan Hever," Aharit davar: Al hayav veyetsirato shel Avraham Ben-Yitshak," in Avraham Ben-Yitshak, *Kol hashirim*, 107.

46. See Hever, "Aharit davar," 101.

47. Leah Goldberg, *Pegishah im meshorer: Al Avraham Ben-Yitshak Sone* (Merhavyah: Sifriyat Po'alim, 1952).

48. Ibid., 5.

49. Goldberg, "Avraham Ben-Yitzhak," *Ketavim*, 232.

50. Kronfeld, *On the Margins of Modernism*, 239n23).

51. On the poetic dialogue between Goldberg and Ben-Yitzhak see Natasha Gordinsky,"Crossing the Spectrum of Solitudes: Lea Goldberg's Lyrical Conversation with Avraham Sonne," *Naharaim*, 7, nos. 1–2 (2013): 75–110.

52. Cf. also my earlier reading of Emma Lazarus's poem "The New Colossus" in the previous chapter, where silence and passivity are invoked to generate a powerful and declarative stance entirely different from the one employed by Goldberg and Ben-Yitzhak. Speaking with "silent lips" and lifting the lamp of "imprisoned lightening," Lady Liberty commands an entire harbor ("between two cities") with her "mild eyes."

53. See Gilbert and Gubar, *The Madwoman in the Attic*, especially the chapter "The Queen's Looking Glass: Female Creativity, Male Images of Women, and the Metaphor of Literary Paternity."

54. Margolin, *Lider*, 101–13.

55. For other readings of the Mari poems cf. Novershtern, " 'Who Would Have Believed That a Bronze Statue Can Weep,' " Barbara Mann, "Of Madonnas and Magdalenes," and Kathryn Hellerstein, *A Question of Tradition: Women Poets in Yiddish, 1586–1987* (Stanford: Stanford University Press, 2014) and "Translating as a Feminist."

56. Hellerstein, "Translating as a Feminist," 198.

57. This poem is in dialogue with Rainer Maria Rilke's 1899 poem "Der Wahnsinn" (*Rilke: Selected Poems*, 24–25) with its refrain "Wer bist du denn, Marie?" ("Who are you then, Mary?"). The beggar woman image of Rilke's poem is also echoed in Margolin's poem "Mari vil zayn a betlerin" ("Mary and the Beggar") in the same cycle. Rilke's poem appeared in Yiddish translation

by Itsik Manger, under the title "Shigoen" ("Madness") in Manger's journal *Getseylte verter* 1, no. 2 (August 1929): 2. Significantly, these first issues of the journal are replete with references to Jewish literary engagement with Christian imagery. Manger chastises *di klasiker*, the "first family" of Yiddish literature, for ignoring their surroundings: "Here we remain, my dear, standing for a moment, to think, perhaps there are deeper reasons we need to uncover, to understand why the Christ figure is missing (even decoratively) from the realistic landscapes of Mendele and Sholem Aleichem, and from the visionary landscapes of Y. L. Peretz" ("Driter briv to X. Y.," *Getseylte verter* 1, no. 4 [September 1929]: 2). Leah Goldberg, on the other hand, in her activation of the landscape of the cross, certainly falls in line with Manger's demands for modern Jewish poetry.

58. Translated by Shirley Kumove, in Anna Margolin, *Drunk from the Bitter Truth: The Poems of Anna Margolin*, trans. and ed. Shirley Kumove (Albany: State University of New York Press, 2005), 184.

59. Translated by Shirley Kumove, *Drunk from the Bitter Truth*, 194.

60. Hellerstein uses Margolin's correspondence with her son and his father, together with Reuven Ayzland's account of Margolin's life in *Fun undzer friling*, to read the mother-child relationship in the poems of the *Mari* cycle (*A Question of Tradition*, 311).

61. Letter from Na'aman Stavski/Stavi to Anna Margolin, RG 1166, Box 1, Folder 2, YIVO Archives, YIVO Institute for Jewish Research, New York, NY. Translation mine.

62. In the introduction I discuss how Yocheved Bat-Miriam takes on a name that reverses the Biblical genealogy, where Yocheved is the mother of both Miriam and Moses.

63. A recent documentary about Palestinian poet Mahmud Darwish includes footage of Darwish recounting how he was expelled from school in the seventh grade for reading a poem about the Nakba during an official visit of this same military governor (*Write Down, I Am an Arab*, directed by Ibtisam Mara'ana Menuhim, Ibtisam Films, 2014).

64. For example, in Harshav's *Language in a Time of Revolution* and Chaim Rabin's "The National Idea and the Revival of Hebrew," in *Essential Papers on Zionism*, eds. Jehuda Reinharz and Anita Shapira (New York: New York University Press, 1996), 745–62.

65. I will discuss the stakes of the shift away from language transmission via heterosexual reproduction in the following chapters.

FOUR. *HEYS* HAUNTING: POETICS OF LESBIAN HISTORY

1. *The Poems of Emma Lazarus*, Vol. 1, 185–86.
2. Love, *Feeling Backward*, 98.
3. Terry Castle, *The Apparitional Lesbian: Female Homosexuality and Modern Culture* (New York: Columbia University Press, 1993), 2.
4. Elaine Showalter, "Pale Denizens of the Night," review of *The Apparitional Lesbian: Female Homosexuality and Modern Culture* by Terry Castle, *Times Literary Supplement*, June 3, 1994, 6.
5. Carla Freccero, "Queer Spectrality: Haunting the Past," in *A Companion to Lesbian, Gay, Bisexual, Transgender, and Queer Studies*, ed. George Haggerty and Molly McGarry (Malden, MA: Blackwell Publishing, 2007), 196.
6. Margolin, *Lider*, 128.
7. Translated by Shirley Kumove, *Drunk from the Bitter Truth*, 233.
8. I am aware of very few other examples, the most explicit being Sholem Asch's *Got fun nekome* (Warsaw: Tsentral, 1913). Bluma Lempel's story "Correspondents" (published in translation in *Found Treasures*, 237–41) is also explicit in its expression of desire, if not consummation. That said, lesbian and homoerotic subtext is not altogether uncommon. There is still so much work to be done to recover queer Yiddish texts and subtexts alike.
9. Novershtern, "'Who Would Have Believed That a Bronze Statue Can Weep,'" 453.
10. Ibid.
11. Carla Freccero, "Queer Spectrality," 194.
12. Ibid.
13. Ibid., 196.
14. Margolin, *Lider*, 10.
15. Translated by Shirley Kumove, *Drunk from the Bitter Truth*, 12.
16. Novershtern, "'Who Would Have Believed That a Bronze Statue Can Weep,'" 456.
17. Ibid.
18. William Abrams, "Kadye Molodovski: A rede gehaltn tsum kaboles-ponim far Kadye Molodovski," *Signal* (November 1935): 3–4.
19. In Kadya Molodowsky, *Der meylekh Dovid aleyn iz geblibn* (New York: Farlag Papirene Brik, 1946), 96–98. There is no English translation of the poem.

20. For further reading, see Andrée Aelion Brooks, *The Woman who Defied Kings: The Life and Times of Doña Gracia Nasi, a Jewish Leader During the Renaissance* (St. Paul: Paragon House, 2002).

21. Translation mine.

22. Freccero, "Queer Times," in *After Sex: On Writing Since Queer Theory*, eds. Janet Halley and Andrew Parker (Durham: Duke University Press, 2011), 21.

23. Freccero, "Queer Spectrality," 196.

24. Molodowsky Collection, RG 703, Box 7, Folder 108, YIVO Archives.

25. Scooler Collection, RG 1262, Box 50, Folder 515, YIVO Archives.

26. Molodowsky Collection, RG 703, Boxes 9–10, YIVO Archives.

27. Kadya Molodowsky, *Nokhn got fun midber: Drame fun yidishn lebn in zekhtsntn yorhundert* (New York: Papirene Brik, 1949).

28. Emma Lazarus, *Song of a Semite: The Dance to Death and other Poems* (New York: Office of "The American Hebrew," 1882), 5–50.

29. Lazarus, *Song of a Semite*, 16.

30. Eve Kosofsky Sedgwick, *Epistemology of the Closet* (Berkeley: University of California Press, 1990), 82.

31. Ibid., brackets in original.

32. Naomi Seidman, "Fag-Hags and Bu-Jews: Toward a (Jewish) Politics of Vicarious Identity," in *Insider/Outsider: American Jews and Multiculturalism*, eds. David Biale, Michael Galchinsky, and Susannah Heschel (Berkeley: University of California Press, 1998), 262.

33. Ibid., 264

34. Freccero, "Queer Spectrality," 200.

35. Arthur Zeiger, "Emma Lazarus: A Critical Study" (PhD diss., New York University, 1951), 86–87.

36. *The Poems of Emma Lazarus*, vol. 1, 185–86.

37. Freccero, *Queer/Early/Modern*, 78.

38. Emma Lazarus, *Poems and Translations: Written between the Ages of Fourteen and Sixteen* (New York: H. O. Houghton and Company, 1866). Esther Schor argues that this reprinting was a reaction to Lazarus's first literary attentions, in the form of a rather negative review in the *New York Times* (Schor, *Emma Lazarus*, 21–22).

39. Original poem found in *Manuscript Notebook*, Emma Lazarus Papers, P-2, Box 1, Folder 1, American Jewish Historical Society, New York, NY. First published in Dan Vogel's, *Emma Lazarus* (Boston: Twayne Publishers, 1980), 89.

40. Paula Bennett, *Emily Dickinson, Woman Poet* (Iowa City: University of Iowa Press, 1990), 173.

41. Vogel, *Emma Lazarus*, 89.

42. Zeiger, "Emma Lazarus," 195.

43. See Edward Wagenknecht's portrait of Emma Lazarus in *Daughters of the Covenant: Portraits of Six Jewish Women* (Amherst: University of Massachusetts Press, 1983), 35.

44. On conventions of the sonnet see Joseph Phelan, *The Nineteenth-Century Sonnet* (New York: Palgrave, 2005).

45. Lisa L. Moore, "A Lesbian History of the Sonnet," *Critical Inquiry* 43, no. 4 (Summer 2017): 814.

46. Anna Seward, *Original Sonnets on Various Subjects: And, Odes Paraphrased from Horace* (London: G. Seal, 1799), 35.

47. Lisa Moore, *Sister Arts: The Erotics of Lesbian Landscapes* (Minneapolis: University of Minnesota Press, 2011).

48. Amy C. Billone, *Little Songs: Women, Silence, and the Nineteenth-Century Sonnet* (Columbus: Ohio State University Press, 2007), 157.

49. Schor, *Emma Lazarus*, 232.

50. Billone, *Little Songs*, 7.

51. Schor, *Emma Lazarus*, 232.

52. D. A. Miller, *The Novel and the Police* (Berkeley: University of California Press, 1988), 207.

53. Moore, *Sister Arts*, 18–19.

FIVE. COMMUNITY ACROSS DISCONTINUITY

1. Audre Lorde, "There are no Honest Poems about Dead Women," *Our Dead Behind Us* (New York: Norton, 1986), 61.

2. Adrienne Rich, *Of Woman Born: Motherhood as Experience and Institution* (New York: Norton, 1986), x.

3. Rich, *A Wild Patience Has Taken Me This Far*, 33. The unusual layout follows that of the original publication, imitating the image of the swooping of the skirts across time, creating a trans-temporal dialogue.

4. See the entire first volume of Bonnie Kime Scott's four-part series *Refiguring Modernism*, titled, *The Women of 1928* (Bloomington: Indiana University Press, 1995).

5. Cook, "'Women Alone Stir My Imagination,'" 718.

6. Korman, *Yidishe Dikhterins*. For extensive consideration of Korman's anthology see Hellerstein, *A Question of Tradition*.

7. *Nice Jewish Girls: A Lesbian Anthology*, ed. Evelyn Torton Beck (Watertown: Persephone Press, 1982).

8. Cook, "'Women Alone Stir My Imagination,'" 718.

9. Ibid., 735.

10. Ibid., 719.

11. Adrienne Rich, "Compulsory Heterosexuality and Lesbian Existence," *Signs* 5, no. 4 (Summer 1980): 649.

12. Adrienne Rich, *Dream of a Common Language* (New York: Norton, 1978), 76.

13. De Lauretis, *The Practice of Love*, 249.

14. Irena Klepfisz and Melanie Kaye/Kantrowitz, "Introduction," *The Tribe of Dina*, eds. Melanie Kaye/Kantrowitz and Irena Klepfisz (Boston: Beacon Press, 1986), 9.

15. Later, more Yiddish texts by women were published in the anthologies *Found Treasures: Stories by Yiddish Women Writer*s, eds. Frieda Forman, et al. (Toronto: Second Story Press, 1994) and *Beautiful as the Moon, Radiant as the Stars: Jewish Women in Yiddish Stories*, eds. Sandra Bark and Francine Prose (New York: Time Warner Publishing, 2003).

16. Kathryn Hellerstein, "Canon and Gender: Women Poets in Two Modern Yiddish Anthologies," in *Women of the Word: Jewish Women and Jewish Writing*, ed. Judith R. Baskin (Detroit: Wayne State University Press, 1994), 136–52.

17. Hellerstein, "Translating as a Feminist," 193.

18. Together with so many others, for example, writing by *Mizraḥim* (Jews from North Africa and the Middle East and their descendants), not to mention works by *Mizraḥi* women writers.

19. Rich, "Compulsory Heterosexuality," 649.

20. Rich, "Split at the Root," 67.

21. Irena Klepfisz, "Forging a Woman's Link in *Di Goldene Keyt*: Some Possibilities for Jewish American Poetry," in *Dreams of an Insomniac: Jewish Feminist Essays, Speeches, and Diatribes* (Portland: Eighth Mountain Press, 1990), 172.

22. Irena Klepfisz, "*Di feder fun harts*/The Pen of the Heart: *Tsveyshprakhikayt*/Bilingualism in Jewish American Poetry," in *Jewish American Poetry: Reflections*,

Poems, Commentary, eds. Jonathan Barron and Eric Murphy Selinger (New England: University Press of New England, 2000), 322.

23. Ibid., 324.
24. Klepfisz, "Forging a Woman's Link in *Di Goldene Keyt*," 172.
25. Klepfisz, "*Di feder fun harts*/The Pen of the Heart," 335.
26. For a wider reading and contextualization of Molodowsky's essayistic work, see Allison Schachter, *Diasporic Modernisms: Hebrew and Yiddish Literature in the Twentieth Century* (Oxford: Oxford Press, 2011).
27. Molodowsky Collection, RG 703, Boxes 9–10, YIVO Archives.
28. Joyce Antler and Sari K. Biklen, *Changing Education: Women as Radicals and Conservators* (Albany: State University of New York Press, 1990), 108.
29. Ibid.
30. While the published pieces acknowledge no sources, a handwritten draft of Molodowsky's Sappho essay does reveal her source to be *The Poems of Sappho* by Maurice Hill, published in 1954 (Folder 114, Box 9).
31. Kadya Molodowsky, "Bagegenishn," *Literarishe bleter* 7, no. 5 (January 31, 1930): 95.
32. The two had in fact recently shared a page in *Literarishe bleter* 5, no. 24 (June 15, 1928): 465.
33. Melech Ravitch, "'Den mir hobn zunshtn keyn andri (mekhaye) in der velt': E. Korman—*Yidishe dikhterins: antologye*" (review). *Literarishe bleter* 5, no. 42 (October 19, 1928): 830–31.
34. Hellerstein's *A Question of Tradition* deals extensively with the anthology, especially in the chapters One and Two.
35. Ibid., 50.
36. Korman's anthology is one of the thousands of titles available online through the National Yiddish Book Center—but the tactile experience lost in downloading it makes very clear the distance between the shelf life and digital versions of the same book. In this transitional moment I feel extremely lucky to have access to both.
37. Korman, *Yidishe Dikhterins*, LXV.
38. Hellerstein, *A Question of Tradition*, 51.
39. Korman, *Yidishe Dikhterins*, vii.
40. This term, coined by Van Wyck Brooks ("On Creating a Usable Past," in *Van Wyck Brooks: The Early Years: A Selection from His Works, 1908–1925*, ed. Claire Sprague [Boston: Northeastern University Press, 1993], 219–26) became central

to New Historicism. In the context of Jewish studies, David Roskies uses the term to indicate shifts in the very method of memory: "Once the search for a usable past was being waged through new venues and institutions [...] the structure of remembrance began to change as well" (David Roskies, *The Jewish Search for a Usable Past* [Bloomington: Indiana University Press, 1999], 3).

41. Hellerstein, *A Question of Tradition*, 45.

42. Quotations marks his.

43. See Avraham Novershtern, "Hakolot vehamak'helah: shirat nashim beyidish bein shtey milḥamot ha'olam," *Bikoret ufarshanut* 40 (2008): 80.

44. Ibid., 82.

45. Ibid., 83.

46. Ibid., 85.

47. Ibid., 86.

48. Ibid., 80.

49. Bonnie Zimmerman, "The Politics of Transliteration: Lesbian Personal Narratives" *Signs* 9, no. 4 (Summer, 1984): 677.

50. Elena Dykewomon, *Beyond the Pale* (Vancouver: Press Gang, 1997). Though this novel was not published until 1997, it is very much a product of Dykewomon's participation in the early lesbian separatist movement. Her adherence to that particular political moment marks her difference from contemporary queer politics, as she herself expressed in her piece with Jyl Lynn Felman, "Forward and Backward: Jewish Lesbian Writers," in *Bridges* 16, no. 1 (Spring 2011): 228–33.

51. The poem appears within the essay "*Di feder fun harts*/The Pen of the Heart, 333.

52. Klepfisz, "*Di feder fun harts*/The Pen of the Heart," 334.

53. Klepfisz, "Forging a Woman's Link in *Di Goldene Keyt*," 172.

54. Ibid.

55. Consider, for example, Malka Heifetz-Tussman (1893–1987), Rajzel Zychlinski (1910–2001), Chava Rosenfarb (1923–2011), and Rivka Basman Ben-Ḥayim (born 1923)—to name but a few.

56. We might compare this to Virginia Woolf's historical account of women's writing in *A Room of One's Own*, where none of her contemporary women writers are acknowledged, as Elizabeth Abel pointed out to me (in a personal communication).

57. The magazine launched in April 1977, and Klepfisz was a founding editor. The magazine is available online at the Lesbian Poetry Archive, http://www.lesbianpoetryarchive.org/conditions.

58. "An Open Letter to the Women's Movement," signed "In sisterhood and struggle," by Evelyn T. Beck, Nancy K. Bereano, Gloria Z. Greenfield, Melanie Kaye, Irena Klepfisz, Bernice Mennis, and Adrienne Rich. April 22, 1982, Subject File: "Jewish Lesbians," The Lesbian Herstory Archives, New York.

59. Irena Klepfisz, "Keynote" (Conference on Jewish Women's Creativity and Scholarship, Mills College, Oakland California, February 26, 2006).

60. This of course was before the now-prevalent celebration of the intersections of "queer" and Yiddish, which Jeffrey Shandler describes in "Queer Yiddishkeit: Practice and Theory," *Shofar: An Interdisciplinary Journal of Jewish Studies* 25, no. 1 (2006): 90–113. While homophobia has not disappeared from Jewish circles, we can certainly note a radical shift in the visibility and prominence of LGBT Jewish topics.

61. Irena Klepfisz, *A Few Words in the Mother Tongue: Poems Selected and New (1971–1990)* (Portland: Eighth Mountain Press, 1990).

62. At the closing of the present book I received three new poems by Klepfisz, which have yet to be published.

63. "In Amerika They Call Us Dykes: Lesbian Lives in the 70s—Spring Series and Fall Festival," Center for Lesbian and Gay Studies (CLAGS), The Graduate Center, CUNY, accessed October 23, 2011, http://www.70slesbians.org/.

64. Elizabeth Freeman, "Packing History, Count(er)ing Generations," *New Literary History* 31, no. 4 (Autumn 2000), 729.

65. Beck is not only a figure to be studied for her Jewish lesbian work, she is also "known as the 'grandmother' of Yiddish at the Modern Language Association, where she started the Yiddish section in 1972, years before the current Yiddish revival" (Liora Moriel, "Evelyn Torton Beck," *Jewish Women: A Comprehensive Historical Encyclopedia*, Jewish Women's Archive, March 1, 2009, http://jwa.org/encyclopedia/article/beck-evelyn-torton).

66. Bonnie J. Morris, "Valuing Woman-Only Spaces," *Feminist Studies* 31, no. 3 (Fall 2005): 628. Morris was referring specifically to the Michigan Womyn's Music Festival, which was then still, in her words, "miraculously thriving," while being criticized by the "next, more radical waves." A decade after this article was written, and five years after the CUNY conference, the Michigan Womyn's Festival shut down. The fact that they chose to end this important project rather than open it to trans women is heartbreaking, from both a trans and lesbian perspective.

67. Bonnie J. Morris, *The Disappearing L: Erasure of Lesbian Spaces and Culture* (Albany: State University of New York Press, 2016), 5.

68. Ibid., 3.

69. Ibid., 4.

70. Kaitlin Noss beautifully transformed her personal experience at the conference into a critical analysis and political program in her article, "Queering Utopia: Deep Lez and the Future of Hope," *WSQ: Women's Studies Quarterly* 40, no. 3 (2013): 126.

71. Ibid., 126.

72. Nishant Shahani, *Queer Retrosexualities: The Politics of Reparative Return* (Bethlehem: Lehigh University Press, 2012), 2.

73. Linda Garber, *Identity Poetics: Race, Class, and the Lesbian-Feminist Roots of Queer Theory* (New York: Columbia University Press, 2001), 7.

74. Ibid., 1.

75. In Eve Kosofsky Sedgwick, *Tendencies* (Durham: Duke University Press, 1993), 252–66.

76. Freeman, "Packing History, Count(er)ing Generations," 729.

77. Ibid., 728.

78. Nealon, *Foundlings*, 96.

79. Rich, "Granddaughter," in *A Wild Patience Has Taken Me This Far*, 37.

80. Rich, "Introduction to the Poetry of Irena Klepfisz," 13.

81. Adrienne Rich, *The Fact of a Doorframe* (New York: Norton, 2002), 198.

82. Linda Garber, *Identity Poetics*, 138.

SIX. TRANSLATING GENERATIONS: IRENA KLEPFISZ

1. Klepfisz, *A Few Words in the Mother Tongue*, 224.

2. Maeera Schreiber, *Singing in a Strange Land: A Jewish American Poetics* (Stanford: Stanford University Press, 2007), 173.

3. Klepfisz, *A Few Words in the Mother Tongue*, 223.

4. Robert Alter, *The Book of Psalms: A Translation with Commentary* (New York; London: W. W. Norton & Company, 2009), 474.

5. Klepfisz, "Der fentster/The Window," in *A Few Words in the Mother Tongue*, 216.

6. Gloria Anzaldúa, *Borderlands/La Frontera: The New Mestiza* (San Francisco: Aunt Lute Books, 1987), 54.

7. In *Singing in a Strange Land*, Maeera Schreiber has dedicated a beautiful chapter to lament and exile in the writing of both Klepfisz and Adrienne Rich,

which also offers a description of the relation between Klepfisz and Anzaldúa as "a two-way mirror" of "mutual illumination" (173).

8. On their connection, see also Jane Hedley, "Nepantilist Poetics: Narrative and Cultural Identity in the Mixed-Language Writings of Irena Klepfisz and Gloria Anzaldúa," *Narrative* 4, no. 1 (January, 1996): 36–54.

9. Klepfisz, *A Few Words in the Mother Tongue*, 228–29.

10. Ibid., 228.

11. Hellerstein, *A Question of Tradition*, 433. For a detailed updated account of Shtok's life, see Helene Kenvin, "Fradel Shtok: Author and Poet," JewishGen KehilaLinks, September 13, 2015, http://kehilalinks.jewishgen.org/skalapodol/FradelShtok.html.

12. As I discussed in the introduction, Hellerstein explores this conflict, both in feminist scholarship and in Yiddish women's poetry, in " 'A Word for My Blood.' "

13. For readings of Dropkin's poetics, see Janet Hadda's chapter "The Eyes Have It: Celia Dropkin's Love Poetry" and Kathryn Hellerstein's "From 'Ikh' to 'Zikh': A Journey From 'I' to 'Self' in Yiddish Poems by Women," both in the groundbreaking collection *Gender and Text in Modern Hebrew and Yiddish Literature*. See also Sheva Zucker, "The Red Flower: Rebellion and Guilt in the Poetry of Celia Dropkin," *Studies in American Jewish Literature*, vol. 15 (1996): 99–117. For more recent readings of Dropkin's poetry, see article in Polish by Agnieszka Legutko, " 'Cyrkowa dama': poezja Celii Dropkin czytana z perspektywy genderowej," *Nieme dusze* (2010): 207–42, as well as Hellerstein's *A Question of Tradition*.

14. Celia Dropkin, "Di tentserin," in *In heysn vint: Lider* (New York: John J. Dropkin, 1959). "The Dancer" translated by Shirley Kumove, in *Found Treasures*, 193–202.

15. Tabatshnik refuted this claim already in 1965, showing that Morris Winchevsky published a sonnet as early as 1892. Still, Tabatshnik gives Shtok her due credit, stating that Shtok was "the first to write real poetry in Yiddish in the form of sonnets" (Avrom Tabatshnik, "Fradel Shtok un der yidisher sonet," *Dikhter un dikhtung* [New York: n.p., 1965], 506).

16. Margolin, Lider, 10. See discussion in chapter 3.

17. Translated by Shirley Kumove, *Drunk from the Bitter Truth*, 12.

18. "The Fact of a Doorframe," in *Poems: Selected and New, 1950–1974* (New York: Norton, 1974). The collection *The Fact of a Doorframe: Poems Selected and New 1950–1984* was published by W. W. Norton in 1984.

19. On the construction of poetic personas in Yiddish and Hebrew poetry by women see Brenner, "Slippery Selves."

20. See Dan Miron, *A Traveler Disguised: The Rise of Modern Yiddish Fiction in the Nineteenth Century* (Syracuse: Syracuse University Press, 1996).

21. Cited in Kronfeld's *The Full Severity of Compassion*, 172.

22. Anita Norich, "A Response from Anita Norich," 215.

23. Ibid.

24. Diana Fuss, *Identification Papers: Readings on Psychoanalysis, Sexuality, and Culture* (New York: Routledge, 1995), 10.

25. Ibid.

26. Klepfisz, *A Few Words in the Mother Tongue*, 225.

27. In *The Passing Game: Queering Jewish American Culture* (Syracuse: Syracuse University Press, 2009), Warren Hoffman traces how the encounter with American terminology of homosexuality made Yiddish-speaking audiences less tolerant of homosexual content (referring specifically to Sholem Asch's play *Got fun nekome* [*God of Vengeance*]). My own research into Yiddish sexology and its close ties to European and American sexology leads me to doubt the notion of a Yiddish culture existing free of "foreign" notions of homosexuality.

28. Jeffrey Shandler, Adventures in *Yiddishland: Postvernacular Language & Culture* (Berkeley: University of California Press, 2006), 166.

29. Ibid.

30. Klepfisz, "Khaloymes/Dreams in Progress: Culture, Politics and Jewish Identity," in *Dreams of an Insomniac*, 187–211.

31. Ibid., 209.

32. Ibid.,

33. Carolyn Dinshaw, "Temporalities," 115.

34. Rich, "Origins and History of Consciousness," in *Dream of a Common Language*, 7.

35. Maeera Shreiber makes the connection between Yiddish as common and Rich's *Dream of a Common Language* in "The End of Exile: Jewish Identity and Its Diasporic Poetics," *PMLA* 113, no. 2 (March 1998): 238. My interest here is in what it means to create something in common out of something that is not common or shared at all.

36. Elizabeth Freeman, "Introduction," *GLQ: A Journal of Lesbian and Gay Studies* 13.2 (2007): 162.

37. Hellerstein, "'A Word for My Blood.'"
38. In Molodowsky, *Der meylekh Dovid aleyn iz geblibn*, 86–87.
39. Hellerstein, "'A Word for My Blood,'" 51.
40. Irena Klepfisz, "Women without Children/Women without Families/Women Alone," in *Dreams of an Insomniac*, 8.
41. Irena Klepfisz, "Di yerushe/The Legacy: A Parable about History and Bobe-mayses, Barszcz and Borsht and the Future of the Jewish Past," *Prairie Schooner* 71, no. 1 (Spring 1997): 8.
42. Ibid., 9.
43. Seidman, *A Marriage Made in Heaven*, 9.
44. Rich, *Dream of a Common Language*, 76.
45. Irena Klepfisz, "Forging a Woman's Link in Di Goldene Keyt," 171.

CODA. QUEERING THE PRESENT OF JEWISH LITERARY HISTORY

1. Klepfisz, *Periods of Stress*, 20.
2. Dan Miron, *From Continuity to Contiguity*, 38.
3. Ibid., 411.
4. Dan Miron's work has very much shaped the field of Hebrew literary scholarship. He has published multiple works of literary scholarship each year starting in 1957, excluding only the years 1963, 1965–68, 1974, 1980, 1985, and 1988.
5. Irena Klepfisz, "*Di feder fun harts*/The Pen of the Heart," 333.
6. Ibid., 334.
7. Though Jewish power is more than fluent in English, and indeed much of the politics ensuring the persistence of the Occupation take place in English.
8. The Israeli human rights watch organization B'Tselem has published testimonies of incarcerated Palestinian youth who admitted to throwing rocks in the hopes of receiving a high school education in an Israeli prison.
9. Ayelet Ben-Yishai has also offered examples of the particular ways Palestinian students employ this history as a means of participation in Israeli academic discourse (Ayelet Ben-Yishai, "Sifrut haḥalukah: Al pedagogiah vepolitikah behashva'ah bein Hodu leYisrael." *Te'oriah uvikoret* 44 (2015): 9–28).
10. For the sake of this experiment, I translated the poem into Hebrew, and my friend and colleague Zahiye Kundus translated it into Arabic.

אני גר כאן עם משפחתי
היהודים באים. אני זורק אבנים.
אני צועק: הייל היטלר!
חבר נורה בכדור גומי.
לוקחים אותו לבית חולים. הוא
יחיה אבל יהיה נכה.
אימי בוכה: מתי זה ייגמר?
אני? אני מבסוט שהבית ספר סגור
מה אני צריך ללמוד?
אני אוהב לראות אותם מתחבאים
מאחורי הקירות. להפיל את היהודים!
תחי פלסטין!

اسكن هنا مع عائلتي
اليهود قادمون. اقذف بالحجارة.
أصرخ: هايل هتلر!
صديق أصيب برصاص مغلف بالمطاط
يأخذونه الى المستشفى
سوف يعيش، لكن عاجزاً
أمي تبكي: الى متى؟
وأنا مبسوط أن المدرسة مغلقة
لماذا أدرس أصلا؟
تسعدني رؤياهم مختبئون
من وراء الجدار. اسقطوا اليهود!
تحيى فلسطين!

11. Dan Miron, *From Continuity to Contiguity*, 276.
12. Butler, *Gender Trouble*, 22.
13. Kronfeld, *On the Margins of Modernism*, 54.
14. Butler, *Gender Trouble*, 26.
15. Miron, *From Continuity to Contiguity*, 313.
16. Dan Miron, "Is There Really One Modern Klal yisroel Literature?" in *The Image of the Shtetl and Other Studies of Modern Jewish Literary Imagination* (Syracuse, NY: Syracuse University Press, 2000), 355.
17. Anita Norich, "Under Whose Sign? Hebraism and Yiddishism as Paradigms of Modern Jewish Literary History," *PMLA* 125, no. 3 (May 2010), 777.

18. Judith Butler, *Bodies That Matter: On the Discursive Limits of "Sex"* (New York: Routledge, 1993).

19. Ibid., ix.

20. Dinshaw, "Temporalities," 109.

21. Dan Miron, *Harpayah letsorekh negi'ah* (Tel Aviv: Am Oved, 2005). The Hebrew version contains a mere 171 pages, compared to the 519 pages in English. The differences between them are fascinating, but unfortunately I am not able to attend to them here in full.

22. Miron, *From Continuity to Contiguity*, 306.

23. Miron, *Harpaya letsorekh negi'ah*, 163.

24. Miron has in fact made invaluable contributions to the study of Jewish women writers in both Hebrew and Yiddish, namely through his study *Imahot meyasdot, aḥayot ḥorgot*. However, none of the women writers discussed in this study are used in his new theorization, which relies on the same canonical male writers past theories have turned to (such as Sholem Aleichem, Franz Kafka, and S. Y. Abramovitsh). In an interesting twist, Miron uses the fact that Yiddish women writers were active where Hebrew women writers were absent to argue against the reading of Jewish literature as one system.

25. Miron, *From Continuity to Contiguity*, 417.

26. Dan Miron "Ahavah hateluyah badavar: Toldot hitkablutah shel shirat David Fogel," in *Aderet leBinyamin*, vol. 1, ed. Ziva Ben-Porat (Tel Aviv: Porter Institute and Hakibuts Hame'uḥad, 1999), 29–98.

27. See especially Kronfeld's article, "The Joint Literary Historiography of Hebrew and Yiddish," in *What and Where Are Jewish Languages?* eds. Joshua L. Miller and Anita Norich (Ann Arbor: Frankel Institute for Advanced Judaic Studies, 2016), 15–35, and her book *On the Margins of Modernism*; Naomi Seidman, *A Marriage Made in Heaven*; Michael Gluzman, *The Politics of Canonicity: Lines of Resistance in Modernist Hebrew Poetry* (Stanford: Stanford University Press, 2003); Yael Chaver, *What Must Be Forgotten*; Jordan Finkin, *A Rhetorical Conversation: Jewish Discourse in Modern Yiddish Literature* (University Park, PA: Pennsylvania State University Press, 2010); Allison Schachter, *Diasporic Modernisms*; and Lital Levy "Reorienting Hebrew Literary History: The View from the East," *Prooftexts* 29, no. 2 (2010): 127–72.

28. Lital Levy and Allison Schachter, "Jewish Literature/World Literature: Between the Local and the Transnational," *PMLA* 130, no. 1 (January 2015): 92–109.

29. Ibid., 93.
30. Eve Kosofsky Sedgwick, *Epistemology of the Closet*, 11.
31. Ibid., 10.
32. Muñoz, *Cruising Utopia,* 1. Since the writing of these words, Muñoz's passing has dealt a cruel blow to optimistic queer utopianism, at the same time reaffirming how very much queer theory matters.
33. Ibid., 18.
34. Klepfisz, "Di feder fun harts," 334.
35. Ibid.
36. Jack Halberstam, *The Queer Art of Failure* (Durham: Duke University Press Books, 2011), 124.
37. As the book itself is titled, ibid.
38. Yerushalmi, *Zakhor*, 101.
39. Jack Halberstam, "The Anti-Social Turn in Queer Studies," *Graduate Journal of Social Science* 5, no. 2 (2008): 153.
40. Ibid.

BIBLIOGRAPHY

Abrams, William. *"Kadye Molodovski: A rede gehaltn tsum kaboles-ponim far Kadye Molodovski." Signal* (November 1935): 3–4.

Alcalay, Ammiel. *After Jews and Arabs: Remaking Levantine Culture.* Minneapolis: University of Minnesota Press, 1993.

Alter, Robert. *The Book of Psalms: A Translation with Commentary.* New York; London: W. W. Norton & Company, 2009.

Amitay, Einat. "Mi himtsi' et Kadya Molodovski be'ivrit?" *Yoman masa leḥeker 100 shnot tarbut leyeladim bakibutsim.* May 2, 2011. http://tarbut-yeladim.blogspot.ca/2011/05/blog-post.html.

Antler, Joyce, and Sari K. Biklen. *Changing Education: Women as Radicals and Conservators.* Albany: State University of New York Press, 1990.

Anzaldúa, Gloria. *Borderlands/La Frontera: The New Mestiza.* San Francisco: Aunt Lute Books, 1987.

Asch, Sholem. *Got fun nekome.* Warsaw: Tsentral, 1913.

Ayzland, Reuven. *Fun undzer friling: Literarishe zikhroynes un portretn.* New York: Inzl, 1954.

Bailin, Carole. *To Reveal Our Hearts: Jewish Women Writers in Tsarist Russia.* Cincinnati: Hebrew Union College Press, 2000.

Balbuena, Monique. *Homeless Tongues: Poetry and Languages of the Sephardic Diaspora.* Stanford: Stanford University Press, 2016.

Bark, Sandra, and Francine Prose, eds. *Beautiful as the Moon, Radiant as the Stars: Jewish Women in Yiddish Stories.* New York: Time Warner Publishing, 2003.

Barzilai, Maya, and Katra Byram. "The Challenge of Lyric Address in War Poems by Yitzhak Laor and Ingeborg Bachmann." *Yearbook of Comparative and General Literature* 53 (2007): 155–68.

Baskin, Judith R., ed. *Women of the Word: Jewish Women and Jewish Writing.* Detroit: Wayne State University Press, 1994.

Bat-Miriam, Yocheved. *Maḥatsit mul maḥatsit: Kol hashirim.* Tel Aviv: Hakibuts Hame'uḥad, 2014.

———. *Meraḥok.* Tel Aviv: The Hebrew Writers' Association, 1932.

———. *Shirim.* Tel Aviv: Sifriyat Po'alim, 1972.

Ben-Yishai, Ayelet. "Sifrut haḥalukah: Al pedagogiah vepolitikah behashva'ah bein Hodu leYisrael." *Te'oriah uvikoret* 44 (2015): 9–28

Ben-Yitzhak, Avraham. *Kol hashirim.* Edited by Hannan Hever. Tel-Aviv: Hakibuts Hame'uḥad, 1992.

Benjamin, Walter. *Illuminations.* Edited by Hannah Arendt. New York: Schocken Books, 1968.

Bennett, Paula. *Emily Dickinson: Woman Poet.* Iowa City: University of Iowa Press, 1991.

Bernstein, Michael André. *Foregone Conclusions: Against Apocalyptic History.* Berkeley: University of California Press, 1994.

Biale, David. *Blood and Belief: The Circulation of a Symbol between Jews and Christians.* Berkeley: University of California Press, 2007.

Bialik, H. N. "Ḥevley lashon." In *Kol kitvey H. N. Bialik*, 197–201. Tel Aviv: Dvir, 1965.

Billone, Amy Christine. *Little Songs: Women, Silence, and the Nineteenth-Century Sonnet.* Columbus: Ohio State University Press, 2007.

Bloch, Ariel, and Chana Bloch. *The Song of Songs: A New Translation.* Berkeley: University of California Press, 1995.

Bloomfield, Elana. "Conceiving Motherhood: The Jewish Female Body in Israeli Reproductive Practices." *Intersections* 10, no. 2 (2009): 227–69.

Bluvshteyn, Rachel. "Ivria." *Davar* 6, no. 5 (November 14, 1930).

Boyarin, Daniel, and Jonathan Boyarin. *Border Lines: The Partition of Judeo-Christianity.* Philadelphia: University of Pennsylvania Press, 2004.

———. "Diaspora: Generation and the Ground of Jewish Identity." *Critical Inquiry* 19, no. 4 (1993): 693–725.

———. *Unheroic Conduct: The Rise of Heterosexuality and the Invention of the Jewish Man.* Berkeley: University of California Press, 1997.

Brenner, Naomi. "Slippery Selves: Rachel Bluvstein and Anna Margolin in Poetry and in Public." *Nashim: A Journal of Jewish Women's Studies & Gender Issues* 19 (Spring 2010): 100–33.

Brooks, Andrée Aelion. *The Woman who Defied Kings: The Life and Times of Doña Gracia Nasi, a Jewish Leader during the Renaissance.* St. Paul: Paragon House, 2002.

Brooks, Van Wyck. "On Creating a Usable Past." In *Van Wyck Brooks: The Early*

Years: A Selection from His Works, 1908–1925, edited by Claire Sprague, 219–26. Boston: Northeastern University Press, 1993.

Brown, Wendy. *Politics out of History*. Princeton: Princeton University Press, 2001.

Butler, Judith. *Bodies That Matter: On the Discursive Limits of "Sex."* New York: Routledge, 1993.

———. *Gender Trouble: Feminism and the Subversion of Identity*. New York: Routledge, 1999.

———. "Imitation and Gender Insubordination." In *The Gay and Lesbian Studies Reader*, edited by Henry Abelove, Michèle Aina Barale, and David M. Halperin, 307–20. London: Routledge, 1993.

Castle, Terry. *The Apparitional Lesbian: Female Homosexuality and Modern Culture*. New York: Columbia University Press, 1993.

Chamberlain, Lori. "Gender and the Metaphorics of Translation." *Signs* 13, no. 3 (Spring, 1988): 454–72.

Chametzky, Jules, ed. *Jewish American Literature: A Norton Anthology*. New York: Norton, 2001.

Chaver, Yael. *What Must Be Forgotten: The Survival of Yiddish in Zionist Palestine*. Syracuse: Syracuse University Press, 2004.

Cohen, Tova. "Portrait of the 'Maskilah' as a Young Woman." *Nashim* 15 (2008): 9–29.

Cohen, Tova, and Shmuel Feiner. *Kol almah ivriyah: Kitvey nashim maskiliot bame'ah hat'sha'-esreh*. Tel-Aviv: Hakibuts Hame'uḥad, 2006.

Cook, Blanche W. "'Women Alone Stir My Imagination': Lesbianism and the Cultural Tradition." *Signs* 4, no. 4 (Summer 1979): 718–39.

Cook, Roger F. *A Companion to the Works of Heinrich Heine*. Columbia, SC: Camden House, 2010.

Curtis, Gregory. *Disarmed: The Story of the Venus de Milo*. New York: Vintage Books, 2003.

De Lauretis, Teresa. *The Practice of Love: Lesbian Sexuality and Perverse Desire*. Bloomington: Indiana University Press, 1994.

Dinshaw, Carolyn. *Getting Medieval: Sexualities and Communities, Pre- and Postmodern*. Durham, NC: Duke University Press, 1999.

———. "Temporalities." In *Middle English, Oxford Twenty-First Century Approaches to Literature*, vol. 1, edited by Paul Strohm, 107–23. Oxford: Oxford University Press, 2007.

Dinshaw, Carolyn, Lee Edelman, Roderick A. Ferguson, et al., "Theorizing Queer Temporalities: A Roundtable Discussion." *GLQ: A Journal of Lesbian and Gay Studies* 13, no. 2 (2007): 177–95.

Dropkin, Celia. *In heysn vint: Lider.* New York: John J. Dropkin, 1959.

Dykewomon, Elana. *Beyond the Pale.* Vancouver: Press Gang, 1997.

Dykewomon, Elana, and Jyl Lynn Felman. "Forward and Backward: Jewish Lesbian Writers." *Bridges* 16, no. 1 (Spring 2011): 228–33.

Edelman, Lee. *No Future: Queer Theory and the Death Drive.* Durham: Duke University Press, 2004.

Eisenstein, Miriam. *Jewish Schools in Poland, 1919–39: Their Philosophy and Development.* New York: King's Crown Press, 1950.

Emerson, Ralph Waldo. *Essays.* Boston: J. Munroe, 1841.

Finkin, Jordan D. *A Rhetorical Conversation: Jewish Discourse in Modern Yiddish Literature.* University Park: Pennsylvania State University Press, 2010.

Fishman, Joshua A. *Yiddish: Turning to Life.* Amsterdam: John Benjamins, 1991.

Forman, Frieda, Ethel Raicus, Sarah Silverman Swartz, and Margie Wolf, eds. *Found Treasures: Stories by Yiddish Women Writers.* Toronto: Second Story Press, 1994.

Freccero, Carla. *Queer/Early/Modern.* Durham: Duke University Press, 2006.

———. "Queer Spectrality: Haunting the Past." In *A Companion to Lesbian, Gay, Bisexual, Transgender, and Queer Studies*, edited by George Haggerty and Molly McGarry, 194–213. Malden, MA: Blackwell Publishing, 2007.

———. "Queer Times." In *After Sex: On Writing Since Queer Theory*, edited by Janet Halley and Andrew Parker, 17–26. Durham: Duke University Press, 2011.

Freeman, Elizabeth. "Introduction." *GLQ: A Journal of Lesbian and Gay Studies* 13.2 (2007): 159–76.

———. "Packing History, Count(er)ing Generations." *New Literary History* 31, no. 4 (Autumn 2000): 724–44.

Fuss, Diana. *Identification Papers: Readings on Psychoanalysis, Sexuality, and Culture.* New York: Routledge, 1995.

Garber, Linda. *Identity Poetics: Race, Class, and the Lesbian-Feminist Roots of Queer Theory.* New York: Columbia University Press, 2001.

Gilbert, Sandra M., and Susan Gubar. *The Madwoman in the Attic: The Woman Writer and the Nineteenth-Century Literary Imagination.* New Haven: Yale University Press, 1984.

Gluzman, Michael. "The Exclusion of Women from Hebrew Literary History." *Prooftexts* 11, no. 3 (1991): 259–78.

———. *The Politics of Canonicity: Lines of Resistance in Modernist Hebrew Poetry.* Stanford: Stanford University Press, 2003.

Goldberg, Leah. *Ketavim.* Merḥavyah: Sifriyat Po'alim, 1972.

———. *Ne'arot ivriyot: Mikhtevey Le'ah Goldberg min haprovintsiah, 1923–1935.* Edited by Yfaat Weiss and Giddon Ticotsky. Bnei Brak: Sifriyat Po'alim, 2009.

———. *Pegishah im meshorer: Al Avraham Ben Yitsḥak Sone.* Merchavyah: Sifriyat Po'alim, 1952.

———. *Yomaney Leah Goldberg.* Edited by Rachel Aharoni and Aryeh Aharoni. Bnei Brak: Sifriyat Po'alim, 2005.

Gordinsky, Natasha. "Crossing the Spectrum of Solitudes: Lea Goldberg's Lyrical Conversation with Avraham Sonne." *Naharaim* 7, 1–2 (2013): 75–110.

Grinberg, Uri Tsvi. "Uri Tsvi farn tseylem INRI." *Albatros* 2 (Warsaw, 1922): 3.

Hadda, Janet. "The Eyes Have It: Celia Dropkin's Love Poetry." In *Gender and Text in Modern Hebrew and Yiddish Literature*, edited by Naomi B. Sokoloff, Anne Lapidus Lerner, and Anita Norich, 93–112. New York: Jewish Theological Seminary of America, 1992.

Halberstam, Jack/Judith. "The Anti-Social Turn in Queer Studies." *Graduate Journal of Social Science* 5, no. 2 (2008): 140–56.

———. *In a Queer Time and Place.* New York: New York University Press, 2005.

———. *The Queer Art of Failure.* Durham: Duke University Press Books, 2011.

Halperin, Liora R. *Babel in Zion: Jews, Nationalism, and Language Diversity in Palestine, 1920–1948.* New Haven: Yale University Press, 2014.

Harshav, Benjamin. *Language in a Time of Revolution.* Berkeley: University of California Press, 1993.

———. *The Meaning of Yiddish.* Berkeley: University of California Press, 1990.

———. *The Polyphony of Jewish Culture.* Stanford: Stanford University Press, 2007.

Havelock, Christine Mitchell. *The Aphrodite of Knidos and Her Successors: A Historical Review of the Female Nude in Greek Art.* Michigan: University of Michigan Press, 2007.

Hedley, Jane. "Nepantilist Poetics: Narrative and Cultural Identity in the Mixed-Language Writings of Irena Klepfisz and Gloria Anzaldúa." *Narrative* 4, no. 1 (January 1996): 36–54.

Hellerstein, Kathryn. "Canon and Gender: Women Poets in Two Modern Yiddish Anthologies." In *Women of the Word: Jewish Women and Jewish Writing*, edited by Judith R. Baskin, 136–52. Detroit: Wayne State University Press, 1994.

———. "From 'Ikh' to 'Zikh': A Journey from 'I' to 'Self' in Yiddish Poems by Women." In *Gender and Text in Modern Hebrew and Yiddish Literature*, edited by Naomi B. Sokoloff, Anne Lapidius Lerner, and Anita Norich, 113–43. Cambridge: Harvard University Press, 1992.

———. "Kadya Molodowsky." In *Jewish Women: A Comprehensive Historical Encyclopedia*, Jewish Women's Archive. March 20, 2009. https://jwa.org/encyclopedia/article/molodowsky-kadya.

———. *A Question of Tradition: Women Poets in Yiddish, 1586–1987*. Stanford: Stanford University Press, 2014.

———. "Translating as a Feminist: Reconceiving Anna Margolin." *Prooftexts* 20, nos. 1–2 (2000): 191–208.

———. "'A Word for My Blood': A Reading of Kadya Molodowsky's 'Froyen-lider' (Vilna 1927)." *AJS Review* 13, nos. 1–2 (1988), 47–79.

Hever, Hannan. "Aḥarit davar: Al ḥayav veyetsirato shel Avraham Ben-Yitshak." In *Avraham Ben-Yitshak, Kol hashirim*, edited by Hannan Hever, 75–111. Tel-Aviv: Hakibuts Hame'uḥad, 1992.

Hobsbawm, Eric. "Introduction: Inventing Tradition." In *The Invention of Tradition*, edited by Eric Hobsbawm and Terence Ranger, 1–14. Cambridge: Cambridge University Press, 2012.

Hochberg, Gil. *In Spite of Partition: Jews, Arabs, and the Limits of Separatist Imagination*. Princeton: Princeton University Press, 2007.

Hoffman, Matthew. *From Rebel to Rabbi: Reclaiming Jesus and the Making of Modern Jewish Culture*. Stanford: Stanford University Press, 2007.

Hoffman, Warren. *The Passing Game: Queering Jewish American Culture*. Syracuse: Syracuse University Press, 2009.

Honig, Edwin. *The Poet's Other Voice*. Cambridge: University of Massachusetts Press, 1985.

Howe, Irving, and Eliezer Greenberg, eds. *A Treasury of Yiddish Poetry*. New York: Holt, Rinehart and Winston, 1969.

Howe, Irving, Ruth Wisse, and Khone Shmeruk, eds. *The Penguin Book of Modern Yiddish Verse*. New York: Viking, 1987.

Hyman, Paula. *Gender and Assimilation in Modern Jewish History: The Roles and Representations of Women.* Seattle: University of Washington Press, 1995.

"In Amerika They Call Us Dykes: Lesbian Lives in the 70s—Spring Series and Fall Festival." Center for Lesbian and Gay Studies (CLAGS), The Graduate Center, CUNY. Accessed October 23, 2011. http://www.70slesbians.org/.

Irshai, Ronit. "Be Fruitful and Multiply." In *Fertility and Jewish Law: Feminist Perspectives on Orthodox Responsa Literature*, 25–52. Translated by Joel A. Linsider. Waltham, MA: Brandeis University Press, 2012.

Jelen, Sheila. *Intimations of Difference: Dvora Baron in the Modern Hebrew Renaissance.* Syracuse: Syracuse University Press, 2007.

Johnson, Barbara. *Mother Tongues: Sexuality, Trials, Motherhood, Translation.* Cambridge: Harvard University Press, 2003.

Kaplan, Marion A., and Deborah Dash Moore. *Gender and Jewish History.* Bloomington: Indiana University Press, 2011.

Kartun-Blum, Ruth. *Bamerchak hane'elam: Iyunim beshirat Yokheved Bat-Miriam.* Ramat Gan: Sifriyat Makor, 1977.

———. "Vegadol minir'eh halo-nir'eh: Al shirat Yokheved Bat-Miriam." In *Yocheved Bat-Miriam, Maḥatsit mul maḥatsit: Kol hashirim*, edited by Yocheved Bat-Miriam, 481–521. Tel Aviv: Hakibuts Hame'uḥad, 2014.

———. "Imi, Yokheved Bat-Miriam: Re'ayon im Dr. Mariassa Bat-Miriam Katzenelson." *Sadan* 2 (1996): 153–63.

Kay, Devra, trans., ed., and commentary. *Seyder Tkhines: The Forgotten Book of Common Prayer for Jewish Women.* Philadelphia: Jewish Publication Society of America, 2004.

Kaye/Kantrowitz, Melanie, and Irena Klepfisz, eds. *The Tribe of Dina.* Boston: Beacon Press, 1986.

Kenvin, Helene. "Fradel Shtok: Author and Poet." JewishGen KehilaLinks. September 13, 2015. http://kehilalinks.jewishgen.org/skalapodol/FradelShtok.html.

Kime Scott, Bonnie. *Refiguring Modernism, Vol. 1: The Women of 1928.* Bloomington: Indiana University Press, 1995.

Klepfisz, Irena. *Dreams of an Insomniac: Jewish Feminist Essays, Speeches, and Diatribes.* Portland: Eighth Mountain Press, 1990.

———. "Di feder fun harts/The Pen of the Heart: Tsveyshprakhikayt/Bilingualism in Jewish American Poetry." In *Jewish American Poetry: Reflections, Poems,*

Commentary, edited by Jonathan Barron and Eric Murphy Selinger, 320–47. New England: University Press of New England, 2000.

———. *A Few Words in the Mother Tongue: Poems Selected and New (1971–1990)*. Portland: Eighth Mountain Press, 1990.

———. "Keynote." Conference on Jewish Women's Creativity and Scholarship, Mills College, Oakland California, February 26, 2006.

———. "Di mames, dos loshn/The mothers, the language: Feminism, Yidishkayt, and the Politics of Memory." *Bridges* 4, no. 1 (Winter/Spring 1994): 12–47.

———. *Periods of Stress*. New York: Out & Out Books, 1975.

———. "Di yerushe/The Legacy: A Parable about History and Bobe-mayses, Barszcz and Borsht and the Future of the Jewish Past." *Prairie Schooner* 71, no. 1 (Spring 1997): 7–12.

Korman, Ezra. *Yidishe Dikhterins: Antologye*. Chicago: L. M. Shtayn, 1928.

Kosofsky Sedgwick, Eve. *Epistemology of the Closet*. Berkeley: University of California Press, 1990.

———. *Tendencies*. Durham: Duke University Press, 1993.

Kramer, Aaron. "The Link between Heinrich Heine and Emma Lazarus." In *The Burning Bush: Poems and Other Writings (1940–1980)*, edited by Thomas Yoseloff, 210–17. New York: Cornwall Books, 1983.

Kronfeld, Chana. *The Full Severity of Compassion: The Poetry of Yehuda Amichai*. Stanford: Stanford University Press, 2015.

———. "The Joint Literary Historiography of Hebrew and Yiddish." In *What and Where Are Jewish Languages?*, edited by Joshua L. Miller and Anita Norich, 15–35. Ann Arbor: Frankel Institute for Advanced Judaic Studies, 2016.

———. *On the Margins of Modernism: Decentering Literary Dynamics*. Berkeley: University of California Press, 1996.

Kumove, Shirley. "Drunk from the Bitter Truth: The Life, Times and Poetry of Anna Margolin." In *From Memory to Transformation: Jewish Women's Voices*, edited by Sarah Silberstein Schwartz and Margie Wolfe, 35–48. Toronto: Second Story Press, 1998.

Lazarus, Emma. "By the Waters of Babylon: Little Poems in Prose," *Century Illustrated Monthly Magazine* 33 (March 1887): 801–3.

———. Emma Lazarus Papers, P-2. American Jewish Historical Society, New York, NY.

———. *Poems and Ballads of Heinrich Heine*. New York: Hurst & Co., 1881.

———. *Poems and Translations: Written between the Ages of Fourteen and Sixteen*. New York: H. O. Houghton and Company, 1866.

———. *The Poems of Emma Lazarus, Vol. I: Narrative, Lyric, and Dramatic.* Boston and New York: Houghton, Mifflin and Company, 1889.

———. *The Poems of Emma Lazarus, Vol. II: Jewish Poems and Translations.* Boston and New York: Houghton, Mifflin and Company, 1889.

———. "The Poet Heine." *Century Illustrated Monthly Magazine* 29 (December 1884): 210–17.

———. *Selected Poems.* Edited by John Hollander. New York: Library of America, 2005.

———. *Songs of a Semite: The Dance to Death and Other Poems.* New York: Office of "The American Hebrew," 1882.

Legutko, Agnieszka. "'Cyrkowa dama': poezja Celii Dropkin czytana z perspektywy genderowej." *Nieme dusze* (2010): 207–42.

Levy, Lital. *Poetic Trespass: Writing between Hebrew and Arabic in Israel/Palestine.* Princeton University Press, 2014.

———. "Reorienting Hebrew Literary History: The View from the East." *Prooftexts* 29, no. 2 (2010): 127–72.

Levy, Lital, and Allison Schachter. "Jewish Literature/World Literature: Between the Local and the Transnational." *PMLA* 130, no. 1 (January 2015): 92–109.

Lorde, Audre. *The Black Unicorn: Poems.* New York: W. W. Norton, 1978.

———. *Our Dead Behind Us.* New York: Norton, 1986.

Love, Heather. *Feeling Backward: Loss and the Politics of Queer History.* Cambridge: Harvard University Press, 2007.

Manger, Itzik. "Driter briv to X. Y." *Getseylte verter* 1, no. 4 (September 1929): 2.

Mann, Barbara. "Of Madonnas and Magdalenes: Reading Mary in Modernist Hebrew and Yiddish Women's Poetry." In *Leket: Yidishe shtudyes haynt, Jiddistik heute, Yiddish Studies Today*, edited by Marion Aptroot, Efrat Gal-Ed, Roland Gruschka, and Simon Neuberg, 49–68. Düsseldorf: Düsseldorf University Press, 2012.

———. "Picturing the Poetry of Anna Margolin." *MLQ: Modern Language Quarterly* 63:4 (2002), 501–36.

Margolin, Anna. Anna Margolin Collection, RG 1166. YIVO Archives, YIVO Institute for Jewish Research, New York, NY.

———. *Anna Margolin: Lider.* Edited by Avraham Novershtern. Jerusalem: Magnes Press, 1991.

———. *Drunk from the Bitter Truth: The Poems of Anna Margolin.* Edited and translated by Shirley Kumove. Albany: State University of New York Press, 2005.

———. *Lider.* New York: Oriom Press, 1929.
Menuhim, Ibtisam Mara'ana, dir. *Write Down, I Am an Arab.* Documentary film about Mahmud Darwish. Ibtisam Films, 2014.
Millen, Rochelle L. *Women, Birth, and Death in Jewish Law and Practice.* Waltham, MA: Brandeis University Press, 2004.
Miller, D. A. *The Novel and The Police.* Berkeley: University of California Press, 1989.
Miron, Dan. "Ahavah hateluyah badavar: Toldot hitkablutah shel shirat David Fogel." In *Aderet leBinyamin*, vol. 1, edited by Ziva Ben-Porat, 29–98. Tel Aviv: Porter Institute and Hakibuts Hame'uḥad, 1999.
———. *From Continuity to Contiguity: Toward a New Jewish Literary Thinking.* Stanford: Stanford University Press, 2010.
———. *Harpayah letsorekh negi'ah.* Tel-Aviv: Am Oved, 2005.
———. *The Image of the Shtetl and Other Studies of Modern Jewish Literary Imagination.* Syracuse: Syracuse University Press, 2000.
———. *Imahot meyasdot, aḥayot ḥorgot: Al shtey hathalot bashirah ha'EretsYisra'elit ha-modernit.* Tel Aviv: Hakibuts Hame'uḥad, 1991.
———. "KesheYokheved Bat-Miriam kiblah al atsmah et din hakni'ah." *Haaretz*, October 13, 2014. https://www.haaretz.co.il/literature/study/1.2455476.
———. *A Traveler Disguised: The Rise of Modern Yiddish Fiction in the Nineteenth Century.* Syracuse: Syracuse University Press, 1996.
Molodowsky, Kadya. "Bagegenishn." *Literarishe bleter* 7, no. 5 (January 31, 1930): 95.
———. *Der meylekh Dovid aleyn iz geblibn.* New York: Farlag Papirene Brik, 1946.
———. Kadia Molodowsky Collection, RG 703. YIVO Archives, YIVO Institute for Jewish Research, New York, NY.
———. *Khezhvndike nekht.* Vilna: B. Kletskin, 1927.
———. *Nokhn got fun midber: Drame fun yidishn lebn in zekhtsntn yorhundert.* New York: Farlag Papirene Brik, 1949.
———. *Paper Bridges: Selected Poems of Kadya Molodowsky.* Translated, introduced and edited by Kathryn Hellerstein. Detroit: Wayne State University Press, 1999.
Moore, Lisa L. "A Lesbian History of the Sonnet," *Critical Inquiry* 43, no. 4 (Summer 2017), 813–38.
Moore, Tracy. *Sister Arts: The Erotics of Lesbian Landscapes.* Minneapolis: University of Minnesota Press, 2011.

———, ed. *Lesbiyot: Israeli Lesbians Talk about Sexuality, Feminism, Judaism and Their Lives.* London: Cassell, 1995.

Moriel, Liora. "Evelyn Torton Beck." *Jewish Women: A Comprehensive Historical Encyclopedia.* Jewish Women's Archive. March 1, 2009, http://jwa.org/encyclopedia/article/beck-evelyn-torton.

Morris, Bonnie J. *The Disappearing L: Erasure of Lesbian Spaces and Culture.* Albany: State University of New York Press, 2016.

———. "Valuing Woman-Only Spaces." *Feminist Studies* 31, no. 3 (Fall 2005): 618–30.

Muñoz, José Esteban. *Cruising Utopia: The Then and There of Queer Futurity.* New York: New York University Press, 2009.

Myers, David. *Resisting History: Historicism and Its Discontents in German-Jewish Thought.* Princeton: Princeton University Press, 2003.

Nealon, Christopher S. *Foundlings: Lesbian and Gay Historical Emotion before Stonewall.* Durham: Duke University Press, 2001.

Niger, Samuel, and Jacob Shatzky. *Leksikon fun der nayer yidisher literatur.* New York: Alveltlekher Yidisher Kultur-Kongres [1956], 1981.

Niranjana, Tejaswini. *Siting Translation: History, Post-Structuralism, and the Colonial Context.* Berkeley: University of California Press, 1992.

Norich, Anita. "A Response from Anita Norich." *Prooftexts* 20, nos. 1–2 (Winter/Spring 2000): 213–18.

———. "Under Whose Sign? Hebraism and Yiddishism as Paradigms of Modern Jewish Literary History," *PMLA* 125, no. 3 (May 2010): 774–84.

Noss, Kaitlin. "Queering Utopia: Deep Lez and the Future of Hope." *WSQ: Women's Studies Quarterly* 40, no. 3 (2013): 126–45.

Novershtern, Avraham. "Hakolot vehamak'helah: shirat nashim beyidish bein shtey milḥamot ha'olam," *Bikoret ufarshanut* 40 (2008): 61–146.

———. " 'Who Would Have Believed That a Bronze Statue Can Weep': The Poetry of Anna Margolin." *Prooftexts* 10, no. 3 (1990): 435–67.

"An Open Letter to the Women's Movement." April 22, 1982. Subject File: "Jewish Lesbians," The Lesbian Herstory Archives, New York.

Pardes, Ilana. "Yocheved Bat-Miriam: The Poetic Strength of a Matronym." In *Gender and Text: Feminist Criticism and Modern Hebrew and Yiddish Literature*, edited by Naomi B. Sokoloff, Anne Lapidus Lerner, and Anita Norich, 39–63. New York: The Jewish Theological Seminary of America, 1992.

Parush, Iris. *Reading Jewish Women: Marginality and Modernization in Nineteenth-Century Eastern European Jewish Society.* Waltham: Brandeis University Press, 2004.

Phelan, Joseph. *The Nineteenth-Century Sonnet.* New York: Palgrave, 2005.

Pratt, Norma Fain. "Anna Margolin's Lider: A Study in Women's History, Autobiography, and Poetry." *Studies in American Jewish Literature* 3 (1982): 11–25.

Rabin, Chaim. "The National Idea and the Revival of Hebrew." In *Essential Papers on Zionism*, edited by Jehuda Reinharz and Anita Shapira, 745–62. New York: New York University Press, 1996.

Ravitch, Melech. " 'Den mir hobn zunshtn keyn andri (mekhaye) in der velt': E. Korman—Yidishe dikhterins: antologye" (review). *Literarishe bleter* 5, no. 42 (October 19, 1928), p. 830–31.

Reitter, Paul. "Heinrich Heine and the Discourse of Mythology." In *A Companion to the Works of Heinrich Heine*, edited by Roger F. Cook, 201–28. New York: Camden House, 2002.

Rich, Adrienne. "Compulsory Heterosexuality and Lesbian Existence." *Signs* 5, no. 4 (Summer 1980), 631–60.

———. *Dream of a Common Language.* New York: Norton, 1978.

———. *The Fact of a Doorframe: Poems Selected and New 1950–1984.* New York: Norton, 1984.

———. "Introduction to the Poetry of Irena Klepfisz." In *A Few Words in the Mother Tongue: Poems Selected and New (1971–1990)*, by Irena Klepfisz, 13–25. Portland: Eighth Mountain Press, 1990.

———. *Of Woman Born: Motherhood as Experience and Institution.* New York: Norton, 1986.

———. *Poems: Selected and New, 1950–1974.* New York: Norton, 1974

———. "Split at the Root: An Essay on Jewish Identity." In *Nice Jewish Girls: A Lesbian Anthology*, edited by Evelyn Torton Beck, 67–88. Watertown: Persephone Press, 1982.

———. *A Wild Patience Has Taken Me This Far: Poems, 1978–1981.* New York: Norton, 1981.

Rilke, Rainer Maria. *Rilke: Selected Poems.* Edited and translated by C. F. MacIntyre. Berkeley: University of California Press, 2001.

Roskies, David. *The Jewish Search for a Usable Past.* Bloomington: Indiana University Press, 1999.

Rugoff, Kathy. "Sappho on Mount Sinai: Adrienne Rich's Dialogue with Her Father." In *Multicultural Literatures through Feminist/Poststructuralist Lenses*, edited by Barbara Frey Waxman, 1–21. Knoxville: University of Tennessee Press, 1993.

Schachter, Allison. *Diasporic Modernisms: Hebrew and Yiddish Literature in theTwentieth Century*. Oxford: Oxford Press, 2011.

Schor, Esther. *Emma Lazarus*. New York: Schocken, 2006.

Scooler, Zvee. Zvee Scooler Collection, RG 1262. YIVO Archives, YIVO Institute for Jewish Research, New York, NY.

Seidman, Naomi. "Fag-Hags and Bu-Jews: Toward a (Jewish) Politics of Vicarious Identity." In *Insider/Outsider: American Jews and Multiculturalism*, edited by David Biale, Michael Galchinsky, and Susannah Heschel, 254–68. Berkeley: University of California Press, 1998.

———. *Faithful Renderings: Jewish-Christian Difference and the Politics of Translation*. Chicago: University of Chicago Press, 2006.

———. *A Marriage Made in Heaven: The Sexual Politics of Hebrew and Yiddish*. Berkeley: University of California Press, 1997.

Seward, Anna. *The Collected Poems of Anna Seward*. Edited by Lisa L. Moore. New York: Routledge, 2015.

———. *Original Sonnets on Various Subjects: And, Odes Paraphrased from Horace*. London: G. Seal, 1799.

Shahani, Nishant. *Queer Retrosexualities: The Politics of Reparative Return*. Bethlehem: Lehigh University Press, 2012.

Shandler, Jeffrey. *Adventures in Yiddishland: Postvernacular Language & Culture*. Berkeley: University of California Press, 2006.

———. "Queer Yiddishkeit: Practice and Theory." *Shofar: An Interdisciplinary Journal of Jewish Studies* 25, no. 1 (2006): 90–113.

Shomroni, Amir. " 'In Yisroel un tsurik: Al nesibot akiratam me'Artsot Habrit leYisrael veazivatam beḥazarah shel Kadya Molodowsky veSimḥah Lev le'or haperek ha'aḥaron shel zikhronoteiha ha'otobiografiim 'Mayn elterzeydns yerushe,' shelo pursam veshenimtsa ganuz be'arkhiyonah beYIVO beNyu York." Unpublished article.

Showalter, Elaine. "Pale Denizens of the Night." Review of *The Apparitional Lesbian: Female Homosexuality and Modern Culture*, by Terry Castle. *Times Literary Supplement*, June 3, 1994, 6.

Shreiber, Maeera. "The End of Exile: Jewish Identity and Its Diasporic Poetics." *PMLA* 113, no. 2 (March 1998): 273–87.

———. *Singing in a Strange Land: A Jewish American Poetics*. Stanford: Stanford University Press, 2007.

Sokoloff, Naomi, Anne Lapidus Lerner, and Anita Norich, eds. *Gender and Text in Modern Hebrew and Yiddish Literature*. New York: JTSA, 1992.

Somerville, Siobhan B. "Queer." In *Keywords for American Cultural Studies*, edited by Bruce Burgett and Glenn Hendler. New York University Press. Accessed October 27, 2017. http://keywords.nyupress.org/american-cultural-studies/essay/queer/.

Stein, Sarah Abrevaya. *Making Jews Modern: The Yiddish and Ladino Press in the Russian and Ottoman Empires*. Bloomington: Indiana University Press, 2003.

Tabatshnik, Avrom. "Fradel Shtok un der yidisher sonet," *Dikhter un dikhtung*. New York: n.p., 1965, 505–8.

Tchernichovsky, Shaul. *Shirim*. Jerusalem and Tel Aviv: Schocken, 1957.

Thomas, Brook. *The New Historicism and Other Old-Fashioned Topics*. Princeton: Princeton University Press, 1991.

Torton Beck, Evelyn, ed. *Nice Jewish Girls: A Lesbian Anthology*. Watertown: Persephone Press, 1982.

Tsamir, Hamutal. *Beshem hanof: le'umiut, migdar vesubyektiviyut bashirah hayisra'elit bishnot haḥamishim vehashishim*. Tel Aviv: Keter, 2006.

Turniansky, Chava. "Introduction." In *Glikl bas Yuda Leib, Glikl: Memoirs 1691–1719*, edited and translated by Chava Turniansky. Jerusalem: Zalman Shazar Center for Jewish History, Ben-Zion Dinur Center for Research in Jewish History, Hebrew University, 2006.

———. "Meydlekh in der altyidisher literatur." In *Jiddische Philologie: Festschrift für Erika Timm*, edited by Walter Röll and Simon Neuberg, 7–20. Tübingen: Max Niemeyer Verlag, 1999.

Vogel, Dan. *Emma Lazarus*. Boston: Twayne Publishers, 1980.

Wagenknecht, Edward. *Daughters of the Covenant: Portraits of Six Jewish Women*. Amherst: University of Massachusetts Press, 1983.

Weingrad, Michael. "Jewish Identity and Poetic Form in 'By the Waters of Babylon,'" *Jewish Social Studies* 9, no. 3 (Spring–Summer 2003): 107–20.

Weinreich, Uriel et al., eds. *The Field of Yiddish: Studies in Yiddish Language, Folklore, and Literature*. New York: Linguistic Circle of New York, 1954–1993.

Weissler, Chava. *Voices of the Matriarchs: Listening to the Prayers of Early Modern Jewish Women*. Boston: Beacon Press, 1998.

Whitman, Ruth, ed. and trans. *An Anthology of Modern Yiddish Poetry*. New York: October House, 1966.

Wittgenstein, Ludwig. *Philosophical Investigations*. West Sussex: Wiley-Blackwell, 2009.

Wolosky, Shira. "An American-Jewish Typology: Emma Lazarus and the Figure of Christ," *Prooftexts* 16, no. 2 (May 1996): 113–25.

Yerushalmi, Yosef Hayim. *Zakhor: Jewish History and Jewish Memory*. Seattle: University of Washington Press, 1982.

Young, Bette Roth. *Emma Lazarus in Her World: Life and Letters*. Philadelphia: Jewish Publication Society, 1995.

Zeiger, Arthur. "Emma Lazarus: A Critical Study." PhD diss., New York University, 1951.

Zierler, Wendy. *And Rachel Stole the Idols: The Emergence of Modern Hebrew Women's Writing*. Detroit: Wayne State University Press, 2004.

———. "Yokheved Bat-Miriam (Zhelezhniak)." In *Jewish Women: A Comprehensive Historical Encyclopedia*. Jewish Women's Archive, March 1, 2009. https://jwa.org/encyclopedia/article/bat-miriam-yokheved.

Zimmerman, Bonnie. "The Politics of Transliteration: Lesbian Personal Narratives." *Signs* 9, no. 4 (Summer, 1984): 663–82.

Zucker, Sheva. "Ana Margolin un di poezye fun dem geshpoltenem ikh." *YIVO bleter* 47 (February 1991): 173–98.

———. "Kadye Molodowsky's 'Froyen-lider' ('Women's Songs')." *Yiddish* 9, no. 2 (1994): 44–52.

———. "The Red Flower: Rebellion and Guilt in the Poetry of Celia Dropkin." *Studies in American Jewish Literature* 15 (1996): 99–117.

INDEX

Bold page numbers refer to figures

Abel, Elizabeth, xxv–xxvi, 160n56
Abraham (Biblical), 75
Abramovitsh, S.Y., 115, 167n24
Abrams, William, 73
Abu-Na'aman. *See* Stavski, Moshe
Adrienne Cooper Dreaming in Yiddish award, 101
affective genealogy, xv
Aleichem, Sholem, 115–16, 153n57, 167n24
Allah, 94
alliteration, xix, 85
Aphrodite of Melos, 35
See also Venus de Milo
Amazons, 98
anachronism, xx, 13, 19, 37–38, 57, 135
anti-Semitism, 13, 35, 58, 100–101, 127, 148n40
    See also blood libel; Hitler, Adolf; Khurbn; Nazis; pogroms; Portugal: expulsion of Jews; Sho'ah; Spain: expulsion of Jews
Anzaldúa, Gloria, 121, 162n7
    Borderlands/La Frontera, 110–11
Apollo, 148n33
apostles, 48
apparitional lesbian, 65, 82
    See also ghosts; haunting; queer spectrality

Arabic (language), xxii, 61–62, 126, 128–30, 132–33, 165n10
Arabs, 126, 129
Aramaic (language), 29
Asch, Sholem
    Got fun nekome, 155n8, 164n27
Ashkenazi Jews, xxviii, 25, 129, 132
atemporality, 19
Australia, 95
Ayzland, Reuven, 39
    Fun undzer friling, 149n50, 154n61

backshadowing, 57
backward future, xv, 42, 57–58, 63
Bat-Miriam, Yocheved, xi–xvi, xviii–xx, xxii, xxx, 43, 56, 62, 150n10, 154n62
    Meraḥok, xvii
    "Miriam," 137n5
Bat-Miriam Katzenelson, Mariassa, xv
Baudelaire, Charles
    "Little Poems in Prose," 26
Beck, Evelyn Torton, 102, 104, 161n65
    Nice Jewish Girls, xxviii, 90–93, 100, 107
Bedouins, 130
Belarus, xiii, 27
    Bereza Kartuska, 3
Belgium
    Antwerp, 75

Ben-Ḥayim, Rivka Basman, 160n55
Bennett, Paula, 85
Ben-Yishai, Ayelet, 165n9
Ben-Yitzhak (Sonne), Avraham, 153n52
　"Ashrey hazor'im" ("Happy Are the Sowers"), 58–59
Berkeley, CA, xxix
　Asklolat Berkeley/Berkeley school of thought, 133
Bernstein, Michael André, 57
Bialik, H.N., xxx
Bialik Prize, xvi
Bible, xvi, xviii, xxii, 19, 47, 53, 56, 75, 78, 80, 97, 120, 128, 137n5, 138n17, 154n62
　2 Samuel 1:26, 33
　Esther, 78
　Exodus, xiii, 25
　Genesis
　　1:28, 140n30
　　19:7, 33
　Habakkuk 2:3, 51
　Isaiah 51:17, 49
　Job 30:29, 33
　John 19:28, 49
　Luke 7:45, 48–49
　New Testament, 48, 51, 55, 59
　Psalm 137, 109–11
　Song of Songs
　　4:9–10, 33
　　4:12, 33
　　5:1, 33
Bikhovska, Elisheva, 43
Bikoret ufarshanut (Criticism and Interpretation), 97
Billone, Amy Christine, 87
binaries, xx, xxviii, 16, 24, 48, 51, 88, 104, 130–34, 147n21
binding, 4–5, 8, 10–11, 17, 75, 97
Binding of Isaac (akeyde), 75

biology, xii–xiii, xx, xxx, 5, 10–11, 57, 91, 122
birth, xix, xxiii, 59, 90–91
birthright, 18, 90
Bloch, Chana, 33
blood, xii, 1–5, 8–11, 16–17, 22, 49, 56, 72, 76, 81–82, 123
blood libel, 34
Bloom, Harold, 18
Bloomfield, Elana, 151n24
Bluvshteyn, Rachel, 43, 150n7
　"Ivria," xvii–xx
bobe-mayses, 34
Boyarin, Daniel, 151n19, 151n33
Brenner, Naomi, 141n7
Brinker, Beebo, 98
B'Tselem, 165n8
butch/femme communities, 21
Butler, Judith, xxiii, 15, 30–31, 133
　Bodies That Matter, 131
　Gender Trouble, 130

Caesar Augustus, 28, 31, 33–34
California, 99, 104
　Bay Area, 145n60
Canaan, 26
canon, xvi, 42, 65, 132, 167n24
Castle, Terry, 65, 82
castration, 91
Catholicism, 92
Catullus, 86
celibacy, 50
Center for Jewish History, 84
Century Illustrated Monthly Magazine, 36
chain of reception, 17
Chain of Tradition (shalshelet hakabalah), 17
Chamberlain, Lori, 13–14
Chaver, Yael, 141n7
Chekow, Arnold, **20–21**

Chicanas, 110, 121
children, xiv, 5, 15–16, 30, 44, 49, 52, 59–60, 99, 102, 120–21, 127, 129, 154n60
    father/daughter relationships, 100
    father/son relationships, 18, 61–62
    grandchildren, 1, 16–18, 105
    mother/daughter relationships, xiii, xv, 62
    mother/son relationships, xv–xvi, xxiv, 27, 61
    reproductive futurity and, xxiii–xxv, 50, 122
children's poetry, 3–4
Christ, 26, 29, 31, 34–35, 45, 47–49, 53–56, 80, 152n31, 153n57
    Imitatio Christi, 57
Christianity, xxviii, 29, 34–35, 47–59, 61–62, 67, 78, 80, 135, 151n18, 151n26, 153n57
    See also Catholicism; Inquisition; Protestantism
chronology, xxiii, xxvii–xxviii, 55, 71
classism, 104
Claudius I, 33
Cliff, Michelle, 91
colonialism, 25
coming out, 21, 79, 100–101
Communism, xiv, 73
Conditions, 100, 161n57
Constantinople, 74–75, 78
contemporaneity, 19, 22, 42, 99
    noncontemporaneous-contemporaneity, 20, 24, 90, 102, 131
continuum of memory, 17
Converso Jews, 79
Cook, Blanche, xxvi, 90
creativity, 5, 13, 59, 69, 111, 122
Crivelli, Carlo
    "Saint Magdalene," 46–47, 49, 80
cross-identification, 151n33

CUNY Center for Lesbian and Gay Studies (CLAGS)
    In Amerika They Call Us Dykes: 1970s Lesbian Lives conference (2010), 90, 102–6

Danzig, 71
Darwish, Mahmud
    Write Down, I Am an Arab, 154n64
Davar, xvii
De Lauretis, Teresa, 91
Dickinson, Emily, 85
Dinshaw, Carolyn, xix, 19, 22, 24, 121, 131
Di Vilde Khayes, 100
Dropkin, Celia, 150n7
    "Di tentserin" ("The Dancer"), 111
Druze, 130
Dykewomon, Elana, 102
    Beyond the Pale, 98, 160n50

Edelman, Lee, xiii
Edelman, Marek, 100
Egypt, 19, 25–26
Eliot, George, 36, 76
Emerson, Ralph Waldo
    "Spiritual Laws," 24–26
enchanted circle of Jewish tradition, 19, 22
English (language), xxiii, xxv, 21, 27–28, 32–33, 131
    gender in, xxvii, 116, 147n21
    Israeli occupation of Palestine in, 165n7
    Jewish women's poetry in, xx, xxvii–xxix, 21, 26, 41, 92–93, 99–101, 107–16, 119–21, 126–29, 134
    relationship to Yiddish, xxvi–xxix, 14–16, 99–101, 107–9, 112–21, 126–28, 134
    translation and, 6, 12–16, 119–21, 155n19, 167n21

enjambment, 12, 85, 113–14, 120
Enlightenment, 31, 147n24
eroticism, xvii–xviii, xxv, 67–68, 70, 80, 82, 85–87, 103
    homoeroticism, 31, 33–34, 48, 134, 155n8
    See also sexuality
Esther (Biblical), 78–80
ethnicity, 132
    sexuality and, 79–80
Europe, xxi, 27, 29, 34–35, 44, 133, 164n27
    Eastern, xxviii, 36, 42–43, 52–53, 55, 62, 98
    See also individual countries
expectancy, xi, xxi–xxii, xxix, xxx, 2–3, 11, 43, 52, 92, 119, 124, 136
    queer, xii–xvi, xx, xxvii–xxviii, 23, 41–42, 48–49, 51, 56, 63, 106
    See also waiting
Ezra, Abraham, 26

Faderman, Lillian, 104
failure, xv, xxvi, 88, 111, 125
    queerness of, 135–36
family resemblance, 18, 115
fascism, 148n40
    See also Hitler, Adolf; Khurbn; Nazis
feeling backward, xv
Feinberg, Leyb, 35
Felman, Jyl Lynn, 160n50
femininity, xiv, 13, 21, 29–30, 34, 50, 53, 69, 97, 110, 120, 143n25
feminism, 5, 116, 132, 135, 163n12
    Chicana, 110
    feminist literary criticism, xxii, 5–6, 97–98
    feminist poetics, 23
    feminist sex wars, 90
    feminist translation, 6, 13–15, 22

    Jewish, 93, 99, 107, 139n24
    lesbian feminism, 21, 104–6
    recovery and, xxvii, xxix, 13, 91
    relationship to queerness, 102–4
    waves, 102
    See also women's liberation movement
fertility, 5, 49, 140, 151n23
    See also motherhood; reproduction
foremothers, xxv, xxvii, 4–5, 10–11, 17, 21, 76, 89, 93, 101, 103, 105, 122–23
    See also grandmothers; motherhood
Forverts, 77, 93–94
foundling texts, xii–xiv
Found Treasures, 92
France
    French Revolution, 27
    Paris, xiv, 27, 35, 146n16
Fraye arbeter shtime, 28
Freccero, Carla, 56, 66, 71, 76
Freeman, Elizabeth, 104–5, 121
French (language), 35
Freud, Sigmund, 103
Fuss, Diana, 116
futurity, xvi, xxviii, 4, 11–12, 24, 37–39, 55–56, 65, 77, 84, 124, 127
    antifuturity, 52, 103
    backward future, xv, 42, 57–59, 63
    Jewish, xxi–xxiii, 43, 50, 53, 62–63, 136
    language and, xxiv–xxvi, xxx, 53, 62–63, 107, 123, 125, 135–36
    queerness and, xii–xiii, xv, xx, xxv, 17, 22, 29, 41, 51, 63, 76, 103–4, 134
    reproductive, xiii, xv, xx, xxiii–xxv, 31, 33–34, 42, 50, 57, 71, 122–23

Galicia
    Skale, 111

Index

Garber, Linda, 104, 106
gay panic, 48–49
gender, 27, 55, 62, 67, 79, 103, 111, 132, 139n24, 152n32
  gender binaries, 24, 104, 130, 147n21
  gender fluidity, 29–31
  in language, xiv, xxi–xxiii, xxvii, 5, 13–14, 19, 29–31, 43, 46–47, 56, 68, 82, 86, 89–99, 107, 114–16, 121–24, 134, 136, 139n26, 139n28, 143n25, 147n21, 152n27, 167n24
  temporality of, xxiii–xxiv, 30–31
  translation and, 14–15
  See also femininity; masculinity; women's liberation movement
gender studies, 96
genealogy, xx, xxx, 11, 42, 62–63, 96, 116, 123, 154n62
  affective, xv
  lesbian, 86, 104–5
  literary, 96
  multilingual, 42
  queer, xxv, 65, 86, 104–5
General Foods, 149n45
generation trap, 103
German (language), 29–30, 32, 44, 58, 77, 115, 128, 134, 147n24, 148n40
Germany, 36, 44, 147n24
  Berlin, 43, 46
  Leipzig, 71
Getseylte verter, 154n58
ghosts, xxviii, 65–66, 71, 74–77, 79–83, 88–89
  See also apparitional lesbian; haunting; queer spectrality
Gibbs, Joan, 104
Gilbert, Sandra M., 18
Gilder, Richard Watson, 36

Glaykhhayt, 94
Glikl of Hameln, 93, 139n28
Gluzman, Michael, 18
God, 49, 74, 76–77, 94, 112, 148n33
Goldberg, Leah, xxviii, 24, 42–44, 61–63, 67, 81, 149n48, 150n15, 151n18, 152n33, 153n52, 153n57
  "Beminzar Pazaislio" ("In the Pazaislio Monastery"), 49–51
  "Ḥalom na'arah" ("Dream of a Girl"), 45–49, 68, 80, 150n13
  "Madonot al parashat derakhim" ("Madonnas at a Crossroads"), 51–60
  Pegishah im meshorer (Meeting with a Poet), 58
  "Pieta," 48
  Taba'ot ashan (Smoke Rings), 50, 150n13
Gordon, Stephen, 98
grandmothers, 1, 3–4, 8–10, 16, 18, 79, 115, 122, 161n65
graven images, 32
Greece
  Athens, 28
Greek (language), 30
Greek antiquity, xxviii, 31–37, 67, 134
  See also Greek Empire; Greek mythology
Greek Empire, 31–37, 135
  See also Greek antiquity
Greek mythology, 27, 34, 37, 69
Grinberg, Uri Tsvi
  "Uri Tsvi farn tseylem INRI" ("Uri Zvi Before the Cross INRI"), 152n29
Gubar, Susan, 18

Hadda, Janet, 141n7
Halberstam, Jack, 15, 135–36, 143n40
Hammer, Barbara, 104

Hasan-Rokem, Galit, 151n16
Hasidic Jews, xiii
haunting, xxviii, 4, 11, 48, 65–83, 88, 95, 120, 122
　See also apparitional lesbian; ghosts; queer spectrality
Hazaz, Nahum (Zuzik), xv–xvi
Hebrew (language), xxv, 27, 49, 126, 131, 148n33, 150n9, 151nn25–26, 152n28, 165n4, 165n10, 167n21
　Biblical, xvi, xxii, 111, 120
　Diasporic Hebrew, xxi
　gendering of, xxi–xxiii, xxvii, 5, 13–14, 19, 46, 56, 143n25
　Hebrew modernism, 32, 42, 44, 58
　Jewish women's poetry in, xii–xiv, xvi–xvii, xix–xxiii, xxvi–xxviii, 3–4, 24, 42, 43–46, 52–54, 59, 139n26, 150n7, 167n24
　Modern, xiii, xvi, xxvi, 128
　relationship to Yiddish, xxi, xxiv, xxvi, xxx, 3, 14, 29, 42–43, 53, 61–62, 111, 120–21, 125, 128–30, 132–33, 141n4, 143n25
　revival of, 54
　role in Jewish identity, xxx, 13
　role in Zionism, 54, 62–63, 129–30, 132
Hebrew literature, xvi, xxi, 49, 62, 125
The Hebrew Octoberists, xiv
Hebrew University, xxi
hegemony, xii, xxx, 55, 130, 132, 135
Heifetz-Tussman, Malka, 160n55
Heine, Heinrich, 26–27, 35, 37, 80, 146n16
Hellerstein, Kathryn, 13–15, 22, 30, 33, 59, 92, 95, 97, 122, 141n3, 141n7, 142n18, 154n60, 163n12
　A Question of Tradition, 96, 98, 159n34

translation of Molodowsky, 5–6, 9–10, 12, 141n1
hemshekh, xxiv, 122–23
hermeneutic friends, xv, xvii
hermeneutics, xix, 49, 121
Hess, Tamar, 151n16
heteronormativity, xv, xx, xxiv–xxvi, 13, 15–16, 29, 31, 42, 56–57, 71, 103, 107, 123, 136
heterosexuality, 21, 71, 79, 90–91, 103, 130, 154n65
Hever, Hannan
　On the Margins of Modernism, 58
historicism, xix–xx, xxiv, 71
　New Historicism, 159n40
historiography, xxvii, 62
　Jewish, 19
　queer, xxix, 121
Hitler, Adolf, 126–28, 135
　See also Khurbn; Nazis; Sho'ah
Hobsbawm, Eric, 140n34
Hoffman, Matthew, 54
Hoffman, Warren, 164n27
Hollander, John, **20**–21, 144n57, 145nn58–59
homoeroticism, 31–34, 33–34, 48, 134, 155n8
homophobia, 100–101, 119, 161n60
homosexuality, 48, 67, 164n27
　See also lesbian continuum; lesbian feminism; lesbian genealogy; lesbian haunting; lesbian history; lesbian movement; lesbian publishing; lesbian relation to queerness; lesbians; lesbian separatism; queerness
Honig, Edwin, 145n58

identity politics, 93, 104–5, 116
Imitatio Christi, 57

immigration, xiv, 4, 25, 28, 36, 44, 54, 62, 80, 98, 104, 111
impossibility, xii, xiv–xviii, 5, 30, 49, 65, 89, 99, 109–10
In Amerika They Call Us Dykes: 1970s Lesbian Lives conference (2010), 90, 102–6
inheritance, xx, xxii, xxv, xxx, 5, 42, 92, 103, 105
Inquisition, 77
intergenerationality, xxviii, 13, 15–16, 21, 71–73, 102, 105, 115
intertextuality, xvi, xxviii, 1, 15, 48–49, 53, 55, 59, 61, 69
Intifada
   First, 127
   Second, xxi
Isaac (Biblical), 75
Israel, xvii, xxiv, xxix, 3–4, 26, 44, 54, 92, 97, 99, 125, 140n37, 145n60, 165n9
   education system, xxi, 136
   Galilee, 62
   language politics, 62–63, 129–32, 135–36, 141n4, 165n7
   Nazareth, 29–30, 35, 45, 52, 55, 58
   occupation of Palestine, xxvi, 100, 126–30, 132, 165nn7–8
   Tel Aviv, xxix, 27, 43
   See also Intifada; Israel/Palestine; Jerusalem
Israelites, 54
Israel/Palestine, xxi, xxvi, xxix, 126, 129, 136, 145n60
   See also Intifada; Israel; Palestine
Israel Prize, xvi
Italy
   Ferreira, 78
   Venice, 75, 78

Jerusalem, xxix, 26, 94, 109–10

West Jerusalem, xxi
Jesus. *See* Christ
Jewish Americans, xiii–xxiv, xxvi, 23, 25, 65, 126
Jewish diaspora, xxi, 29, 54, 62, 111, 131, 136
Jewish feminism, 93, 99, 107, 139n24
Jewish imagism, 32, 53
Jewish literary complex, xxvi, 125–26, 130–32
Jewish literature, xxii, xxiv, xxvi, xxx, 21, 43, 55, 125–26, 130, 132–36, 167n24
   See also Hebrew literature; Yiddish literature
Jewish Theological Seminary
   The Eternal Light program, 149n45
Jewish Voice for Peace (JVP), 145n60
Johnson, Barbara, 15
Judas (Biblical), 48
Judeo-Arabic (language), xxi

Kabbalah, 26
Kafka, Franz, 167n24
Kaiser Friedrich Museum, 45–46
Kartun-Blum, Ruth, 138n13
Kay, Devra, 139n28
Kaye/Kantrowitz, Melanie, 91
Khurbn, 62, 75, 99–100, 129, 135
   See also Hitler, Adolf; Nazis; Sho'ah
kinship, 15, 71, 96
   See also family resemblance
Klepfisz, Irena, xxvii, xxix, 18, 88, 93–94, 102, 105, 125, 141n7, 144n57, 160n57, 161n62, 162n7
   "Der Soyne/The Enemy: An Interview in Gaza," 99–100, 126–29, 132–35
   "Di rayze aheym/The journey home," 108, 114
   "Di tsung/The tongue," 107–11

Klepfisz, Irena (cont'd)
  "Etlekhe verter oyf mame-loshn/A Few Words in the Mother Tongue," 101, 107–8, 116–20
  "Fradel Shtok," 107–8, 111–15
  "Khaloymes/Dreams in Progress," 120–21
  The Tribe of Dina, 91–92, 95, 107
  "Women without Children," 122–23
Klepfisz, Michał, 100
Korman, Ezra
  Yidishe dikhterins, xxviii, 6, 10, 43, 89–90, 92, 95–97, 142n19, 159n36
Korn, Rokhl, 94, 150n7
kosher, 3–5, 8–11, 10, 122
Kronfeld, Chana, 14, 18, 58–59, 130, 133
Kundus, Zahiye, 166n10

Ladino (language), xxi–xxii
Landau, Mina, 49
Lazarus, Emma, xxviii, 48, 51, 76, 93, 102, 149n45, 152n31, 156n38
  "Assurance," 84–88, 90
  "By the Waters of Babylon," 25, 27, 78, 80
  A Dance to Death, 77–79
  "Echoes," 23, 84
  Emma Lazarus (play), 36–37
  "Epochs," 24, 41
  "Magnetism," 65, 81–83
  "The New Colossus," 25–26, 36–37, 153n52
  "Only a Dream," 83–85, 88
  "Venus of the Louvre," 26–28, 35–39, 80
  "Will o' the Wisp," 84
Lazarus, Josephine, 79
Lebanon, 100
Lebanon War, 90

Lebnsboym, Rosa. *See* Margolin, Anna (Rosa Lebnsboym)
Leksikon fun der nayer yidisher literatur, 44
Lempel, Bluma
  "Correspondents," 155n8
Lenin, Vladimir, 94
lesbian continuum, 17, 106
lesbian feminism, 21, 104–6
lesbian genealogy, 86, 104–5
lesbian haunting, 65–89, 120
lesbian history, xx, xxiv–xxvi, xxviii–xxix, 13, 17–19, 66, 80, 82, 88, 91–93, 98–106, 111, 123–24
lesbian literature, xxiv–xxvi, 102
lesbian movement, xxiv–xxvi, xxix, 18–19, 93, 100–101, 103, 121
lesbian publishing, 90–92, 100
lesbian relation to queerness, 102–6, 123
lesbian separatism, 102, 160n50
Levin, Khane, 94
Levy, Lital, 133
lezbianke, 101, 117–19
literary history, xvi, xxii, xxvii, xxx, 18, 42, 89, 133
Lithuania, 44
  Kovno, 49
Lithuanian (language), 44, 49
logocentrism, xxiii
Lorde, Audre, 41, 89
loshn-koydesh (holy tongue), 29, 147n24
Louvre Museum, 26–28, 35–37, 39, 80, 146n16
Love, Heather, xv, 42, 57, 65
Luria, Esther, 94–95
Lynch, Michael, 104

Madonna, 50–57, 59
  See also Virgin Mary

Magdalene, Mary, 46–49, 80
mame-loshn/mother-tongue, xxi, 61, 101, 107–9, 117, 120–21
Mandatory Palestine, xxviii, 61
Manger, Itsik, 154n58
Mann, Barbara, 30, 32, 42, 52, 53, 141n7, 148n32
Margolin, Anna (Rosa Lebnsboym), xxviii, 23, 36–39, 41–44, 48–50, 53, 55, 62–63, 69, 88, 92, 94–95, 102, 120, 148n33, 148n37, 149n50, 150n15, 154n60
  "Ikh bin geven a mol a yingling" ("I Was Once a Boy"), 27–35, 45, 47, 54, 57–58, 67, 134–36
  Lider, 39
  Mari cycle, 59–61, 153n57, 154n60
  "Maris tfile" ("Mary's Prayer"), 59
  "Mari un der prister" ("Mary and the Priest"), 59
  "Mari un di gest" ("Mary and the Guests"), 60–61
  "Mari vil zayn a betlerin" ("Mary and the Beggar"), 153n57
  "Mayn shtam redt" ("My Ancestors Speak"), 71–73, 114–15
  "Oyf a balkon ("On a Balcony"), 66–71
  "Vos vilstu, Mari?" ("What Do You Want, Mary?"), 59–60
marriage, 24–25, 27, 33, 56, 77
  translation and, 14
martyology, 32
masculinity, 29, 37, 47, 69, 110, 119
matrilineality, 1, 5, 13, 116
Mendelsohn, Moses, 26, 80
Mendes Nasi, Doña Gracia, 74–78
Menuhim, Ibtisam Mara'ana
  Write Down, I Am an Arab, 154n64
Messiah, 54
messianism, 49

Christian, 56–57
secular, 53–55
Zionist, 53–57, 63
See also Second Coming of Jesus
metaphor, xxiii, 5, 10, 12–15, 18, 33, 122, 131
methodology, of book, xx, 25
Michigan Womyn's Music Festival, 161n66
Middle East, 61, 158n18
See also individual countries
Miller, D.A., 88
Mills College, 99–100
Miłosz, Czesław, 108
Minkin, Sarah Anne, 145n60
Miranda Warning, 106
Miriam the Prophetess (Biblical), xiii, 137n5, 154n62
Miron, Dan, xvii, xxii–xxiii, xxvi, 130, 132–33, 140n39, 165n4, 167n24
  From Continuity to Contiguity, 125–26, 131
  Imahot meyasdot, aḥayot ḥorgot (Founding Mothers, Stepsisters), xxi, 167n24
misogyny, 13, 29, 69, 97
  See also patriarchy
Mizraḥim, 158n18
Modernah, 44, 54
modernism, 18, 59, 96
  Hebrew, 32, 42, 44, 58
  Jewish, 42, 51, 54
  Yiddish, xxi, 3–4, 32, 42, 54, 62
Modern Language Association, 161n65
Molodowsky, Kadya, 88, 92–93, 95–97, 121, 141n4, 149n45, 159n30
  Adrienne Rich's relationship with, xxvii, 6, 8, 10, 12–13, 16–18, **20**–22, 100, 102, 106, 122, 142n19

Molodowsky, Kadya (cont'd)
"Bagegenishn" ("Encounters"), 94, 99
Der meylekh Dovid aleyn iz geblibn (Only King David Remained), 75
"Dona Gratsye Mendes," 74–76
"Dona Gratsye Mendes: Ir tifer gloybn un vunderlekh lebn" ("Doña Gracia Mendes: Her Deep Belief and Wondrous Life"), 77–78
Dray momentn in lebn fun Dona Gratsye Mendes Nasi (Three Moments in the Life of Doña Gracia Mendes Nasi), 76–77
Emma Lazarus, 36–37
"Froyen-lider" ("Women's Poems/Songs"), xxvii–xxviii, 2–6, 12–13, 20–22, 71–74, 76, 120, 122
Kathryn Hellerstein's work on, 5–6, 9–13, 22, 141n1, 141n3, 142n18
Khezhvndike nekht, 6, 10–11, 142n19
"Mayne kinder" ("My Children"), 122–23
Nokhn got fun midber (After the God of the Desert), 77
Moore, Lisa, 86
Sister Arts, 87–88
Morris, Bonnie, 161n66
The Disappearing L, 102–3
Moscow State University, xiv
Moses (Biblical), xiii, 19, 80, 154n62
motherhood, 15–17, 25–26, 37, 54–55, 59, 91, 93, 103, 115, 122, 126–27, 154n60, 154n62
mother/daughter relationships, xiii, xv, 62
mother/son relationships, xv–xvi, xxiv, 27, 61
See also foremothers; grandmothers

mother tongue, xiii, xxi–xxii, xxv–xxvi, 49–51, 61, 101, 107–8, 116, 120–21
"Etlekhe verter oyf mame-loshn/A Few Words in the Mother Tongue," 101, 107–8, 116–20
Moznaim, xvii
multiculturalism, 91, 93
Muñoz, José Esteban, xx, 134, 168n32
Myers, David, xxiv, 140n34

Name of the Father, 13
nationalism, xxiii, 42, 54–55, 57, 125, 151n23
See also Zionism
National University of Kharkov, xiv
National Yiddish Book Center, 101, 159n36
Nazis, 35, 37, 50, 62, 99, 128, 135
See also Khurbn; Sho'ah
Nealon, Christopher, xii, xiv–xv, 105
New Historicism, 160n40
New Jew, 62
Newton, Esther, 104
New York City, 84, 93, 96, 102
Klepfisz's time in, xxvii, xxix, 107, 110
Lazarus's time in, 25, 35–36, 76
Lower East Side, 36
Luria's time in, 94
Margolin's time in, xxviii, 27, 35–36, 43
Shtok's time in, 111
New York Times, 156n38
Niger, Sh., 143n25
nigunim, 4–5, 11, 73
Niranjana, Tejaswini, 14
Norich, Anita, 14–15, 97, 115–16, 131, 141n7
North Africa, 158n18
Noss, Kaitlin, 103, 162n70

Novershtern, Avraham, 70, 73, 96–99

Odessa University, xiv
Oedipal drama, 91
open secret, 88
optimism, 57, 63, 168n32
Orientalism, 61

Pagans, 29, 57
Palestine, xiv, xxix, 27, 44, 52, 54, 61–62, 154n63, 165nn8–9
    Gaza, 99–100, 126–29, 134
    Israeli occupation, xxvi, 100, 126–30, 132, 165n7, 165nn7–8
    Mandatory Palestine, xxviii, 61
    See also Intifada; Israel/Palestine; Jerusalem
Pappenheim, Bertha, 151n33
passivity, 37, 53, 56, 59, 61, 72, 153n52
    See also submission
Passover, 19
patriarchy, 4, 13, 18–19, 48, 58, 79, 103, 105, 116, 132
    See also misogyny
Pazaislio Monastery, 49
pederasty, 32
Peretz, Y.L., 154n58
pessimism, xxviii, 35, 51
Petrarch, 86
phallocentrism, 91, 103
phallus, 48
Pharisees, 48
Pinkerfeld, Anda, 150n7
Pirkey Avot, 17
pogroms, 25, 54, 78
Poland, xxix, 150n7, 150n9
    Warsaw, 4, 6, 27, 43, 94, 99–100
Polish (language), xxii, 44, 150n7
Portugal, 74–75
    expulsion of Jews, 25, 76

Pratt, Norma Fain, 97, 141n7
prayer, 5, 11, 59, 72, 78, 94, 97, 114, 139n28
proleptic mourning, 57
pro-Semitism, 80
Protestantism, 93
psychoanalysis, 91
Purim, 79

queer art of failure, 135–36
queer expectancy, xii–xvi, xx, xxvii–xxviii, 23, 41–42, 48–49, 51, 56, 63, 106
    See also waiting
queer genealogy, xxv, 65, 86, 104–5
    See also lesbian genealogy
queer generations, 102
queer historical impulse, xix, 24
queer history, xxiii–xxiv, xxviii, 19, 23–24, 29–30, 34, 43, 45, 84, 131, 134, 136
queer lines, xxviii, 1, 16, 41
queerness's relationship to feminism, 102–4
queerness's relation to lesbianism, 102–6, 123
queer reading practices, xv–xvi, 13
queer spectrality, 65–66, 71–83, 76, 88
    See also apparitional lesbian; ghosts; haunting
queer studies, xv
    queer theory, xiii, xxiv, 22, 79, 106, 125, 130–31, 133–34, 168n32

Raab, Esther, 43
racism, 104
Ravitch, Melech, 95
Raz, Yosefa, 151n16
Reinhard, Richard
    Der Tanz zum Tode, 77

Reitter, Paul, 146n1
reproduction, 5, 56, 63, 103, 116, 130, 152n33, 154n65
    reproductive futurity, xiii, xv, xx, xxiii–xxv, 31, 33–34, 42, 50, 57, 71, 122–23
    See also children; fertility; foremothers; motherhood
resurrection, 49, 54, 83
rhyme schemes, 30, 69, 87, 147n25, 151n25
Rich, Adrienne, xxviii, **20**, 88, 93–94, 101, 145n60, 157n3, 162n7
    "Compulsory Heterosexuality and Lesbian Existence," 90
    Dream of a Common Language, 21, 90, 121
    "The Fact of a Doorframe," 115
    "For Julia in Nebraska," 1, 16
    "Granddaughter," 16–17, 105–6
    "Hattie Rice Rich," 17
    "Mary Gravely Jones," 17
    relationship with Kadya Molodowsky, xxvii, 6, 8, 10–13, 16–18, **20**–22, 100, 102, 105, 106, 122, 142n19
    "Split at the Root," 92
    "Transcendental Étude," 90–91, 123
    Of Woman Born, 89, 122
Rilke, Rainer Maria
    "Archaic Torso of Apollo," 148n33
    "Der Wahnsinn," 154n58
Romance languages, 29
Roman Empire, 31–35, 39, 57, 67, 134–35
    See also Roman mythology
Roman mythology, 27
Rosenfarb, Chava, 160n55
Roskies, David, 160n40
Rugoff, Kathy, 13

Russia, 54
    Königsberg/Kalingrad, 27
    Moscow, xiv
    Odessa, xiv, 4, 27, 43
Russian (language), xiv, xxii, 4, 27, 35, 44, 150n7

San Francisco Jewish Community Center (JCC), 145n60
Sappho, 86, 93–94, 159n30
Schachter, Allison, 133
Schor, Esther, 87, 156n38
Schreiber, Maeera, 108
    Singing in a Strange Land, 163n7
Schulman, Sarah, 95–96
Scooler, Zvee, 37, 77
Scott, Bonnie Kime, 18
Second Coming of Jesus, 49, 53
Second Commandment, 32
secularism, xxii, 31, 43, 53, 62–63, 110, 123, 150n9
secular messianism, 53
Sedgwick, Eve, 133
    Epistemology of the Closet, 79
    "White Glasses," 104
Seidman, Naomi, xiii, 13, 15, 79, 143n25
Sephardic Jews, xxviii, 25
Seward, Anna
    "Sonnet xxxiii," 87
sexology, 164n27
sexuality, xv–xvi, xxv, 10, 21, 25, 68, 71, 88, 91, 103, 132, 164n27
    ethnicity and, 79–80
    feminist sex wars, 90
    gendered, 4, 31, 48, 51, 67, 79, 85, 105, 130
    temporality and, xiv, 45, 82
    translation and, 12–15
    See also celibacy; eroticism; heteronormativity;

heterosexuality; homoeroticism; homosexuality
shalshelet hakabalah. *See* Chain of Tradition (shalshelet hakabalah)
Shandler, Jeffrey, 120, 161n60
Sho'ah, 129
   See also Hitler, Adolf; Khurbn; Nazis
Shomroni, Amir, 141n4
Shreiber, Maeera, 121, 164n35
Shtok, Fradel, 92, 163n15
   Erzeylungen, 111
   Klepfisz's poem about, 107–8, 111–16
   For Musicians Only, 111
Shumiatcher, Esther, 94
Signal, 73
Sinister Wisdom, 91
sisterhood, 101–2
Slavic languages, 29
Smith, Charlotte, 86–87
Socrates, 28, 31–35
Song of the Sea, xiii
sonnets, 23, 35, 84, 86–88, 111, 163n15
South Africa, 95
Soviet Union, xv, 95
   See also Russia
Spain
   expulsion of Jews, 25–26, 75–76
Spanish (language), 110
Stalin, Joseph, 62
Statue of Liberty, 38–39
   Lazarus's "The New Colossus" on, 25–26, 36–37, 153n52
Stavi, Na'aman, 61–62
Stavski, Moshe (Stavi), 61–62
Steiner, George
   model of translation, 13–14
Stowe, Harriet Beecher, 93
straight panic, 48–49

submission, 48, 50, 79
   See also passivity
Svive, 4, 11
synecdoche, 32, 68
Szold, Henrietta, 93

Tabatshnik, Avrom, 163n15
Talmud, xxii
Tarbut movement, 150n7, 150n9
Tatour, Dareen, xxix
Tchernichowsky, Shaul
   "Before the Statue of Apollo," 148n33
Tehiyah, 54
temporal drag, 104–5
temporality, 15, 32, 38–39, 61, 70, 84, 91, 95–96, 102, 114, 122, 130, 133, 152n32
   atemporality, 19
   cross-temporal community, xxvii–xxviii, 4, 22, 76, 90, 98, 101, 157n3
   cyclical, 19, 35, 57–58, 88, 135
   disruption of, xxviii, 4, 13, 16, 24–25, 27, 30, 34, 41, 49, 55–57, 62, 71, 75, 81–83, 110, 123
   gendered, xxiii–xxiv, 30–31, 55
   language choice as temporal choice, xxvi
   normative, 41, 66, 71, 82
   progressive, xiii, xx, xxiv, 20, 23, 31, 33–34, 42, 57, 67, 119–20, 136
   queerness and, xiii–xvi, xix–xxi, xxiv–xxx, 4, 13, 17–20, 22–25, 51, 56, 66–67, 76, 78, 89–90, 98, 104–6, 131, 136
   sexuality and, xiv, 45, 82
   See also backshadowing; backward future; contemporaneity; expectancy; feeling backward; futurity; haunting; lesbian history; queer historical impulse; reproduction: reproductive futurity; waiting

tense, xiv–xvi, xix, 4, 105, 127
Texas, 26
Three Graces, 69
Ticotsky, Giddon, 49–50
transgression, 32, 50–51, 54, 95, 151n18
    temporality and, xxviii, 4, 13, 16, 24–25, 27, 30, 34, 41, 49, 57, 62, 81–82, 110, 123
    translation as, xxvii, 13–14, 16
translation, xii, xiv, xxviii, 3, 26, 32, 37, 46, 61, 71, 73, 77, 84, 96–98, 101, 113–14, 119–21, 123, 128–29, 131, 134, 142n13, 142n21, 148n40, 155n19
    Alter's translation of Psalm 137, 109–10
    Bloch's translation of Song of Songs, 33
    Catallus's translation of Sappho, 86
    Feinberg's translation of Margolin, 35
    feminist, xxvii, 6, 13–15, 22
    Hellerstein's translation of Margolin, 30, 142n19
    Hellerstein's translation of Molodowsky, 5–6, 9–12, 22, 141n1
    Kundus's translation of Klepfisz, 165n10
    lesbian, xxv, 6, 17
    Manger's translation of Rilke, 153n57
    Pardes's translation of Bat-Miriam, 137n5
    queer, xxvii, xxix, 13, 16, 22, 107, 115
    Rich's translation of Molodowsky, 6, 8–13, 16, 20–22, 142n19
    Steiner's model of, 13–14
    as transgression, xxvii, 13–14, 16
    Weiman-Kelman's translation of Bat-Miriam, 137n1
    Weiman-Kelman's translation of Goldberg, 150n15
    Weiman-Kelman's translation of Klepfisz, 165n10
A Treasury of Yiddish Poetry, 6, 21
Tsukunft, 94
Turkey, 77
Turniansky, Chava, 139n28
Tynyanov, Yuri, 115

Ukraine
    Kharkov, xiv
    Kiev, 26, 71
Ulinover, Miriam, 94
ultra-Orthodox Jews, xxv, 110
United States, xxv, 4, 28, 141n4
    See also individual cities and states
University of Pennsylvania, xxix
University of Toronto, xxix
usable pasts, 96, 159n40
utopia, 63, 168n32

Venus, 26–28, 35–39, 80, 146n16
Venus de Milo, 27, 35–39, 146n16
Virgin Mary, 34, 47, 53–55, 54, 59–60, 153n57
    See also Madonna
Vogel, Dan, 86

waiting, 3, 9, 37, 54, 59–60, 85, 92, 96
    queerness and, xii–xv, xix, xxx
    in vain, 41–42, 51–56, 63
    See also expectancy
Wamsley, Rachel, 151n16
War of 1948, xv–xvi, 62
Warsaw Ghetto Uprising, 100
WATV, 149n45
Weingrad, Michael, 26
Weinreich, Max, 101

Weiss, Yfaat, 49–50
Weissler, Chava, 139n28
Whitman, Ruth, 96
Winchevsky, Morris, 163n15
Wittgenstein, Ludwig, 18
Wolosky, Shira, 151n32
women's liberation movement, 13, 17
  See also feminism
Woolf, Virginia
  A Room of One's Own, 161n56
Wordsworth, William, 87
Write Down, I Am an Arab, 154n64

Yale Series of Younger Poets award, 21
Yerushalmi, Yosef Haim, 17, 22, 39, 96, 135–36
  Zakhor, 19
Yiddish (language), xiii, xxii, 30, 33, 41, 77–78, 88, 92, 105, 141n1, 141n7, 147n24, 150n7
  association with diaspora, xxi, 111
  as composite language, 29
  critical potential of, 125–36
  gender politics of, xxi–xxiii, xxvii, 13, 43, 89–99, 107, 114–16, 121–24, 134, 136, 139n26, 139n28, 143n25, 167n24
  Old Yiddish, 139n28
  precarity of, xxx, 14, 22
  queerness and, xxv–xxvi, xxix, 65–69, 99, 107, 119–24, 155n8, 164n27
  relationship to Arabic, 128–30
  relationship to English, xxvi–xxix, 14–16, 99–101, 107–9, 112–21, 126–28, 134

relationship to Hebrew, xxi, xxiv, xxvi, xxx, 3, 14, 29, 42–43, 53, 61–62, 111, 120–21, 125, 128–30, 132–33, 141n4, 143n25
relationship to Spanish, 111
revival, 161n65
translation and, 6, 10–16, 22, 96, 119–21, 142n19, 142n21, 153n57
Yiddish modernism, xxi, 3–4, 32, 42, 54, 62
  See also National Yiddish Book Center
Yiddish literature, xxi, xxiii, xxv, 6, 36, 43–44, 92, 97, 115, 139n28, 143n25, 153n57
Yiddish studies, 5–6, 101, 161n65
YIVO (Institute for Jewish Research), 36, 77, 93
Yocheved (Biblical), xiii, 154n63

Zeiger, Arthur, 80, 86
Zhelezniak, Yocheved. *See* Bat-Miriam, Yocheved
Zilberg, Rivke. *See* Molodowsky, Kadya
Zimmerman, Bonnie, 98
Zionism, xxvi, xxx, 50, 53, 56, 58, 151n23
  role of Hebrew language in, 54, 62–63, 129–30, 132–34
Zucker, Sheva, 141n7
Zychlinski, Rajzel, 160n55
Żydowski Instytut Historyczny (ZIH), 98–99

Printed by Libri Plureos GmbH in Hamburg, Germany